BETWEEN

GOD AND

THE PARTY

BETWEEN

Religion and Politics

GOD AND in

Revolutionary Cuba

THE PARTY

JOHN M. KIRK

University of South Florida Press

Tampa

Library of Congress Cataloging in Publication Data

Kirk, John M.
Between God and the party: religion and politics in revolutionary
Cuba / John M. Kirk.
p.   cm.
Bibliography: p.
Includes index.
ISBN 0-8130-0879-4
1. Church and state—Cuba—History—20th century.
2. Cuba—Church history. 3. Cuba—Politics and
government—1959–. I. Title.
BR645.C9K57—1988
322'.1—dc19   87-16006

Printed in the U.S.A. on acid-free paper ∞

University Presses of Florida is the central agency for
scholarly publishing of the State of Florida's university system,
producing books selected for publication by the faculty editorial
committees of Florida's nine public universities: Florida A&M
University (Tallahassee), Florida Atlantic University (Boca
Raton), Florida International University (Miami), Florida State
University (Tallahassee), University of Central Florida
(Orlando), University of Florida (Gainesville), University of
North Florida (Jacksonville), University of South Florida
(Tampa), University of West Florida (Pensacola).

Orders for books published by all member presses should
be addressed to University Presses of Florida, 15 NW 15th Street,
Gainesville, FL 32603.

In memory of my father, Edward Hamilton Kirk,

and

my father-in-law, Roy Campbell Ness,

"Two of Nature's Gentlemen," with love and respect.

Contents

Tables

Preface

Few institutions have a richer historical tradition in Latin America than the Catholic church, which for 460 years has colonized the entire continent. And few historical developments in recent times have had as far reaching influence throughout Latin America as the Cuban Revolution, led by Fidel Castro for thirty years. When these two diverse historical strands intertwined, an extraordinary, fiery relationship resulted, as one would expect. The ensuing social polarization, religious divisions, unrelenting opposition of the church hierarchy to the revolution's goals (and to friendship with the Soviet Union), outspoken denunciations of the church by the revolutionary government (which deported dozens of priests and encouraged many others to leave), followed by a long—and extremely slow—process of rapprochement and general fence-mending, is fascinating material indeed. For many years, though, this area has been generally neglected by academics.

This work derives from my fascination with the role of the church, and the importance of the Cuban Revolution. Attracted by the spirit of *aggiornamento* that developed out of Vatican II, and following several research trips to Cuba, this project began to take shape during a sabbatical year (1984–85), and developed with further visits to Cuba in 1987 and 1988.

Many people have aided its progress: Roland Laneuville (of the Québec-based Missions Etrangères, and himself a missionary with many years' experience in Cuba) helped enormously in the initial stages of the project. In Cuba many church representative, academics, and government delegates gave generously of their time, including

Eliselia Díaz and Reinaldo González of ICAP, José Felipe Carneado, director of the recently established office of religious affairs of the PCC's Central Committee, Archbishop Jaime Ortega Alamino of Havana, and nuns and clergy in the Archdiocese of Havana (in particular the sisters of the Santovenia residence for senior citizens and some of the staff of the San Carlos y San Ambrosio Seminary, including René David). A special debt of gratitude is owed to Msgr. Carlos Manuel de Céspedes, secretary-general of the Cuban Episcopal Conference, who in a balanced and fair way tried to explain the development of church-state relations and to correct an over-simplified understanding. Among Protestant clergy, grateful thanks are expressed to the staff and students of the Seminario Evangélico at Matanzas and to Sergio Arce Martínez, Rafael Cepeda, Adolfo Ham and René Castellanos of the Consejo Ecuménico Cubano. Enrique López Oliva of the University of Havana was a mine of information; he gave generously of his time and allowed the use of his own research material. Noted Cuban historian Jorge Ibarra read an earlier draft of the work and made helpful suggestions, while writers Cintio Vitier and Fina García gave me clear insights into the church's role. Many other revolutionaries and Christians (the two terms not being mutually exclusive, it must be remembered) in Cuba, too numerous to list, deserve recognition for the many hours spent explaining their interpretation of the religious ethic. Cubans from many walks of life, who have become good friends during the research trips spent in the "Pearl of the Antilles" also warrant recognition: René and Ineloy Rey, Frank and Onalaima Istueta, Rigoberto and Carmen Martínez and their daughter Frances, Raúl Domínguez, Orlando and Miriam Muñiz, Roberto Luis Núñez, and Néstor Gómez, for example. In addition, Ramón Castro Ruz was a source of information on the prerevolutionary church in Oriente. He and his wife, Alicia, are to be commended for their support, and their generosity and friendship are much appreciated. A special debt of gratitude is owed to Israel Echeverría of the Biblioteca Nacional "José Martí" for suggestions, advice, and aid at the library in the field trips of 1984 and 1985.

In North America, many colleagues have been helpful as the various drafts of this study have appeared. Among these, special recognition should be accorded Lou Pérez of the University of South Florida for invaluable suggestions and a valued friendship, and Meg Crahan of Occidental College, who provided useful advice. Jordan Bishop of the College of Cape Breton drew upon his many years as a priest in Latin America to offer some useful comments on theological matters.

"Infrastructure" for the project came in various shapes and sizes. Funding from the Social Sciences and Humanities Research Council of Canada (SSHRC) followed a seed grant from the Canadian Association of Latin American and Caribbean Studies (CALACS). Library materials in North America were provided by the helpful librarians at the Atlantic School of Theology and the Inter-Library Loan Office at Dalhousie University. Typing was undertaken by Wanda Hebb and Pat LaMoyne in a smooth and efficient manner. Finally, my wife, Margo, and children Lisa, Michael, and Emily put up with me when I was buried under mounds of pastoral letters, political analyses, and church documents. To all, my respect and gratitude.

The material is of course both controversial and provocative, and flies in the face of my mother and father's counsel not to talk about religion or politics (and here they're both covered). For better or worse I take full responsibility for the interpretation encountered here (as well as for the translations from Spanish, undertaken to furnish a wider understanding for English-speaking readers). As the church-state rapprochement continues, slowly but steadily, in revolutionary Cuba, I hope that it will provide some room for thought and challenge people from all ideological perspectives to reevaluate their interpretations.

Introduction

Consider the relationship of religion and politics in modern Latin America, and far from peaceful images are likely to spring to mind: the Vatican's ongoing struggle with the concept of liberation theology and its exponents such as Leonardo Boff and Gustavo Gutiérrez; the tense standoff in Nicaragua, where priests such as Fernando and Ernesto Cardenal, Miguel d'Escoto, Uriel Molina, and many others are engaged in an increasingly bitter polemic with the country's hierarchy, personified in the leadership of Cardinal Obando y Bravo; the recent courageous stand in the face of martial law of (now retired) Cardinal Silva in Chile, reminiscent of actions of church leaders in Poland and in the Philippines under the Marcos regime; the phenomenon of "guerrilla priests" in revolutionary Central America as well as in conservative areas of South America. In Brazil's harsh Northeast or on Colombia's rich coffee-growing slopes, in Managua's Barrio Riguero or Mexico City's sprawling slums, controversy continues over the relative influence of religion and politics.

If one were asked to list Latin American countries where the debate over the proper relationship between religion and politics rages the hottest, many names would tumble out automatically: all of Central America except Costa Rica and perhaps Panama, as well as Brazil, Pinochet's Chile, Colombia, and Mexico. Missing from anyone's list, though, would be Cuba. Whatever else one can say about the church in revolutionary Cuba, in matters of ecclesiastical or political importance it is scarcely a pacesetter—hence the benign neglect.

There are many reasons for this neglect. The Cuban church has never been particularly strong. Because the revolution preceded the momentous Second Vatican Council (1962–65), neither the Cuban church nor Cuba's revolutionary government came to terms with the changes stemming from the papacies of John XXIII and Paul VI. The church's urban-centered activities, in particular its many and highly respected private schools catering to the urban middle class, had little impact on Cuba's populace at large. Bitter disputes arose in the wake of radical social policies adopted by the revolutionary government. The ensuing antagonistic diplomatic relations with the United States and Cuba's economic dependence on the Soviet bloc led to embittered relations, mutual recriminations, and actual hostilities. Compound this historical background with media misinformation, and it is no wonder that many Christians visiting Cuba are amazed to discover any vestiges of organized religion at all.

While there is every reason to imagine that in contrast to its traditional posture in Latin America the church in Cuba will continue to lack in popular support and to exert little political influence, such a view fails to recognize some important political currents at play in revolutionary Cuba. Too often scholars have been fascinated with the more dramatic examples of Nicaragua's Ernesto Cardenal, Brazil's lively Dom Helder Camara or Cardinal Arns, Colombia's Camilo Torres, or El Salvador's Oscar Romero; their research has usually concentrated on the areas where these and other eminent church representatives have become embroiled in dangerous struggles to harness their religious beliefs to the service of Latin America's long-suffering population. Cuba by comparison is a sluggish backwater, offering little to the scholar pursuing the tangle of political and religious life. As a result, the extensive discussions of the church in Latin America have for the most part neglected the church in contemporary Cuba.

Nevertheless the church in Cuba invites our attention, both from a historical perspective (much of the tension present in revolutionary Nicaragua existed around similar issues in Cuba during the early 1960s) and from that of the rapprochement between church and government leaders in the mid-1980s. This book seeks to fill some of the gaps in our knowledge of the church in the last three decades.

Trying to piece together a solid analysis of the church in revolutionary Cuba reminds one of the schizophrenic nature of *lo real maravilloso*, the blend of the fantastic and the real that the late Cuban writer Alejo Carpentier employed so successfully.[1] Examples abound: The Partido Comunista de Cuba (PCC) maintains that organized religion, by its very nature, is out of place in communist society and will in time disappear totally—yet every year more than a hundred thousand persons make a pilgrimage to Saint Lázaro's shrine on his saint's day to request favors, and almost 60 percent of all funerals at Havana's Colón Cemetery are preceded by a religious ceremony. Fidel Castro has been painted by his detractors as a fiery, dogmatic Marxist-Leninist for the last thirty years, yet his position on the role of religion (indeed on the contribution of religion) has been remarkably consistent, and welcoming, since long *before* the development of liberation theology. All the older leaders of the PCC (including Fidel, educated at the prestigious Jesuit college Belén in Havana) received their education at private Catholic schools, while most of the Catholic hierarchy attended state schools. Finally, in a country with, it is often thought, a total disinterest in organized religion, people have recently lined up in the thousands to buy the latest best-seller, *Fidel y la religión* by Brazilian cleric Frei Betto (by early 1988, more than a million copies had been sold). Any one of these phenomena is worthy of detailed attention; together they present a fascinating paradox to the student of modern-day Cuban affairs and the role of the church in Latin America. Just what *is* happening to religion in revolutionary Cuba? This study contributes one interpretation of these phenomena that are unparalleled in Latin American history.

Despite the best intentions to report objectively, this book will undoubtedly be viewed as controversial. On the one hand this result stems from the very nature of the material—in a work on any political aspect of contemporary Cuba, one may claim with some certainty that it is impossible not to present what others will see as a biased view. On the other hand, the rise of religious fundamentalism and of polarization within the Christian church—especially the Catholic church of Latin America—adds to the polemical nature of this topic. Contributing to this debate are diverse elements such as the swing toward political conservatism in North America, the difficulty many exiles have in looking objectively or dispassionately on events in the *patria*, and the advantages, and disadvantages, of the author's geographical and temporal distance from the events described. It is hoped, though, that the book will be received in the spirit in which it is written, one of respect for the Christian faith and its difficult passage—the fault of government and church alike—in Latin America's first socialist revolution. Now is not the time for reminiscing about what might have been in Batista's Cuba and before John XXIII's modernizing bombshells: rather, what is appropriate to study is the painful development of the Cuban church as it has sought to join the mainstream of the post–Vatican II church.

The work proper is divided into two sections. In the first the origins of the church in Cuba are described; in the second the focus is on specific developments in clearly defined periods of the revolutionary process. In the first part (chapters 1 and 2) the role of the church in colonial

Cuba and during the first sixty years of "independence" (i.e., up to
1959) is studied; its thesis is that the church, with the notable exception of the "golden century" of 1750–1850, was generally out of the
mainstream of colonial life. Indeed, in many ways the lack of solid missionary work that is a constant throughout most of evangelical life in
Cuba can be traced directly from this period. This generally unflatter-
ing portrayal (with several notable exceptions, indicated in the book)
is continued in the second chapter.

Two great revolutionary struggles would influence Cuba's subsequent development. Chapter 2, which deals with the church's role
from 1898 to 1959, examines the role of the church on the verge of
both those sweeping social movements and shows that—again with
some exceptional clerics playing a major role—the mainstream church
in both cases simply misread the historical epoch, or at least opted for
the "comfortable pew" in the face of the unknown. Seeking to protect
its own respectability and modest wealth, the church wanted to maintain the sociopolitical status quo; it tried to remain above the political
realm, while in fact its positions reinforced the existing government.
In sum, at these two moments of fundamental social change, the
church gambled—and lost, badly.

The first part of the book attempts to prepare the reader for the central case history of the church in revolutionary Cuba, which forms the
bulk of the work. Armed with an understanding of the often inglorious
origins of the church's role, the reader may better appreciate the dynamics at play within church and political circles as the Batista dictatorship was overthrown.

The second part of the book is a historical account of precisely how
the relationship between the church and the revolutionary government unfolded over the next quarter century. With extensive reference
to periodical literature and church documents, this central sector examines the stormy relationship of religion and politics against the
background of a rapidly polarizing society. It examines the church's
response to this unusual historical phenomenon—Latin America's
first socialist revolution—and also studies the revolutionary government's often repressive and generally critical approach to the religious
phenomenon. One of the conclusions posited concerns the lack of pre-
paredness shown by each "hierarchy" to understand the views of the
other.

Other themes examined in this section are the basis of the church's
support, the positions taken by the hierarchy over this period of almost
three decades, the church's search for an identity in a country where
it was never popularly acclaimed and its subsequent existence on the
margins of society, the division between the clergy (often along Cuban-

Spanish lines) over the "social question," and the strategies adopted by the church to find a niche in Cuban society. Finally, as indicated in chapter 7, important developments have been brewing in Cuba since the mid-1980s. Given the political and religious instincts of Fidel Castro and John Paul II and the general polarization of religious life throughout Latin America, these developments may well produce not only a historic rapprochement but also a model for constructive engagement in the Americas.

While not exhaustive, this work constitutes a useful comparison if studied in conjunction with recent works by Cuban exiles (in particular, see the bibliography for the studies by former Acción Católica director Manuel Fernández and those of Pablo M. Alfonso and Juan Clark), with Hageman and Wheaton's important critical anthology, as well as with studies by Mateo Jover Marimón, Celso Montero Rodríguez, Manuel P. Maza, Walfredo Piñera Corrales, Raúl Gómez Treto, or Margaret E. Crahan. This work is intended in some ways to represent an updating of the landmark study of another Canadian scholar, Leslie Dewart's *Christianity and Revolution: The Lesson of Cuba* (1963).

A note on this book's focus may be in order: while concentrating on the Catholic church for obvious historical reasons, where appropriate the study touches upon aspects of the Protestant church's development. (Readers are encouraged to consult Margaret E. Crahan's many thoughtful works for a more detailed study of Protestantism in Cuba.) Taking note of pertinent similarities and differences between the two, it is hoped, will add a dimension to the reader's perception of the Catholic church—generally referred to as "the church."

This study has grown out of a desire to fill a void in the study of Cuban history. Historians in contemporary Cuba have traditionally tended to play down the importance of the church's role in their national culture while their colleagues abroad concentrate on countries where that role has been more dramatic. My contention is that the study of the controversial relationship of Cuban revolutionary and religious politics, set in the midst of the development of Latin America's first Marxist-Leninist government, has all the fascination of Carpentier's *lo real maravilloso*—heady stuff, indeed.

One

1

The Colonial Period,

1492–1898

I do not know a land . . . called Christian which is so utterly lost, laymen and clergy alike.

Francisco Calvillo y Avellaneda,

pious resident of Bayamo in the 1570s

Throughout colonial times, the Catholic Church would be the legitimizer of the Spanish administration and its policies. The church would bless the destruction of the Indian customs which were sensed to be contrary to Catholic faith. The church would approve the repartimientos *and the* encomiendas, *and in general it would sustain ideologically the Spanish conquest as something providential, a manifest destiny that the divinity had bestowed on the Catholic kings after the conquest of Granada.*

Manuel P. Maza,

"The Cuban Catholic Church:
True Struggles and False Dilemmas"

Whatever else one may think about the history of the church in Cuba during the colonial period, it can hardly be called dull. Encompassing close to four centuries, this period contained numerous developments and crises, along with accompanying tragedies and triumphs more in keeping with television melodrama than with ecclesiastical history. Yet many of these events would directly reflect upon later developments in revolutionary Cuba, particularly with respect to the role played by the church in its relationship with the government of Fidel Castro, and the church's resistance to sweeping social reform. Consequently, if we are to understand fully the position of the church in the revolutionary period, we need to appreciate the crucible in which the church's value system was cast.

Some of these fundamental events revolved around traditional areas of concern, such as the sometimes conflicting roles of the Spanish Crown and the Holy See, or local rivalries between church hierarchy and priests. There were, however, several bizarre developments which would not be out of place in the novels by practitioners of "lo real maravilloso." Fray Bernardo de Mesa, named bishop of Cuba in 1516, for instance, justified the slavery of Indians on the basis of Cuba's geographical situation and lunar cycles.[1] The tenure of Bishop Espada (1802–32) was also a time of great consternation: while progressive church people praised his modernizing influence, others such as Msgr. Pío Bighi, secretary of the Sacred Congregation for Extraordinary Ecclesiastical Affairs, referred to him as a wolf who devastated his diocese "instead of governing it like a Father, debilitated it instead of ministering to his charges, more a seducer of morals than an example of virtuous works."[2] Later in that century, the military imposition of Pedro Llorente as archbishop of Santiago without approval from Rome, and his subsequent excommunion, recalled a similar schism in the 1840s.[3]

Despite these extraordinary incidents, however, the church in Cuba developed roughly along the lines encountered elsewhere in Spanish America. The church was of course a major colonizing agent, whose personnel were appointed by the Spanish Crown and whose policies were intended to dovetail with the rapid conquest and settlement by Spanish forces. The church stuck resolutely to its mission, religiously (in the literal and figurative senses of the word) defending Spanish interests and the status quo, even when it became obvious—particularly after the wars of independence broke out on mainland Latin America between 1810 and 1820—that the tides of history were coursing swiftly in a radically different direction.

This deliberate disregard for historical trends and the firm support of the *madre patria*, Spain, in the face of rapidly changing circumstances can be interpreted as the hallmark of the Catholic church in Cuba. Consistently, the church realized too late that the evolving historical reality demanded a more sensitive, and more localized, appreciation and consequently watched the slow ebbing of what moral authority it had. The tragedy of the church during this period is that it sought to perpetuate its role by clinging to a set of rules designed in Madrid for the benefit of the Spanish colonial structure, at the same time punishing or neglecting its only potential source of spiritual and moral regeneration, as well as of temporal power, the outspoken and often nationalistic Cuban churchmen who sought to make their church move with the times.

Forging an Identity: The First Two Centuries

The issue of Cuba's indigenous people illustrates that, with a few exceptions such as Father Las Casas and Antonio de Montesinos, the church in Cuba deliberately ignored the moral questions inherent in the legalized slavery of the native people through Spain's *encomienda* system, largely because—as was the case throughout Latin America—raising such questions would have threatened their temporal interests. Writing in 1938, Juan Martín Leiseca excused this ecclesiastical conduct, claiming that slavery was in fact "an age-old crime which humanity has to bear on its back. That stain had long permeated the environment." While many ecclesiastics did ignore the moral dimension of this question, he noted, they persevered nonetheless in their "work of indoctrination, profoundly interested in the eternal salvation of those souls.'"[4] A more dispassionate approach offers a somewhat different view.

In *The Spanish Struggle for Justice in the Conquest of America*, Lewis Hanke emphasizes the concern of both the Crown and the church to define in legal terms their rights and obligations regarding the peoples and riches of the New World.[5] He stresses the hostility that arose between the well-meaning clergy and the *reyes católicos* (Catholic monarchy) on the one hand and the settlers on the other, between the demands upon the *encomenderos* of the 1512 Laws of Burgos for housing, for religious instruction, and for respect for the Indians on the one hand, and the settlers' goals of wealth and power on the other.[6] Clerical spokesmen, including Las Casas, "Protector of the Indians," and Montesinos, quickly realized that their cause was hopeless. The geographical distances between settlements and difficulties in communicating with Spain, the ultralegalistic and imperialistic concerns of the Crown, and the greed of the Spanish settlers combined to still their opposition. The conspiracy of silence that they joined led to the total destruction of the native peoples within forty years.[7] The reasons for this conspiracy of silence shed interesting light on the conduct of church spokesmen. Both Crown and church wrestled with moral concerns and monetary gains and in the end subordinated the former to the latter, although they continued to grapple with legalistic formulas (at times sincere, especially in the case of Queen Isabel) with which to justify their eventual conduct. In his subsequent transcript of the entry of 11 November 1492 in the diary of Columbus's first journey, Las Casas noted the two of the explorer's suggestions regarding the ingenuous natives:

> And so Your Highnesses should decide to make them Christian, since I believe that if you initiate this process, you will soon succeed in converting a multitude of peoples to our Holy Faith. Moreover, in so doing you will acquire vast domains and riches, all to fall under the dominion of Spain—since without doubt there are immense sums of gold in these lands.[8]

Unfortunately for the Indians, these "immense sums of gold" carried the day, not only because Spain badly needed these funds but also because their potential protector, the church, rapidly realized where its vested interests lay and in essence ignored the Indians' plight. To a large degree this should not be surprising if one remembers that the church representatives were paid not by their congregation or even Rome but by the Spanish Crown. Fernando V had reached an understanding with Pope Alexander VI according to which a tax of colonists' profits (the *diezmo*) was collected by the Crown and then transferred for the maintenance of the church in the colonies. (Later Fernando obtained from Alexander's successor, Pope Julio II, the right to nominate and appoint bishops in dioceses of the colonies.) This system of *Patronato* guaranteed the Crown domination of church activities, since it controlled the funds for their development and also had the right to appoint bishops, who would of course be expected to comply with recommendations from Madrid. Royal authority thus held sway, dramatically, over moral concerns, and in general the church in Cuba—particularly for the first century of its foundation—adhered closely to its expected role as respectful servant of the Crown. Father Las Casas and his supporters notwithstanding, the social conscience of the church was skillfully anesthetized.

The first century of the church's existence in Cuba was inauspicious. The country was large, communication was difficult, and the population was comparatively small and scattered. By 1608, almost a century after Cuba was discovered, its population was only about 20,000. It rose to 30,000 by 1622 and 50,000 by 1700—still only one inhabitant per two square kilometers.[9] Lacking the gold and silver found in Mexico and South America, Cuba was rapidly relegated to backwater status, a place for the fleet to rest and take on provisions before continuing in search of fortune in the Aztec and Inca empires. The resultant lackluster quality of church representatives who arrived in Cuba, and the general dearth of interest in the country shown by Madrid, failed to stir up any meaningful activity. The backwater soon became stagnant.

Early references to ecclesiastical life are rare, although it is known from a letter to Diego Colón from the king on 25 July 1511 that Diego Velázquez had taken four friars along on his expedition to conquer Cuba.[10] In 1516, Fray Bernardo de Mesa was named bishop of Cuba and the bishopric was established, but Mesa resigned the position that same year; his successor, a Flemish priest, Fray Juan de Wite, resigned in 1525 without even having traveled to his diocese. This extremely shaky foundation and, more important, the apparent lack of interest in firmly establishing a diocese in a clearly strategic locale augured ill for the development of the church in Cuba.

Equally detrimental to the nascent church, bickering and rivalry emerged, both between church and government representatives and among churchpeople. Quarrels in the first category generally sprang from the administration of the diezmos, the tithes that many colonial administrators were loathe to pass along to their church colleagues. Graft and corruption were widespread, and many colonial administrators, having been obliged to purchase their offices in Spain, were keen not only to recoup their initial investment as expeditiously as possible but also to turn a handsome profit. The clergy, few in number and widely scattered, offered a tempting target for abuse, and the resultant expropriation of funds intended for the maintenance of clergy and church institutions, as well as for hospitals and schools, was widespread.

More debilitating from the church's perspective, friction abounded within Mother Church, the beginnings of a tradition sustained throughout Cuban ecclesiastical history with a steady stream of invective among dioceses, bishops, and regular clergy. Ismael Testé, for instance, quotes from a letter written in 1522 by Fray Francisco de Avila of the Franciscan order to the Spanish emperor to complain about the local bishop, "who after he came here, was so distressed at both our presence and construction of the monastery I have mentioned, that he desired to completely thwart it—in this way showing, both by word and through all the means at his disposal, how he wanted to make us depart from the Island."[11] Some thirty years later, to take one of many examples, a strong rivalry developed in Havana between the Dominicans and the Jesuits over "territorial rights," since there was only a limited number of souls to whom Catholicism could cater. Irene Aloha Wright has commented with some insight on the disturbing scenario presented by this confusing religious rivalry:

> There was friction between the heads of both monasteries [Jesuit and Dominican] and the bishop, who in selecting incumbents for church offices through the island preferred, they said, "vagabond, apostate" priests; he for his part lamented that the existence of these two monasteries cut down the incomes of his subordinates, for the people could give only so much to religion and it was inconvenient to share it among too many. The governor, at odds with the bishop and by him excommunicated, believed that the guardians of the monasteries should enjoy something of the authority of a court of appeal against such excommunication, since appeal to the bishop's superior, the archbishop of Santo Domingo, was a lengthy procedure.[12]

Throughout the sixteenth and seventeenth centuries, the situation of the church in Cuba was precarious as the discovery of ever-greater riches on the Latin American mainland matched a corresponding drop in church fortunes in Cuba. Cuba's leading churchman at the time, Bishop Diego Sarmiento (1538–45), did modern historians an enormous service when he undertook a pastoral visit of his diocese in 1544, and his extensive report in the form of a letter to the Spanish emperor, dated 25 July of that year, provides an invaluable look at the poverty of the Cuban church.

The situation in regard to personnel was particularly bleak: three priests assisted the cathedral in Santiago de Cuba, in addition to a sacristan and two choir assistants, while other religious services were provided by the nearby Franciscan monastery, where three or four religious lived; in Bayamo two clerics tended the spiritual needs of some "thirty inhabitants married, or soon to be so. In addition there were about four hundred natives [*indios naborias*] with very little interest in matters of the faith." In Puerto del Príncipe the bishop noted the presence of fourteen settlers as well as "235 Indians granted [*encomendados*] to the settlers," who "would be lost, together with the Spanish, if the natives were to be freed," and 160 black and Indian slaves from the Yucatán—all attended by a cleric. Trinidad had been abandoned, and La Zavana with ten settlers had a chaplain; Sancti Spiritus boasted "18 residents, all of whom were married; 58 natives granted to the other inhabitants, 14 blacks and 50 Indian slaves," as well as a chaplain who had been in Cuba for twenty years. Even in Havana there were only 40 Spanish settlers, 120 free Indians, 200 slaves, and a priest and a sacristan. (Bishop Sarmiento closes his letter on an ominous note, explaining that he will shortly return to Spain to give an oral account of his report and promising, "In addition I will provide a response to the calumnies raised against me," setting the scene for increasing tension in Cuba between church and political authorities.)[13]

To worsen an already bad situation, according to Irene Aloha Wright, in the period 1492 to 1586, "there was no moral, corrective force in the clergy; with few individual exceptions the clergy of Cuba through all the period under consideration was ignorant, venal, and licentious."[14] By comparison with the areas previously dominated by the Aztecs and Incas, where church penetration had been swift and lucrative, within two decades of the conquest of Tenochtitlán, center of the Aztec empire, Cuba had been relegated to a position of inferiority in the context of Spanish colonial interests. Had there been larger numbers of "infidel" to convert, and more financial rewards to be reaped, church history in Cuba would undoubtedly have taken a different course.

Still the Cuban church limped along. Nearly twenty-five years after Bishop Sarmiento's report, despite an influx of Spaniards, Bishop Juan del Castillo after an exhausting eight-month tour of his diocese painted a similarly grim picture in 1570: "No church held an apostolic bull, royal letter patent [*cédula real*], nor indeed any source of income other than the tithes [*diezmos*], diminished and badly collected. In addition, in no church was there a register for baptisms, confirmations or weddings. At the church in Santiago, the tithes had not been granted since 1561."[15] To illustrate the irrelevance accorded the Cuban church and the undesirability of an episcopal posting to it, when Bishop Castillo's resignation was accepted in 1580, the colony had to wait twelve years for a successor to be appointed.

At the turn of the seventeenth century, then, the church in Cuba had spread Catholicism to several towns and had made an effort to convert the local Indians, but it was widely seen by Spanish settlers as an impediment to their acquisition of greater wealth. The settlers' indifference made the church's fortunes precarious. Church leaders, who disliked residing in Santiago de Cuba, constantly went to Havana on the slightest pretext, ignoring the spiritual needs of their faithful. The cathedral itself was badly in need of repair and possessed only one small bell for all services.

For roughly the next century, until the 1687 arrival of Bishop Diego Evelino de Compostela, who remained in Cuba for eighteen years, the church there hovered on the brink of disaster. Raids by European pirates, indirection among clerics (many of whom were only barely tolerated by civilian administrators), earthquakes and hurricanes which destroyed Cuba's early wood and *guano* churches, indifference on the part of the Vatican and the Crown, and a set of mediocre church administrators (church records were only initiated in Havana in 1590) all threatened its precarious balance. A burgeoning rivalry between eastern and western Cuba made matters worse. At least two bishops, Bernardino de Villalpando (1561–64) and Juan de las Cabezas Altamipano (1603–11), favored Havana in the west over Santiago de Cuba as the center for the diocese but had little success in persuading the Crown to uphold their position. Finally, Fray Alonso Enríquez de Toledo y Armendáriz (1612–24) made the unilateral decision to move the see to Havana without permission from Madrid or Rome—only to have a royal decree of 1613 force him to turn to Santiago.

The tenure of Fray Alonso Enríquez de Toledo y Armendáriz, named bishop of Cuba in 1611, illustrates the church's situation in microcosm. It had become so bad that, according to one church historian, when the prelate took up his posting there was not even oil to keep the sacramental lamp alight.[16] In the bishop's favor, he did undertake another pastoral visit of his diocese, but he soon took up the traditional rivalry with the Franciscans, fearful perhaps of their influence in Havana. Criticizing them for having left Florida, he noted that they were "not only useless in their convent, but also caused a great deal of scandal in the republic."[17] Moreover, the bishop rapidly fell into disfavor with the civil authorities, in particular Governor Ruíz de Pereda. When the bishop authorized the construction of the convent of San Agustín the governor forbade it, pending a decision on a building permit from the Patronato—a decision that remained pending until 1633. The bishop excommunicated Governor Pereda, then relented, only to excommunicate him again in the wake of a further clash. The governor responded by suspending payments due to the bishopric.

Throughout its history, the development of the Cuban church has been tied closely to the figure of its bishop. Thus, a prelate who supported church interests or built a solid relationship with civil authorities usually prepared the terrain for noticeable progress. Unfortunately, particularly during the first two centuries of Catholicism in Cuba, such bishops were the exception. One such prelate was Bishop Compostela (1687–1704), who showed that, with dynamic guidance and some luck, the church could play a relevant, important role in colonial life.

Luck is important in this equation, since it allowed the bishop to undertake a radical restructuring of church activities. The luck was the happy combination of a notable increase in Spanish immigration, a more benign political administration, and a less contentious prelate. Taking advantage of the wave of Spanish immigrants, the bishop consolidated the church's fortunes by creating some thirty parishes by 1688, carving a distinctive image of the church in colonial society.

One facet of this invigorated church was a deliberate attempt to revamp socially oriented programs, particularly in education. At this time the colonial government took little interest in health care, education, or orphanages, and the church had undertaken to provide such services where circumstances allowed. Unfortunately for the destitute population, the church's haphazard program had produced generally disappointing results. Bishop Compostela changed both program and results dramatically. One of his first actions was to encourage and coordinate efforts in Cuba to provide homes for orphaned children. Emerging triumphant from this campaign, he concentrated his efforts on developing education facilities and encouraging native vocations. In both these aims he was extremely successful, prompting the church to pursue fresh objectives with renewed vigor.

Bishop Compostela saw these goals as both politically strategic and theologically sound. The Colegio San Francisco de Sales, founded in 1688, that of the Bethlehemite Fathers for poor children in Havana, and the San Ambrosio seminary (1689) improved the profile of the Cuban church and at the same time encouraged young Cubans to pursue religious vocations. The result of these enlightened policies can be gauged by comparing the figures of barely a century earlier with those of 1689, when there were 225 secular clerics registered (the majority of whom were Cuban), as well as 204 religious and 100 sisters—figures that would increase in the eighteenth century.[18] Nearly all these religious were situated in the cities—where there were of course more people to tend to but also where larger donations assured the upkeep of churches and clergy. This trend would persist throughout Cuban history—much to the detriment of the church.

Until the middle of the nineteenth century, the church continued to prosper, ultimately catching up to mainland Latin America and asserting itself as a pillar of the community. The field of education represented an obvious avenue down which the church might pursue this image, a goal sought with particular sensitivity by Bishop Gerónimo Valdés (1705–29) and Bishop Pedro Agustín Morell de Santa Cruz (1753–68). During Valdés's tenure the Royal and Pontifical University of San Jerónimo de la Habana was inaugurated in 1724 and assigned to the Dominican order. Given the lack of secular public schools, the church—teaching as it did the children of Spanish settlers as well as those of the government bureaucracy—thus carved out a respectable niche for itself and swelled the ranks of prospective clergy.

The Golden Age, 1750–1850

In his multivolume *Historia eclesiástica de Cuba,* Ismael Testé refers
to the period 1750–1850 as "the golden years of priestly vocations."[19]
Maza confirms this, noting that "towards the end of Morell's episcopal
ministry there were 90 churches in Cuba, about half of them headed
by native Cuban priests. In Havana lived 118 Franciscans, 59 Dominicans, 55 Augustinians, 39 *Hospitalarios,* 32 Mercedarians, 20 Beth-
lehemites, and 9 of the Oratory. Among the religious women, there
were 108 of Saint Claire, 27 *catalinas,* 21 Carmelites and some 45
cofradías and lay associations."[20] At least in the urban centers, the
Cuban church had finally established itself.

Another reason for the rapid popular acceptance of the church in the
second half of the eighteenth century was the people's perception of
its prelates as patriotic. This characteristic was particularly admired
by the population of Havana in the wake of the seizure of that city by
British forces in 1762 and 1763. Bishop Morell de Santa Cruz would
not be cowed by the British presence, refusing them—in vain—the use
of a local church for Protestant services, and upon his return from exile
in Florida he was well received by the people of Havana. Ironically,
prior to Morell's deportation, the relationship between bishop and governor was again so poor that, when the British took Havana, Governor
Prado issued an order for all religious to leave the city for the safer con-
fines of the interior, apparently considering them more a hindrance
than a help.[21]

When Bishop Santiago José de Hechavarría replaced Morell de Santa
Cruz upon the latter's death in 1768, a milestone in church history
was reached in Cuba. After 250 years, he was the first native-born clergyman to be appointed bishop and one of only a few Cubans to bear
the miter during the colonial period. At a time of great economic
growth in Cuba, following a popular and celebrated prelate,
Hechavarría took office at the same time as a reasonably progressive
Spanish governor, Felipe de Fonsdeviela, Marqués de la Torre. With the
inauguration in 1774 of the highly respected Colegio Seminario San
Carlos y San Ambrosio, the bishop enhanced the respectability and
popular acceptance already achieved by the church.

San Carlos y San Ambrosio (still functioning actively in Old Havana)
was crucial to the development of the church in Cuba. Both a college
and a seminary, the school rapidly developed a reputation as the best
in Cuba. Through its doors passed the children of the elite of colonial
society, who ironically once in its classrooms developed a powerful
sense of nationalism, an awareness of the dignity of Cuba as more

than an appendage of the Spanish empire. (Indeed the school's role in nation building deserves more extensive research than has yet been realized.)

Three members of the school were largely responsible for the development of its nationalistic image: José Agustín Caballero, one of the school's students when it opened in 1774 and later professor of philosophy there; Félix Varela y Morales; and José de la Luz y Caballero, about whom the great Cuban writer-revolutionary José Martí would say, "He was a true *maestro* who in just one generation transformed a people, brought up as slaves, into a nation of heroes, industrious and free. . . . He had learned all that was known during his epoch: not to show that he knew it, but rather to transmit it to his students. In sum, he sowed men."[22]

José Agustín Caballero blazed the trail for his illustrious colleagues, in 1791 terming slavery "the greatest civil evil committed by men,"[23] developing social awareness among his students, and revealing how philosophy offered the tools for social analysis—radical views in a rigid Spanish colony not known for its liberalism. As did Varela and José de la Luz, Father Caballero tried to direct the Cuban church on a prophetic and eminently relevant course, defending the rights of the weak against the abuses of colonial life. While they were successful in raising the consciousness of many, the church as a whole was little affected by their teachings. The church was progressing but, given its newfound respectability, was wary of criticizing the norms of colonial life and thereby setting itself up as a target for the political administration.

Caballero was succeeded in the chair of philosophy by Félix Varela y Morales in 1811, who brought a further modernizing influence to bear upon the elite of young Havana society. The importance of these men should not be underestimated: at times there were 600 students at the Colegio Seminario, most of whom took courses in law and philosophy. Varela, aided by the controversial (and essentially liberal) Bishop Espada of Havana, revolutionized the curriculum, abolishing the use of Latin in philosophy courses, dropping many of the classical tenets that had traditionally formed the backbone of the college's teaching, and introducing the study of chemistry and physics. In 1821 he also instituted the "Chair in Constitutional Matters" (*Cátedra de Constitución*), renamed by him the "Chair in Liberty and the Rights of Man" (*Cátedra de la libertad y de los derechos del Hombre*), preaching in the classes the right of self-determination and sovereignty.

Varela combined skillfully the roles of priest and politician, and, although many of his Spanish colleagues must have found his ideas bordering on sedition, his contribution to the formation of a Cuban *conciencia*, or awareness and commitment, brought respect for the church from nationalist sectors. This change became evident following Varela's brief tenure as a Cuban representative at the Spanish Cortes, or parliament, where he presented two bills, one calling for the abolition of slavery, the other for an autonomous form of government. Such ideas were so poorly received in Spain, particularly in light of the loss of her mainland Latin American colonies, that Varela had to flee Spain after the Cortes was dissolved by Fernando VII and Varela was condemned to death. In exile in the United States, his political thought gradually radicalized, as his newspaper *El Habanero* reflected, yet his ideology remained predicated on his religious search for justice and freedom. With reason he was revered (in the fortuitous phrase of José de la Luz) as "the first person who taught us to really think."[24]

Of the three outstanding nationalists associated with San Carlos, José de la Luz is especially warmly treated by Martí, who shared many of the illustrious teacher's aims and aspirations. For Martí, Luz was the "loving father of the Cuban soul,"[25] a term that equally fits his two predecessors at San Carlos. Like them he saw all of Cuban society sharing a collective sin, slavery, which multiplied the inequities resulting from Cuba's colonial status. Accordingly he lost no opportunity to use his position at San Carlos y San Ambrosio to provide an education "conceived not simply as mere information, but rather as the very formation [of patriots]," to use Cuban poet Cintio Vitier's expression,[26] for the thousands of wealthy students passing through the school's doors.

While these three educators (and to a lesser extent prelates like Bishop Espada) represented the exception rather than the rule within the church sector, their influence and that of San Carlos as an institution for fifty years starting in the 1770s cannot be denied. The respectability of the Colegio Seminario and of Luz's college, El Salvador, provided them a certain immunity that allowed them to inculcate modern liberal ideas into the students, the youthful elite of Havana's colonial society. Their message was a volatile mix of nationalism, modern scientific approaches, and social awareness. Luz explained their goal when he said that "he couldn't in all conscience sit down to produce books—which it is easy to do—because he was devoured by a restless concern and a lack of time for the most difficult task, which is to produce men."[27] It is to their credit that these men, amid the arid scholasticism of the Spanish colonial era, undertook precisely that mission and had such an impact on the *concientización*, or consciousness-raising, of several generations of Cuban society.

One result of the prestige of San Carlos and of these respected teachers' work was a dramatic increase in the number of vocations. One historian has claimed that there were 700 secular and regular priests in Cuba by the late eighteenth century, and in Havana alone, with its 75,518 inhabitants, there were apparently thirty-three churches, ten convents, eight hospitals, two schools, a university, and a seminary.[28] Figures often deceive with their simplicity, however, and in his thoughtful dissertation Manuel P. Maza presents a different evaluation of the quality of church life, noting how "the credibility of the church was undermined by the outright ambitions of many of the pastoral agents, who received large sums of money through tithes and *capellanías* [chaplaincies]."[29] Still, while the church might not be particularly relevant as a dynamic social force, in urban centers it made its presence felt. Indeed, buoyed by increasing numbers of Spanish immigrants, the Vatican split the bishopric in 1787, creating the bishopric of Havana, which extended east to Camagüey, where that of Santiago de Cuba began. Less than twenty years later, in 1803, the diocese of Santiago was promoted to archdiocese, and the following year the bishop of that region was named the first archbishop of Santiago de Cuba.[30]

The Church and Slavery

To a large extent this impressive albeit somewhat superficial growth of the church was the result of a tremendous increase in Cuban sugar production which attracted large numbers of Spanish immigrants, who then needed priests to minister to their spiritual needs. The parallel between Cuban society and its church is instructive, for in spite of the outstanding growth in sugar production, little else was changing. Numerical indices constituted neither social nor religious progress.

Slavery was still the driving force of the Cuban economy, and still the vast majority of profits from the sugar mills were shipped back to the mother country. Nevertheless, the apparent progress in the colony was undeniable, particularly between 1760 and 1790 when increased mechanization and modern mass production techniques increased the sugar yield considerably. One scholar noted that where sugar mills previously employed only a handful of laborers, new mills started at this time "would soon employ well over a hundred," and that where the average sugar plantation in 1762 was about 320 acres (4 *caballerías*), in the 1790s it spread over some 700 acres.[31] In the first decades of the nineteenth century, this trend intensified, as Jorge Ibarra has pointed out. Manpower was provided by way of slaves, and between 1790 and 1820, Cuba imported approximately 227,000 African slaves. By 1841, at the peak of sugar production, the 436,500 slaves in Cuba represented 43.3 percent of the population.[32] The large number of slaves was due, of course, to the expanding sugar industry. The number of sugar mills rose from 400 in 1800 to about 1,000 in 1827 to 1,200 in 1840. The church, eager to retain its rapidly improving social position in a society that was finally in a "boom" phase, refrained from corporate criticism of slavery—criticism that would only alienate the faithful. It sought instead to accommodate.

Working and living conditions on the sugar plantations were nothing short of pathetic, as the church must have known: the average day was sixteen hours of grueling work, broken only for meals. In the *barracón*, or common dormitory, men and women workers, along with their children, lived in misery. Kept alive by landowners desirous of large profits, the slaves received minimal consideration. Even the farce of traditional spiritual teachings and comfort—the least one might expect of a concerned church—were often denied the slaves, and church officials were remarkably lax in evangelizing among them. José Agustín Caballero might rail against the abuses of slavery, but colonial society knew well that the wretched slaves, in Caballero's terms, were the "arms which prop up our riches, furnish our houses, supply our tables, fill our wardrobes, drive our carriages, and allow us to enjoy our abundant pleasures."[33] Little wonder, then, that slave rebellions averaged twelve per year between 1800 and 1820, rising to a total of 584 by 1850.[34] Meanwhile, the church in general took great pains to look the other way, keeping what the Reflexión Eclesial Cubana has termed "a silent complicity in the face of many colonial injustices."[35]

To see how superficial was the church's role at this time, one has only to look at its positions on slavery. Much has been made of the courageous stand taken by the three outstanding intellectuals of the seminary, Caballero, de la Luz, and Varela. Bishop Espada of Havana would continue this line, noting in a stern pastoral letter of 1826 that "slavery was in essence opposed to religion, nature, and indeed any sense of virtue." The slave traders, he added, were "criminals trafficking in human blood."[36] Yet these noble exhortations had minimal impact on the Catholic population, who, despite their bishop's admonitions, continued to hold slaves and exploit them. Although debates did take place concerning the responsibilities and duties of *hacendados* (landowners) to their slaves, and lip service was paid to improving the slaves' conditions, the crucial issue—the justification of the very existence of slavery—was in general conveniently ignored. The Spanish settlers thus participated in religious rituals but turned a deaf ear to the teaching of church leaders when it went against their economic self-interest. Business, after all, was business, and too much religion would only interfere with it.

In part because of church pressure a code was finally drawn up in 1842 (the "Reglamento de esclavos") which outlined owners' obligations toward slaves. On paper these recommendations reflect a sincere concern for the well-being of the slaves, calling for annual donations of clothes by the masters to their charges, special food for nursing mothers, and even child-care facilities. In practice, however, the *reglamentos* were ignored throughout Cuba.

Of particular importance were the first five articles—all dealing with religious matters—since they adhered, however superficially, to Catholicism. Not surprisingly given the religious rationale for the *Conquista,* the first article noted that "Every slaveowner shall instruct [slaves] in the basic principles of the Roman Catholic Apostolic Religion." The thrust of the second article was to explain that these religious classes were of course to be given "at night time, after the day's work has been concluded," after which "they will be made to say the rosary or some other pious prayers." The third article stated that slaves could be used for a maximum of two hours on Sundays and then only to clean, providing that they had met their religious obligations. Article four stipulated that slaveowners were to ensure that, as slaves reached the appropriate ages, "the holy sacraments be administered to them, either when Holy Mother Church has provided for them, or when it should prove necessary." The fifth article, quite unnecessary given the treatment to which slaves were subjected, stipulated that they must show "the necessary obedience to the constituted authorities, the obligatory reverence to priests, and respect for white settlers."[37] Unfortunately for the slaves these goals were almost universally subordinated to the profit motive of their masters and the greed of Madrid. The lobbying of a well-intentioned church minority thus had little impact on their living conditions, largely because "the church was losing its political authority at just the time when a new class of slaveowners had arisen, with less respect for the customary role of the church in society."[38]

It was a time of progress, of modernizing, and ethical questions were simply brushed aside to be discussed later, if at all. Moreover, the slave rebellion in neighboring Haiti in 1791, with its widespread slaughter of white settlers, had proved to many Spanish colonialists that the slaves were barbarians. The massive immigration of white families to Cuba in the wake of the slave uprising, and to a lesser extent that of 1793, after Spain ceded Santo Domingo to France, also contributed both to the apparent economic growth and to a population increase, from 172,620 in the 1774 census to 272,318 by 1795.[39] Yet beneath the burgeoning development of Havana and other cities, all this growth depended solidly on the monoculture sugar economy—which itself depended on slave labor. The abolition of slavery, many thought, in addition to increasing the danger of a massacre of white settlers, also made little business sense.

There are two schools of thought concerning the role of the church with regard to the slavery of the indigenous people and of the Africans brought by force to work in the plantations when many of the native slaves died. The "apologist view" admits that some abuses did take place and that some clergy did ignore the plight of the wretched slaves but claims that, for the most part, the church supported the slaves with spiritual solace and looked after their moral well-being. Typical of spokesmen for this view is Juan Martín Leiseca, who contrasts the church's concern for these unfortunates with that of colonial Spanish authorities, concluding that while "the adventurers of colonization sowed hate and cultivated oppression in all its most repugnant forms toward the wretched American race, [the priests] sowed love instead, consoling the sadness of the abused Indians, illuminated the darkness of their misfortune with the light of hope, and teaching them to love God, persuaded them to hope solely in His infinite goodness for relief of their suffering in the glory of life after death as heavenly recompense."[40]

Although there is a grain of truth to Leiseca's claims, particularly with relation to the early years of colonial sugar development, this interpretation of the church as a force for good on the plantation seems exaggerated. Until the end of the eighteenth century, before the massive sugar boom, the church did have some effect on slaves' lives. However, while this spiritual support sometimes came from a nearby parish, more often the upkeep of the chapel on the plantation and the priest's salary came out of the landlord's pocket. As the sugar industry developed at an astounding rate, even this limited influence vanished, for two reasons. First, the church hierarchy did not like either the relative autonomy of the plantation priests vis-à-vis the bishop or their failure to contribute, as did the regular parish priests, a fixed portion of their income to the prelate. Second, landlords dropped all pretense of trying to win the souls of their slaves: with profits to be made, the slaves' labor represented a means to that end. The result was that the church presence made little difference, for as Eduardo Machado noted in 1864 on the role of the church, "Your ceremonies serve only to stamp the seal of approval on our crimes."[41] While church representatives might not have liked his interpretation, he was right.

Machado's viewpoint reflects the second school of thought, which takes issue with the concept that heavenly rewards recompense the centuries of suffering imposed upon slaves, and which regrets the absence of clergy like Las Casas and Varela to condemn these practices. Representatives of this position accuse churchpeople of both a sin of omission in not condemning slavery and a sin of commission in taking advantage of it. Bishop Espada might fulminate in Havana against the inherent ills of slavery, yet his flock—and many of his fellow religious—profited handsomely from the system.[42]

Not only did clergy take advantage of the captive audience by charging slaves for baptismal, wedding, and burial services,[43] but the church itself owned many sugar mills. The monastery of Santa Clara, for example, owned no less than twenty, while "the Reverend Fathers of Belén [the Bethlehemites] owned the third most productive mill in the harvest of 1804."[44] Apparently, the seminary in Havana also owned two mills. In addition, as noted, many of the owners of the larger sugar mills built chapels on their property and contracted with priests to attend to the spiritual needs of their slaves. As salaried employees these priests would obviously not alienate their employers, instead maintaining by their respectful silence a church that "was a part of the system of slavery. It supported, reinforced, and reflected the status quo. It preached obedience to the white master among the slaves, and propagandized the then-present inequality and suffering as preparation for an equitable afterlife."[45] Finally, the church—with a few exceptions—came to provide such overt support for slavery "that slaves were announced in Church as to be sold 'on the following Sunday, during the celebration of Mass, before the church doors.' Priests were unable to instruct in anything slaves who worked up to twenty hours during the harvest."[46]

As the nineteenth century dawned, the church (in particular the Dominican and Franciscan orders) appeared to be in good shape. In the 1790s, a solid working relationship between church and government authorities, a fresh wave of French immigrants from Haiti and Louisiana, and a fairly stable economy contributed to a modest prosperity for the church. One scholar noted that "all the monastic houses (some 20) had enriched themselves extensively over many generations, owning sugar mills, cattle farms, slaves and large tracts of uncultivated land. (Enemies would calculate that the Dominicans, in about 1830, owned $25 million . . . and the Franciscans and Jesuits $20 million . . ., all in the prosperous west of Cuba.) The secular clergy on the other hand were poor and no one took much notice of them."[47] The church was finally one of the pillars of the community but a pillar that provided no moral or spiritual support to society. Instead it had become a bland, moralizing agency, raising few queries or doubts, preferring to bask in its newfound respectability. This was a position the church would seek to re-create when struggles for justice would break out in 1868–78, in 1895–98, and in 1956–59: all cases when, unprepared for the radical social changes desired by most of the population, the church would again cling to the status quo, prepared to seek mild reforms—but refusing to seek any major social restructuring.

Bishop Espada y Landa: A New and Controversial Approach, 1802–1832

One churchman willing to challenge the status quo was Juan José Díaz de Espada y Landa, bishop of Havana from 1802 to 1832. Although many of his actions were controversial, he saw his role as one of reviving the social awareness of his rather lax clerics. Accordingly he condemned the practice of slavery, criticized the extensive landholding patterns of the colony, and in general emphasized the need for a more modern, liberal approach by Havana's clergy. Needless to say, while he struck a responsive chord in Varela and José Agustín Caballero, the majority of Spanish clergy found Espada too radical. His views provoked dissent, and throughout his tenure constant bickering hindered his progress.

Espada was in many ways the perfect figure to wrest the Cuban church from its self-congratulatory comfort and modest prosperity and make it confront the challenges of the modern era. He pushed his church to respond to the dramatic changes in Europe, such as the wave of the French Revolution and, following the Napoleonic wars, the mood of liberalization in Spain that sought to limit the power of the church. In the support by church authorities of the Spanish forces over the insurgents, in the wars of independence on the South American mainland, Espada saw a grave strategic error—one which he hoped to see avoided by the Cuban church.

The problem with the views of Bishop Espada and his protégés at San Carlos was that they were simply too radical for this last conservative outpost of the Spanish empire. Proud of their Spanish roots, most Catholics still preferred their religion traditional, with prayer and contemplation rather than social action and swift change. Younger people might be inspired by Varela and José de la Luz, but the cement that held the colony together was an austere and grim *españolidad*, a love of things Spanish.

Despite his farsighted plans for the renovating and revitalizing of the church, Espada never fully overcame the deep-seated traditionalism of the people and of his fellow clerics. Unlike them he saw clearly why the wars of independence had taken place elsewhere in Latin America, and therefore he wanted to foment a more progressive interest in church reform. The inevitable clash with Spanish settlers and political administrators was not long in coming, due in part to Espada's brusque and stubborn manner and to a lack of understanding—or perhaps to a lack of desire to understand—on the part of many Spanish Catholics in Cuba.

Espada's many projects to move the church squarely into the Age of Reason, of benefit to the population at large, nevertheless brought widespread opposition in their wake. One example was his suggestion in 1804 to abolish the burial of Catholics in individual churches and instead to construct a cemetery in Havana. By 1806 the work was concluded,[48] and while most people agreed that the existence of a hygienic burial facility was an improvement, many clergy expressed their dismay—not only because this change broke centuries-old traditions of Christian burial but also because they would lose the high burial charges paid to the parish churches. Espada ignored these complaints, considering them petty squabbles typical of a medieval mentality, and urged towns throughout Cuba to build cemeteries outside the town centers.

Bishop Espada was unpopular within the church essentially because he represented a new questioning attitude, a radical approach to his ministry that his fellow clerics, steeped in the traditional, hierarchical structure of the Catholic church and its teachings of resignation and humility, were either unwilling or unable to accept. His expanded pastoral visit to the interior of his diocese in 1804, for instance, caused much dissatisfaction among the clergy because he used the opportunity to make people aware of a vaccine recently introduced in Havana by Dr. Tomás Romay. At his own expense, Espada financed a campaign to spread the news of this medical discovery and instructed his clergy to encourage their parishioners to take the vaccine. This novel behavior—in addition to Espada's heavy-handed instructions—surprised church members, who thought that, however beneficial the goal might be for the faithful, the church's mission lay in ministering to their souls, not their bodies.

The rivalries and petty squabbles that had developed among clergy in Cuba as early as the sixteenth century continued under Espada, to the obvious detriment of the development of the church. The struggle during Espada's tenure revolved around conflicting views of the role of the church held by a progressive minority on the one hand and by the majority of conservative Catholics on the other. This tension highlights one of the constants in Cuban church history, namely, the bitter rivalry among churchpeople. In Espada's case, ferocious opposition came from his fellow bishop Joaquín de Osés y Alzúa, who opposed the 1787 division of the Diocese of Cuba apparently because it affected adversely the economic interests of the Santiago diocese.[49] Osés claimed compensation from Bishop Espada as a result of the division but never received it; as a result he became Espada's outspoken foe.

The divisive nature of these bitter confrontations—quite commonplace in Cuban church history—was of course disquieting. Most disturbing about the Espada case, however, were its duration and the tactics used against him. That Osés continued the complaint with the ecclesiastical tribune of the Audencia in Puerto Príncipe (which decided in favor of Espada) and that Osés then pursued the matter through less formal channels, later denouncing Espada to the Spanish government and the Curia, reveals how deeply ran this particular confrontation. The forces opposed to Espada's thirty-year tenure never relented in their attacks, and as a result at one point Espada was nearly excommunicated.[50] One of his most outspoken foes in this campaign was the bishop of Cartagena, who lived in Havana after fleeing from the rebel forces on the South American mainland and who was determined to bring Espada down—perhaps to replace him as bishop of Havana. He criticized Espada's assistant, Don Francisco Castañeda, as a mason and libertine but saved his most scathing criticisms for the bishop, claiming that "he has been—and continues to be—an eminent constitutionalist and liberal (as indeed are all the individuals in his Curia). Together they took every step possible to develop the *infernal plans of modern institutions*" (emphasis added).[51]

Bishop Espada, perhaps with Pérez Serantes in the twentieth century the most memorable of all Cuban prelates, attempted to modernize the Cuban church despite itself, and his achievements were exceptional. José Martí would later describe Espada as "that Spanish bishop . . . whom all Cubans bear in our heart."[52] At the time of the wars of independence on the mainland, the imperial crisis in Spain (complete with the machinations of Napoleon and Fernando VII), and the struggle over liberal ideas, Bishop Espada's ideas were simply inappropriate for the Cuban context at that time. A bulwark of pro-Spanish values reinforced by clerics fleeing the struggles for independence, served by a conservative clergy with traditional values and a desire to maintain the status quo, Cuba would not accept easily the ideas of Varela, José de la Luz, or Espada. The bishop did leave a legacy that would be of considerable benefit as the nineteenth century progressed, one not only of added wealth and influence through its educational institutions but also of identity (both for the church as a leading social agent and a legacy of identity for the nascent Cuban nation). More than ever before, the church garnered for itself an aura of respectability and wielded extensive power. This newfound authority was to be short-lived, however, as events in Spain overtook the church both in the mother country and in the few remaining colonies—and the church would not recover it for decades.

The Liberal Backlash

The death of King Fernando VII in September 1833 led inevitably to a fresh outbreak of civil strife in Spain over who his successor would be; for the next seven years, struggles between *carlistas* and liberals shook the nation. In theory a contest between two aspirants to a form of absolute monarchy, in practice it became one between the principles of liberalism and of reaction. When a new liberal constitution was introduced in 1837, in the wake of a military revolt, attacks on the church soon followed. To finance the war against the carlistas, the new government helped itself to the church's extensive wealth. Church properties became "national wealth," used both to pay Spain's national debt and to guarantee foreign loans. In March 1836, all monastic property was assumed by the nation, and in July 1837 the government proposed the sale of all secular church property and the abolition of the diezmos.[53] Furthermore, the government forbade many priests to preach, imprisoned many others, and in general imposed its authority ruthlessly to bring the church swiftly to heel. This campaign occurred at a period of internal crisis in the Spanish church: the number of vocations was already dropping, the clergy was incapable of reacting to the traumatic effects of the wars for independence in Spanish America, and many orders were undergoing grave economic difficulties. Added to these difficulties, the new wave of liberalism in the late 1830s had a disastrous effect: in Madrid alone forty-four churches and monasteries disappeared.

To a certain extent the church had been prepared for this onslaught, since church property had been similarly expropriated by legislation in the 1820s—again as a result of a struggle in Spain between liberals and the old order. There had been a seesaw effect as, first, Joseph Bonaparte ordered the expropriation of all church wealth in 1809, a policy supported in 1812 when the Spanish parliament (Cortes de Cádiz) took possession of all convent property. Next, Fernando VII's decree in May 1814 that this property be returned to the church helped to restore the historical balance, only to be upset when the constitutional regime returned in 1820 and resumed the campaign against church wealth. Repercussions of this later episode reached Cuba. For example, the law suppressing religious orders in 1820, which urged the closing of all convents in which there lived less than twenty-five religious, meant that the Franciscans could retain only one of their twenty-three convents in Cuba. In Spain also the church was adversely affected by these sweeping reforms—and even more in the following decade.

This massive upheaval of the Spanish church and the radical political restructuring of the country had a major impact upon the ecclesiastical and administrative organizations of the colony. The Cuban church, which under Espada had been dragged reluctantly into the nineteenth century and which appeared able to modernize somewhat its traditional role, declined rapidly. For fourteen years after the death of Bishop Espada in 1832, Havana was left without a bishop. Meanwhile, Archbishop Civilo Alameda, accused of being a carlista and fearing for his safety, fled from the Santiago diocese, leaving his seat vacant from 1836 to 1851.

The church in Cuba suffered more than the deprivation of its two chief spokesmen, however, for the 1836 and 1838 Spanish laws stripping the church of its "earthly possessions" were rigorously applied by Governor Miguel Tacón (1834–38), who was loathed by most Cubans for his arrogant, heavy-handed approach to colonial administration. Eleven of the twenty convents were taken over by the government, the Dominicans were expelled from the university, and many Catholic schools were closed. A mass exodus of clergy from Cuba resulted. By the middle of the nineteenth century, the Cuban church was devastated. Deprived of spiritual and political leadership, stripped of most of its wealth, and viewed as a social pariah by an inimical government, the Cuban church (more precisely, the Spanish church in Cuba) would subsequently support the desires of Madrid, to the detriment of Cuban interests.

The church faced two crucial issues at midcentury: the serious lack of religious to minister to the spiritual needs of the population and the divided political allegiances of the clergy. Looking first at the latter problem, it became clear that political allegiance in some sense was a generational question, since many young people favored the ideas of Varela and subsequently Luz y Caballero, while more powerful members of the colonial elite and most older clergy thought an alliance with the mother country offered the most encouraging potential for an unfettered church life. In the post-Espada era, after an initial struggle of conscience, the official church won the day, swinging its support solidly behind the mother country, liberalism and all. Under a tacit agreement between Madrid and the colony, token recompense was provided the church in Cuba in return for a respectful attitude from it. In essence the church had sold out after recovering some of the property expropriated in the 1830s. For the rest of the century, and despite the protestations of Cuban-born clergy, it would play the role of moral supporter of the colonial status quo. Yet again the spiritual concerns of this allegedly apolitical body would appear to be imbued with earthly considerations.

The more pressing of the two critical issues for the Cuban church toward the middle of the nineteenth century was also more prosaic—there was an embarrassing lack of native clergy, not surprising in the wake of the savage laws of the late 1830s and the usually harsh treatment of all clergy by the Spanish colonial administration. Stripped of property and prestige, clerical life attracted few adherents. The prevailing Spanish influence meant that native clergy, routinely overlooked in favor of Spanish colleagues, were confused and frustrated. Thus when Msgr. Félix y Solans was named Bishop of Havana in 1874, one of his first goals was to revitalize the San Carlos Seminary which had produced only six priests during the previous twelve years.[54]

A brief study of the number of clergy between 1750 and 1850 (table 1) gives a fair idea of the rise and decline of church fortunes. In 1757, for instance, 46 of the 52 parish priests in Cuba were native-born (almost 92 percent). In addition there were 102 secular priests and several hundred other religious—in all, 561 *eclesiásticos* and 156 women religious.[55] Sixty years later, in 1817, there were slightly more than 1,000 ecclesiastics tending the spiritual needs of a population of approximately 550,000.[56] Yet by 1846, in the wake of the spiritual and economic (and, many would argue, moral) devastation of the Catholic church, while the population had passed one million, the number of ecclesiastics on the island had been reduced by more than half, to 438.[57] In other words, between 1817 (at the height of Espada's tenure) and 1846 (following the liberal reforms initiated by Madrid), the population had doubled but the number of clergy had been halved. (If one com-

Table 1

The Number of Ecclesiastics in Cuba in Relation to Population, 1757–1846

Year	No. of ecclesiastics	Population	Ratio of clergy to population
1757	561	172,620 (1774)	1:307.7
1817	1,000 (approx.)	550,000	1:550
1846	438	1,000,000 (approx.)	1:2283.1

Sources: Drawn from Leiseca, *Apuntes para la Historia Eclesiástica de Cuba*; Hageman and Wheaton, eds., *Religion in Cuba Today*; REC.

Note: Thomas, drawing on census returns, provides some useful comparative figures for the number of ecclesiastics over the next century: 1899, 283; 1907, 380; 1919, 880; 1953, 784 (*Cuba, or the Pursuit of Freedom*, 1128).

pares the 1846 figures with those of 1757, it becomes apparent that while the 1757 population was less than one-fifth that of 1846, the actual number of ecclesiastics was actually greater; moreover, the ratio of clergy to population was greater by a factor of seven in 1757 compared with the 1846 figures—an outstanding difference.)

Father Jerónimo Usera y Alarcón, appointed to head the Santiago de Cuba diocese in 1849, summarized clearly the church's disastrous condition: "The state of this Church is deplorable. . . . The church buildings are poor and decrepit, and the priests reduced to misery." Even so, he found a hint of promise: "The natives here are so devout and docile that once a remedy to these ills is applied, it will be easy to rebuild this weakened foundation." Usera's well-meant observation reveals an honest if somewhat haughty appreciation of "the natives," a view that would hinder the church in its interpretation of the struggle for independence undertaken by Cuba. Usera's observations, moreover, provide insight into the superficial conquests of Catholicism, particularly in the countryside. The slaves, he claims, had remarkably little contact with religion, while there was a "lamentable contrast with the state of gross ignorance held by the poorest classes, especially those employed in rural areas, be they white or colored."[58] Despite occasional missionary campaigns, a century later, in the late 1950s, Father Usera's words would still ring true.

Identity Crisis: Spanish Influence v. Cuban Independence, 1850–1898

While a somber picture has been painted of the church in decline, some bright spots existed. Chief among these was the tenure of Antonio María Claret as archbishop of Santiago (1851–56) and his outspoken attempts to revive church fortunes and receive compensation from the Spanish government for losses suffered by the church. Four times he undertook wide-ranging pastoral visits, writing extensively about the depressing condition of the church, particularly in rural areas: "I swell with indignation as I witness the criminal abandonment of the people and clergy of this bishopric by the Spanish government. . . . At times in order to survive their misery, the poor priests have to go to the miserable huts of blacks hoping to eat their yams and bananas."[59]

The prelate was not content merely to preach to and convert rural settlers, although his vigor in these *visitas* was legendary. For Claret the evangelizing task also included criticizing social injustice and seeking practical solutions for it. To this end he undertook two farsighted projects: the "school-workshop" in Camagüey which combined an academic program with physical labor, and in 1854 a small-scale agrarian reform on the lands previously held by the Dominican fathers outside Bayamo. Although isolated, these incidents showed that the church was capable of innovative social programs as well as the more traditional forms of evangelization (although, to be fair, both Espada and Claret's successor, Osés, had advocated some type of agrarian reform).

Living conditions, particularly in rural Cuba, appalled Archbishop Claret, who criticized both the Spanish government and the sugar mill owners. He was particularly incensed by the widespread common-law relationships between whites and blacks or mulatto Cubans. At this time, interracial marriage was forbidden by the colonial administration so whites and blacks simply lived together. Supporting one of his clergy, Father Adoaín, the archbishop criticized the legislation as "un-Christian," for which he became the target of much criticism by powerful Spanish settlers. Even worse for the Spanish settlers, though, was his constant preaching of the equality of all, whatever their color. A court case was taken up against Claret for this provocation, but charges were dropped when, in the wake of no less than fifteen assassination attempts against him, he returned to Spain. Again powerful colonial interests had insisted that the church should save the souls of its flock—and leave their physical condition alone.

In this arid colonial atmosphere, anyone who strayed from the Spanish norm was bound to encounter tremendous pressure to conform (witness the assassination attempts against Archbishop Claret and the continuous pressure against Archbishop Espada). As a result, when the stirrings of national consciousness began in the 1850s and several isolated Cuban uprisings against the Spanish government took place, the church dutifully ignored the situation, preferring to improve its material base rather than to risk engendering the wrath of Madrid. Exceptions occurred, particularly as civil war broke out in 1868, but for the most part the church took pains to stay neutral—and of course was nothing of the kind.

The first major uprising against the colonial government, in Camagüey in 1859, ended in the arrest and sentencing to death of seven of the participants. Most clergy were content to ignore their plight, although recently arrived Archbishop Claret pleaded for clemency on behalf of the rebels. Ultimately he was ignored and four insurgents were killed, but unlike the majority of his colleagues he had tried. The clerical norm of the day, then, was to avoid antagonizing the Spanish administration, to lead a "spiritual" existence, and to attempt to reestablish a religious presence, mainly in urban centers. The stage was set for a program that would dominate the church's weltanschauung for the next century: retreat into the spiritual womb, supported by reduced rents from commercial activity. Reduced benefits were clearly preferable to none at all.

This urban-based pietism led to an unfortunate and unsavory church presence. Visitors to Cuba from 1850 on repeatedly commented on the church's demoralized state. Religious festivities were only excuses for excessive merrymaking; with the diezmos abolished, many secular clergy were poor. One historian quotes a priest "en route for a Sunday cockfight" who claimed they were so impoverished that the "very ministers at the altar must sell the holy things for money."[60] A feature of priestly life widely commented on was the practice of clerics living openly with women.[61] To put it mildly, the church was providing poor social and religious leadership and of course was thereby at least partially responsible for its diminished social standing.

The practice of religion on the Lord's day provides another gauge of the depth of popular religious sentiment. Writing in 1854, Maturin M. Ballou criticized the traditions in all Catholic countries, reserving his harshest judgment for Cuba, where the "impression made by the Sabbath ceremonies of the church strikes us as evanescent, and as of such a character as to be at once obliterated by the excitement of the worldly pleasures that follow."[62] He disliked the din in the capital, the noise of military music, the loud church bells, and he was amazed that the stores were open, the organ grinders and monkey shows commonplace, the lottery ticket sellers omnipresent—so different from the New England Sundays to which he was accustomed. Even allowing for cultural differences and local color, his views were extremely critical of the lax Christian spirit, for which he laid much of the blame on the clergy:

> The character of this class of men has of former years been a scandal to the island, and the stories that are told by respectable people concerning them are really unfit to print. They led lives of the most unlimited profligacy, and they hesitated not to defy every law, moral or divine. . . . Many persons traced the bad conditions of public morals and the increase of crime just previous to Tacón's governorship directly to this ruling influence.
>
> A fearful condition when those who assume to lead in spiritual affairs proved the fountainhead of crime upon the island, themselves the worst of criminals.[63]

Five years later, Richard Dana's journal, *To Cuba and Back*, confirmed these impressions of a church without any religious identity and apparently offering lax moral influence: "There were only about half a dozen persons at mass" at the Havana cathedral "and all but one of these were women."[64] At the Jesuit College, Belén, although there was a larger attendance, significantly the vast majority were women. Dana's account describes a powerless, somewhat insignificant and distant church, in poor financial and psychological shape, seeking desperately to regroup and forge an identity—and failing.

In many ways the logical conclusion of this collective identity crisis, and perhaps the single most important reason for this generally lax moral standard, was the poor example set by clergy. Fearful of another massive government intervention, lacking decisive prelates to encourage them, and catering to a population that held their position in little regard, the clergy drifted, uncertain of itself and its future. The result was a vicious circle, for, held in little esteem, priests often behaved in an unbecoming fashion, which in turn justified similar behavior by the faithful. As Dana summed it up: "Cuba became a kind of Botany Bay for the Romish clergy. There they seem to have been concealed from the eye of discipline. With this state of things there existed, naturally enough, a vast amount of practical infidelity among the people, and especially among the men, who, it is said, scarcely recognized religious obligations at all."[65]

Between the middle of the nineteenth century and the war of independence (1895–98), the church changed remarkably little, continuing to tread water, searching in an ineffectual way for a mission to pursue, an identity to develop. The wars of 1868–78 and 1895–98 applied the coup de grace to this moribund institution. During this thirty-year period, the church failed either to gauge the depth of nationalist sentiment or to react to it. Having been recompensed to a certain extent by Madrid in 1861 for property confiscated by the liberal government of Mendizábal, church leaders had good reason not to seek out opportunities to confront the colonial authorities. Their newly won gains, following a period of intense government criticism and harassment, were worth retaining. This position was bitterly opposed by the native-born clergy who were clearly marginalized by their Spanish superiors. As in the 1895–98 struggle, tension and ill will developed between Cuban clergy, many of whom supported the insurgents, and their Spanish colleagues, who took Madrid's position. To a certain extent, the church's response to public protest following the brutal repression by Spanish forces was based upon calculated self-interest: many clerics, savoring their relative prosperity, would not risk criticizing the hand that fed them.

This clerical controversy mirrored, in microcosm, a more fundamental reason for the demise of the church during this period—the broader psychological struggle between Spanish and Cuban sentiments, between *peninsular* (literally, born on the Iberian peninsula) and *criollo* (creole, born in the colonies). Developments in the rest

of Spanish America required a new working relationship between
Cuba and the mother country, but such minor modifications as were
reluctantly made only fueled growing social frustration at Spain's
haughtiness.

After the compensation arranged by Madrid in 1861, however, most
clergy (especially those born in Spain) refused to criticize Spanish conduct, much less take up the cause of the *mambises*, or insurgents. Exceptions included priests like Pedro Nolasco Alberre, eighty-two years
old, who was deported, Francisco Esquembre, who was shot for alleged
treason, and Father Braulio Odio of Santiago, who followed his parishioners into battle. Even Bishop Jacinto María Martínez Sáez, who pro-
tested against a wave of killings, became a victim of this colonial justice. For his pains he was deported in 1869, and when he returned in
1873 was refused permission to disembark. (To remind the church of
its subservient role, the government left the diocese without a bishop
for several years—and the lesson was well taken.)

In sum, inspired by Cuba's patron saint, the Virgin of Charity, and
understanding the nationalist sentiments held by the insurgents, a
vocal minority of Cuba's clergy supported the patriots. Unfortunately,
they were disregarded by their Spanish superiors (as would be the case
in the 1895–98 war): had they been listened to, the development of
church history in Cuba would have been very different.

The thirty-year period leading to the overthrow of the Spanish administration of Cuba thus saw the mainstream church nudged and bul-
lied into supporting the status quo and therefore opposing the struggle
for independence. With the exceptions noted, the church decided to le-
gitimize the Spanish position: "Churches were turned into Spanish
fortresses: Te Deums were sung on the deaths of the Cuban heroes José
Martí and Antonio Maceo."[66] This official position in turn added to
strained relations between Spanish and Cuban clergy, although in general this tension would not translate into extra-church tension. The
Cuban population at large, favoring independence, would not forget the
church's support for the Spanish overlords.

The more mundane reasons for the dramatic decline of church influence during this period included a continued failure to penetrate rural
areas. In 1887, Bishop Ramón Fernández de Pierala wrote upon leaving
Havana: "When at the beginning of our Apostolic Ministry we undertook a trip around the Diocese, one of the things which most caught
our attention and most profoundly afflicted our spirit was the neglect,
if not abandonment, of a large part of our subjects. . . . The most striking feature was the ignorance held by families, towns and entire regions, especially those separated by large distances from major populated areas, of the mysteries, Christian dogma, and even the most

essential rudiments of our religion."[67] Other reasons for the church's waning influence range from the concentration of clergy in private schools based in the cities to the nature of destruction that results from war. Estimates of the numbers killed in this period range as high as 300,000, an amazingly large percentage of the population at that time, and, as one would expect, the civil war curtailed opportunities to develop any program or institution. In addition, since church buildings—because of their strength—were often used as strategic buildings by the warring forces, a large proportion were destroyed. Finally, the church continued to be the center of controversy generated by its own members, as in the unfortunate case of the "Pretender to the Seat" of Santiago, Pedro Llorente, in 1873: imposed by the military as archbishop of Santiago without Rome's approval, he was excommunicated by the Holy See.

Compounding the church's self-inflicted problems, the population at large had little faith in the church's aspirations for future campaigns or in its relevance to their societal well-being: "Cubans have always paid little attention to religious problems and, although they are not atheists, neither are they fanatics. Indeed, their religiosity borders on indifference—an attitude based in part on the fact that many priests acted as Spaniards and not as representatives of God. As a result, religion in Cuba has never been a factor in political upheaval, as has been the case in Mexico, Ecuador and Bolivia."[68] Ruled by an essentially ineffective series of prelates, split internally by Cuban-Spanish tensions, and fearful of taking a prophetic stance, the church on the eve of Cuban independence was in a sorry state.

After the defeat of the colonial forces the Spanish nature of the Cuban church would be emphasized by a series of incidents, each of which reminded Cubans of the conservative posture taken by the church as an institution against the struggle for freedom. The Cuban church's narrow view kept it from even considering the possibility of a Spanish defeat and what that would entail for the church and consequently from making plans to deal with this potential crisis. Instead, the church as a social body tried, Canute-like, to ignore the tides of history and to muddle through as best it could, ingratiating itself into the Spanish system while neglecting its pastoral mission, particularly in rural areas. When the church sought to establish an identity for the first time since Bishop Espada's tenure, it would encounter tremendous difficulties not only because it was short of personnel and money but even more because of the Cubans' indifference and resentment. Once again the Cuban church had proved to be its own worst enemy.

2

The Church in Search of

a Constituency, 1898–1959

The profound alienation between the people and the clergy (hence be-tween the people and the sacraments and the liturgy) began well over a century ago, as Cuba began to acquire a national consciousness and stir from her long colonial lethargy. The Cuban hierarchy and clergy, who had always remained more closely identified with the mother country than with the masses, chose to remain faithful to Spain. . . . The church and the clergy became figures of fun. If one thought of them at all, they were to be ridiculed but to be neither feared nor hated; the feeling remains to this day that organized religion is a matter for women and young children.

Leslie Dewart

The framing of this important stage in Cuba's national development between two revolutionary events is not coincidental. Rather it helps to illustrate how the church in Cuba reacted to the increasing social inequity and racial tension, the massive foreign investment, the political unrest, and the external military intervention that characterized the period. To evaluate the development of the church at this time, it helps to look at the context immediately prior to the "liberation" and "independence" that resulted from the Spanish capitulation in 1898. Moreover, in view of the slowness with which the church reacts to historical change, it is also worthwhile to examine the church's response to the independence struggle throughout Latin America, in particular the role of the church in Cuba at the time of the 1895–98 civil war. One can then better appreciate both the extensive challenges facing the church during the period 1898–1958 and the steps it took to meet them.

What does the church's reaction to the independence struggle on the mainland in the period 1810–25 have to do with events in Cuba in 1895? Part of the answer lies in the constants of Vatican teaching during this period: the spiritual (and political) advice from the Holy See to the Cuban church in 1895 was not dissimilar to the advice given to mainland prelates in 1810. Moreover, Cuban society has always been profoundly Spanish—still true of the Havana of the 1980s. Finally there is the tenacity with which Spain held on to Cuba, her last Latin American colony, after losing the rest of Spanish America. This fervently patriotic and politically myopic vision was even more firmly entrenched as a result of the garrison town mentality, a factor of course heightened by the return to Cuba of the most reactionary Spanish elements fleeing the independence movement on the mainland. As a result of these complementary pressures, the Cuban political administration, as well as that of the church, became "more Spanish than Spain."

This sweeping historical analysis recognizes the extremely important role played by individual religious throughout Latin America and in no way intends to minimize their personal courage and strength of conviction in fighting for their nation's independence. Nevertheless, it must also be recognized that these brave priests and religious were comparatively few and only a handful were members of the church hierarchy, which of course tended to be Spanish-born. Therefore, while not ignoring the contributions of outstanding individuals, this study, in contrast to works by, for example, Leiseca and Testé, which present the church as solidly criolla (identifying with native values) and strongly in favor of independence, reveals a very different picture.

Typical of the attitude cultivated by the church mainstream in colonial Spanish America was that of Fray José María Romo in August 1810, who condemned the movement for independence and called for resignation to God's will as reflected in the political system headed by the monarchy: "Say clearly then that you do not wish to subject your-selves to, nor indeed obey, that divine precept: 'omnis anima Potestatibus sublimioribus subdita sit' [Let every soul be subject to the highest Powers], that you refuse to obey the power of the King and Queen of Spain—given to us by God since the time of the conquest, and through his mercy, saved for us until today; proclaim that you are better able to govern yourselves under your own system than through the power coming from above—but then do not be surprised if we hold forth in our pulpits against such scandalous disobedience, such arro-gance inspired by Lucifer, and such disastrous ambition, which not only debases our Holy Kingdom for the obedient, submissive faithful, but which will also arouse God's justice and bring on all our heads its lightning bolts and anathemas."[1]

At the time of the movement for independence in Spanish America, Pope Pius VII made it obvious that he preferred to deal with the Span-ish monarchy, despite their disagreements, than with a revolutionary junta. For, while Fernando VII of Spain constantly revealed himself to be a distasteful and despotic extremist, crushing liberalism and all its manifestations, criticizing the Vatican for its meddling, and even re-viving the Spanish Inquisition, he nevertheless represented the lesser of two evils when compared with the leaders of the independence movement in Latin America.[2] The Vatican therefore tried to rally sup-port for the troubled Spanish monarchy among the colonial faithful, thereby overstepping strictly spiritual boundaries. Opposed to the dan-gers of revolution (and a potential decrease in Vatican influence), the pontiff urged "fidelity" and "obedience" to Fernando VII. Eight years later, acting on the request of Fernando VII, Pope Leo XII also took up the monarch's support, employing his position as head of the church to pacify revolt and maintain the status quo.[3]

In light of such papal letters and of Fernando VII's ability to request a document of this type, it seems fairly clear that the Spanish monar-chy and the Holy See enjoyed complementary goals as well as excellent working relations. As one of the fundamental rationales for the con-quest and subsequent colonization of Spanish America, religion was a natural ally of the Crown, which depended heavily on spiritual lead-ership in the colonies to guide the faithful down the correct moral and, occasionally, political paths. For its part the Vatican needed the Crown's support to spread its program of evangelization through the New World. Apart from occasional jealousy and bickering and a natu-ral rivalry over financial and political control, for three centuries this relationship had been sound. The movement for independence threatened to destroy this carfully wrought and tended structure, and so, despite reservations concerning Fernando VII's despotism, the Vatican raced to support its longtime ally.

Between this period and the struggle for independence in Cuba in 1868–78 and 1895–98, remarkably little happened to modify the Vatican's interpretation concerning social upheaval and the right to political self-determination. With a few minor amendments, the attitude of Leo XIII in 1895–98, then, resembled that of Pius VII in 1816 and of Leo XII in 1824.

Leo XIII is often viewed by church historians as the first "modern" church leader, "a progressive Pope who never sacrificed principles to expediency."[4] The author of the encyclical *Rerum Novarum* (1891), whose social teachings are still frequently quoted by conservative theologians, Leo XIII recognized the existence of a modern, radically different era and, unlike many of his predecessors, sought to make church teachings more relevant to a rapidly industrializing world.

Despite effusive praise from some quarters concerning his role as statesman and peacemaker, Leo XIII did not pursue a particularly different policy from his predecessors in regard to Cuba. A pragmatist, he recognized established authority in international relations and so supported the Spanish monarchy in its continuing struggle with its rebellious colony, Cuba.[5] True, he claimed that, it was legitimate to oppose an unjust government (as in *Sapientiae Christianae*, 1890), but either he believed that Cuba's colonized government was just or he was prepared to subordinate such feelings to more practical concerns. The result was less effusive support for the monarchy than that shown by his predecessors, yet support nonetheless.

There were practical and personal reasons for Leo XIII to throw his support to Spain: not only did he fear that a defeat of the Spanish forces at the hands of the mambises might precipitate the downfall of the Crown in Spain itself, but he was apparently godfather to the successor to the throne, Alfonso XIII.[6] The end-of-century malaise, in particular, was feared, since many thought it might trigger a Spanish defeat in the colony—with disastrous results for both the Crown and the Vatican. And, while Spanish prestige was in decline, the Vatican preferred to have some influence in Spain rather than none at all. Accordingly, Leo XIII dusted off the policy of his predecessors eighty years earlier, made some minor adjustments to it, and sought to evoke support for the Crown.

In Cuba, the outbreak of civil war in 1895 after decades of simmering struggle polarized the church dramatically, pitting the proinsurgency minority against the overwhelmingly pro-Spanish majority. Commenting on the psychological state of the Cuban church at this time, one historian points out the anachronistic nature of religious life there:

> The breath of modern times, thus, had vivified Cuba no more than it had Spain.
>
> To say that the outlook of the Cuban Church had remained Spanish is no more than to say that it had remained medieval. Medieval is not of itself a pejorative term. There was a time when to be medieval was to be progressive and abreast of the times. But that was seven centuries ago, and time has since gone on.[7]

The church in Cuba aligned itself with a power structure no longer relevant to the contemporary political scene. As a result of having taken sides and despite support from the Holy See, the church's credibility plummeted to an all-time low, and friction continued between church factions during the three years of the civil war. On the very eve of the Spanish defeat, wrote Dewart, "the Bishop of Havana wrote a pastoral letter 'for' civilization, against barbarism, that is, for colonial rule rather than independence. The effects of such a teaching may be easily deduced."[8] In it, Bishop Santander y Frutos denounced U.S. interests and justified the Spanish colonial position, exhorting the faithful to fight for a just cause: "The calamity of war which we thought was reaching its termination has been renewed. . . . Our zealous authorities and armed forces will know how to discharge their duty. As Catholics, we ought to help them with our prayers saying to the Lord with David, 'destroy the nations that desire war.' Justice is on our side. God is with us. The mother of God is also our mother. She helped us in Lepanto and on many other occasions. She will also help us now. Never was it heard that she failed to help those who invoke her. Let us put confidence in God and in our blessed mother and we will not be overcome."[9]

When it became obvious that Spain's imperial days in Cuba were finally over, both bishops requested repatriation to Spain. After them came a wave of Spanish priests, emigrating both to Spain and to the Latin American mainland. With church influence severely curtailed—largely as a result of its clear support for the Spanish cause—it was in the best interests of all to seek to wipe the historical slate clean.

The Church in an "Independent Cuba"

The Treaty of Paris, putting an end to the war, was signed by representatives of Spain and the United States on 10 December 1898. As a result of this agreement, on 1 January 1899 General John Brooke assumed office as military governor of Cuba, to be followed by General Leonard Wood. The nationalist movement was thus severely weakened during Cuba's first years as a republic, her interests subordinated to the interests of the United States. "Cuba Libre" was nothing of the kind. "Independence" existed on paper alone.

During this period of U.S. occupation and control (1899–1902), the Catholic church undertook to reassess its position and to plan a strategy that would allow it to recoup some of its political and financial losses. The church appears to have been successful in both goals, although a closer look reveals that in doing so, it alienated a large section of the population, which saw church leaders as being opportunistic at their expense.

General Brooke's brief tenure as governor brought in some liberal measures intended to strengthen North America's cultural and political influence over the island by substituting civil for religious control. One new law, for instance, eliminated the church monopoly on marriage ceremonies and established civil marriage as the only legally binding act, for which a one-dollar fee was to be charged. The law was understandably poorly received by church officials, who for centuries had controlled this crucial religious and social ceremony. Brooke also made it clear from the outset that church and state were to be totally separated and that no funds would be provided by him for the maintenance of the church. Other steps taken under Brooke (who favored the introduction of Protestantism in Cuba) included prohibiting religious education in public schools and separating religious from the hospitals.

Brooke's successor, General Leonard Wood, was much less harsh in his dealings with the church. Largely through his encouragement and counsel the church was able to find a "breathing space" and redefine its political base. For his part, Wood was keen to enlist the support of the church for his own purposes and so sought to pursue goals that would be mutually beneficial. In this he was successful. For example, Wood amended the civil marriage legislation in August 1900, making civil and church marriage ceremonies equally valid. This move was a major concession to the church, given Brooke's short-lived legislation dealing with this matter, and was well received by the church hierarchy.

Wood also had to deal with matters relating to divorce and annulment (which he transferred from church to civil courts), the secularization of ceremonies, the role of public cemeteries, and compensation for confiscated church property. His pragmatic answer to the cemetery question was to establish civil cemeteries and to allow the church to retain possession of those cemeteries under its control, although these were ultimately to be subject to state jurisdiction.

Compensation for church property proved to be a thorny problem, which aroused—and among certain sectors still arouses—strong feelings. The "Liberal" laws passed in Spain, and subsequently enacted in Cuba, had drastically reduced the holdings of the church as well as the number of clergy on the island. In 1861, an arrangement was worked out according to which "all land the government 'did not need' was handed back to the church; the rest was leased by the state—and rent between then and 1899 had totaled $M21."[10] Since Spain had stopped paying these rents following the U.S. intervention, church leaders demanded compensation from the new state representatives, the interventionist forces, although they had little obligation to do so. Eventually Wood agreed to pay a settlement of 5 percent per annum of the value of church property in question. While theoretically separate, the state thus strengthened the church during the traumatic public backlash of the wars of independence, causing one Cuban to note, "In this way the Catholic clergy of Cuba, and in particular the church hierarchy, began leaning in favor of the North American military occupation, and obtaining concessions from her."[11]

The religious question in these early years of Cuba's independence was more important than is generally thought. True, a discussion on this topic did not touch off as heated a debate as it did in postrevolutionary Mexico, where the clergy had been extremely wealthy and powerful, but it did nevertheless awaken strong feelings, particularly because the church had been so openly pro-Spanish. The 1900–1901 constitutional convention, for example, saw much discussion on the nature and role of religion in the new republic. All delegates agreed that professing one's own religious beliefs was to be an inalienable right, but they were badly split on the nature of church-state ties. Eventually they voted to separate church and state definitively—the first Latin American country to do so. This stand, together with a clause guaranteeing religious freedom, became Article 26 in the 1902 constitution:

> The profession of all religions and of all forms of worship is free, without any other limitation than the respect for Christian morals and public order.
>
> The Church is to be separate from the State, which cannot subsidize—in any case at all—any religious worship ["ningún culto"].[12]

Between 1899 and 1903, the church hierarchy in Cuba underwent a dramatic reorganization. The exodus of Cuba's two Spanish bishops along with a large proportion of the clergy had left the church in a difficult situation. The Vatican responded in 1899 by appointing as the new archbishop of Havana Donato Sbarretti, an Italian who had been auditor at the apostolic delegation in Washington and who in that context had excellent connections with the U.S. government. This appointment infuriated many churchpeople, who had hoped for the appointment of a Cuban. In 1903 two new dioceses were created—Pinar del Río, with twenty parishes, and Cienfuegos, with thirty-five parishes.[13] Both were headed by Cuban prelates. The church thus entered the twentieth century with a fresh administration and a different approach—an English-speaking archbishop in Havana at a time of U.S. military occupation as well as Cuban bishops in the three other Cuban dioceses—to satisfy nationalistic desires and present the new image. When Sbarretti left, he was replaced by another Cuban, Pedro González Estrada, who was assisted by an American, Auxiliary Bishop Broderick. In this way pragmatic nationalistic and international concerns were skillfully balanced by the Vatican, eager to repair the damage caused both by the Spanish hierarchy in the previous thirty years and by its own stance in favor of Spain and against the insurgents.[14]

For the next three decades, the church improved its image in Cuba. The promotion of native-born clergy to high positions, virtually unheard of earlier, became more common. Other gains came through the education offered by religious groups, particularly to the children of the middle class. Although the 1902 constitution determined that public schools would offer a lay education, perhaps one-half of these schools had been closed or destroyed by the civil war. And while there had been a marked exodus of priests and religious from the Catholic school system following the 1895–98 war, those who remained were busy regenerating an interest in their schools. In short, the time for patient reconstruction and image-building had arrived—a challenge skillfully taken up by church leaders.

The Church as a Social Institution, 1902–1940

Following the withdrawal of General Wood in 1902, the church underwent a quiet transformation, seeking to win support especially among the Spanish who had remained in Cuba and among the wealthy urban middle class. Several religious fraternities and religious associations were instituted, particularly in Havana—first the Buen Pastor (1908), the Sagrado Corazón de Jesús (1909), La Milagrosa (1910), and the Damas de Caridad (1910), later La Caridad (1921), La Inmaculada

(1921), El Carmen (1922), and the Santo Angel Custodio (1923). These associations, designated both as contemplative in nature and to help the urban poor in a benign if paternalistic fashion, were symptomatic of the newfound respectability of the church in the first two decades after the war for independence. Together with the prestigious private schools run by the priests and religious, who returned in large numbers once it became clear that they could fulfill a useful role, these associations laid the foundations for a church that became increasingly popular among the middle class as the 1920s progressed.

Spain and the Spanish influence played major roles in rejuvenating the church. A generation had passed since the Spanish colonial administration had been overthrown; the resulting venom and anti-Spanish invective had long since disappeared, and Spanish influence in the last Spanish colony resurfaced. The many Spaniards who now came to make their fortunes in Cuba emerged as a Cuban-Spanish bourgeoisie, strongly Catholic and observant of Christian and philanthropic duties to the less fortunate. They supported the importation from Spain in the late 1920s of Catholic Action, an innovative movement that "opened up decision-making to limited lay input and tended to focus energies on the creation of an idealistic new Christendom which bore little relevance to the Cuban reality."[15]

From the point of view of developing an interest in social concerns, the activities of the Franciscans (especially those from the Basque area of Spain) and the Jesuits were particularly important. In 1931 the latter developed the Agrupación Católica Universitaria, a somewhat elitist group of university students who strove with great energy to proselytize among their peers.[16] Their success lay with the upper middle class, and they played a major role in organizing Catholic university students at the time.

Certain sectors within the church also realized that the church might broaden its new and tenuous base of support, as well as meet its spiritual goals, by making its religious message more applicable to the less fortunate members of Cuban society. In 1919, for example, at the First National Eucharistic Congress, much was said about socio-economic difficulties facing more and more Cubans. The congress concluded that "If, as has been said, the social problem has been created and perpetuated by the present system of capitalist production, let that system be transformed."[17] This interest in social justice held by a limited number of Catholics would expand in the 1940s and 1950s through the activities of Catholic Action groups.

Within twenty to thirty years after the overthrow of the colonial system, the church in Cuba had been transformed: its reactionary policies had been cast away, its schools had educated vast numbers of children, and its religious were serving in hospitals, hostels, and orphanages. The schools were of first importance, since they were responsible in part for molding future influential citizens. The Jesuits had several schools in Cuba as did the Christian Brothers (Lasalle Brothers); other schools were run by the Augustinians, Salesians, Dominicans, Maristas, Ursuline Sisters, Sisters of Charity, Sisters of the Sacred Heart of Jesus, Passionist Sisters, Madres Filipenses, Hermanas de la Caridad del Sagrado Corazón, and a dozen or so other orders. It was a singularly impressive feat in view of the inauspicious state of the church as the twentieth century dawned.

Perhaps the best indicators of the church's achievements lay in its publications and its nature as a patriotic institution. The media controlled directly by the church during the 1930s included an array of journals: the *Boletín Eclesiástico* of the Archdiocese of Havana; *San Antonio* of the Franciscans; *Belén, La Anunciata, El Mensajero* and *Esto Vir* of the Jesuits; *La Salle* of the Christian Brothers; *Don Bosco* of the Salesians; *Rosal Dominico* of the Dominicans; *Aromas del Carmelo* of the Carmelites; *El Mensajero Católico* of the Scolapians; *Mensajes* of the Caballeros de Colón, *Nuestra Hojita* of the Cathedral; and *La Milagrosa* and *Cultura* of the Paulists. The church also controlled religious sections in newspapers such as the *Diario de la Marina, El Mundo,* and *El País.* Concerning the church as a patriotic institution one can cite the example of the establishment of the Asociación Nacional de Caballeros Católicos de Cuba in 1929. Their inspiration ("with a noble desire for Catholic fraternity, and the patriotic cultivation of civic and moral values") and their goal (to demonstrate publicly and practice their beliefs, and to work "for the church and for the Patria") were generally well received among the middle classes. In short, within a generation of the Spanish defeat in 1898 it had become socially acceptable to be a practicing Catholic.

Another indicator of the new church's social popularity between the mid-1920s and mid-1940s was the increased role of affiliated organizations. In addition to more spiritually oriented groups, such as the Caballeros de Colón, Adoradores Nocturnos de la Catedral, Venerable Order Tercera del Carmen, Pía Unión de Santa Teresita de Jesús, Hijas de María, Siervas de María, or the Asociación de la Virgen de la Caridad, this period witnessed the development of church groups in society across the social sprectrum. "Among the most significant associations was the Federación de la Juventud Cubana, founded in 1927–28 by Brother Victorino of the Christian Brothers of La Salle. Through the common efforts of Dr. V. Arenas, the Jesuit P. E. Rivas, the Franciscan Apraiz, the Caballeros Católicos de Cuba were founded in 1929; and in 1931, the Agrupación Católica Universitaria by the Jes-

uit Felipe Rey de Castro. By 1940 the Catholic women teachers had
federated (Federación Nacional de Maestras Católicas) and in 1941 the
Catholic schools formed their own association. Since 1947, the Catholic Action had a representation among the workers, the Juventud
Obrera Católica."[18] The church was clearly succeeding in asserting itself as a relevant component of Cuban society.

This climb to prominence did not of course happen in a vacuum.
The first two decades of the twentieth century saw a dramatic increase
in immigration, especially from the poorer regions of Spain. The national population rose by one-third, from 2,028,930 in 1907 to
2,889,004 in 1919.[19] More foreign investment and profitable development of the sugar industry created an optimistic outlook. The apparent prosperity in the cities, where most of the country's priests and
religious were located, contributed to the popularity of the church,
which ran all the best schools and which elsewhere in Latin America
was a pillar of the community. Philanthropy and token gifts thus flourished alongside a more sincere form of charity among many bourgeois
Catholics. However, for virtually all, the concept of social justice—as
opposed to charity—was largely ignored.

During the first three decades of Cuba's independence, alongside
many examples of political corruption, foreign intervention, and military brutality, one finds remarkably little evidence of church protest.
One searches in vain for consistent church criticism of the U.S. interventions of 1906–9, 1912, or 1917–20, or for church challenge of the
corruption and fraud traditional in the Cuban elections, or for church
censure of the brutality of the Machado dictatorship.

The church deliberately ignored the harsh Cuban reality for two reasons. The first lay in the tradition that politics and religion do not mix,
that churchpeople must not pronounce on political events, however
distasteful. Second, the church simply did not want to endanger its
comparatively recent social acceptability and resulting gains. Setting
the seal on new relationship, the Cuban government established diplomatic relations with the Holy See in 1936, the Vatican opened a nunciature in 1935, and Pius XII appointed the first Cuban cardinal, Msgr.
Manuel Arteaga, in 1946.

The first four decades of church development thus witnessed a dramatic improvement in its fortunes, although many observers have
shown how these developments were not without their limitations.[20]
Evidence that the church's success had its dark side comes from an
unlikely source, church historian Martín Leiseca, in a sympathetic
1938 study, *Apuntes para la Historia Eclesiástica de Cuba*. Leiseca's
extensive preface, "Pages of Honor" (unpaged), praises Catholic
schools, associations, and individuals for their religious and charitable
works. Most of the individuals Leiseca cited share a prestigious social

standing and a strange mixture of paternalism, charity and spiritual and economic benevolence. Of Sra. Ramona Torriente y Madrazo, he wrote: "The poor and the humble, those disowned by Life, found in her the alms to cover daily necessities, the mystical and pious mite to heal the soul's wounds and produce the marvelous action of hope." Based upon the people featured in this part of Leiseca's study, the leading Catholics of the day were white, upper-middle-class lawyers, businessmen, and teachers. Most were either Spanish themselves or the children of Spanish immigrants. Their paternalistic benevolence, subsequently converted into acts of charity, can thus be seen as representing the quintessential Catholic values of the day. Acting as a kind of Rotary Club with religious leanings, they practiced what they preached by raising funds for good works among their peers, believing in the value of what they were doing and pleased to be part of the Catholic renaissance.

Leiseca presented a similarly elitist if well-intentioned description of the leading Catholic schools of the day. Although he recognized that some of the schools—such as the Colegio "La Inmaculada Concepción" of the Sisters of Charity, as well as the Salesians' "Artes y Oficios" and the Jesuits' "Escuela Electromecánica"—accepted children from poorer socioeconomic conditions, most of the schools he featured were rather exclusive. Most taught English ("given the importance it is convenient to apportion to this language in Cuba") and many employed North American nuns to teach these courses. The schools enjoyed excellent facilities for the study of commerce, typing, home economics, and languages. What is telling, however, is what Leiseca omitted. Of the four hundred people photographed in this school section, for example, only two are black. Significantly, they attented the "Escuela del Hogar 'María Auxiliadora'" which took in orphaned or unwanted children. Most of the adults featured were from the social urban elite of Cuba, largely from Havana. The large number of Catholic schools supplemented the church activities of this group, since they represented the future of the church—white, urban, and middle class, with a strong Spanish influence. Thus, while the church had made giant strides in becoming accepted in the social mainstream, there were disquieting signs that its popular base, particularly in rural areas and among blacks, was narrow. The church was once again limiting itself to an elite, albeit economically powerful, minority.

Church Gains in the Forties and Fifties

The decades of the forties and fifties were a period of impressive growth for the church, paralleling the tenure of Manuel Arteaga as archbishop. All of the earlier trends were substantially strengthened in these decades: the popularity of the Catholic school system, the increasingly intimate relationship between church hierarchy and leading government officials, the network of lay Catholic associations, and the slowly awakening interest in practical social projects (in part a response to the spread of Protestant churches). A sociological and psychological profile would have revealed for the first time in Cuban history a Catholic church comparable to that in the rest of Latin America. The church had apparently overcome serious difficulties and caught up with mainstream church practices.

The first test of this newfound respectability came in the Constituent Convention called to draft the 1940 constitution, where Freemason and Protestant groups (perhaps jealous of the church's preeminent educational role and fearful of Catholic efforts to have religious education in all public schools) were determined to emphasize the divisions between church and state and to strengthen the lay nature of the latter. Their plans failed. The church received tacit recognition and support from Fulgencio Batista, which Cardinal Arteaga recognized in his pastoral letter of 16 February 1941: "It would be an example of ingratitude not to express . . . how much I owe to the national authorities . . . at extremely difficult moments, during the constitutional reconstruction of our *Patria*, when we saw a variety of ideologies intensely stirred up. As a result, after passing through the storm we have been able to reach calm and stable waters."[21]

This trend of striking astute, pragmatic alliances with the political masters of the day continued through the 1940s and 1950s, most noticeably during the presidential terms of Ramón Grau and Carlos Prío (1944–52). Church spokesmen regularly attended state functions and received gifts from these political administrations toward building new churches. What may have favored church development in the short run ultimately worked against it: "Most churches attempted to build links with these regimes even in the face of corruption, repression, and maintenance of acute socioeconomic injustices. This further contributed to the low esteem Cubans held for the institutional churches."[22] Within two months of the Batista coup in 1952, similarly warm relations were reestablished between church and government leaders. Indeed, shortly afterwards, the image of the Virgen de la Caridad del Cobre, Cuba's national religious symbol, was carried by military plane on a national pilgrimage. The Virgen de la Caridad is venerated in Cuba with tremendous fervor—something akin to that shown Mexico's Virgin of Guadalupe—and through her presence the church officially conferred its blessing on the coup, despite its absolute overthrow of constitutional practice and the clear rejection of the national will. In return the hierarchy gratefully accepted favors extended by the dictator, often at the behest of his second wife. At the summit of its material and political well-being in this century, the church was increasingly seen in poorer circles as having subordinated its reformist zeal to accommodate the political elite, a viewpoint that would resurface in the first year of the revolution as social polarization rapidly forced Cubans to take sides.

The exception to this generalization about the church hierarchy was Archbishop Enrique Pérez Serantes of Santiago de Cuba, a remarkably outspoken Galician and on several issues a maverick cleric. An acquaintance of the Castro family for many years, he rose to public prominence in 1953 when he spoke out against the atrocities committed by government forces on the fidelistas who had stormed the Moncada barracks in Santiago. Fidel Castro's July 26 Movement was unsuccessful in the attack, and almost all those who were captured shortly afterwards were brutally tortured and killed. In the face of a massive public outcry, the archbishop pressured the military authorities to issue a declaration that none of the assailants was to be killed and took an active role in mediating safe passage for those fidelistas captured by the military and ensuring that they were well treated following their arrest. To a large extent the survival of all the prisoners taken in the wake of the carnage, including ultimately that of Fidel Castro, was due to public protests at the extent and nature of the brutal torturing and also from the archbishop's timely intercession. Pérez Serantes lived in Oriente, the province most neglected by the government in Havana and therefore the one with the highest levels of malnutrition, infant mortality, unemployment, and unsanitary conditions. He was more sensitive than most of his fellow bishops to the suffering of Cuba's rural poor.

Not only was the church divided on the issue of the church's role and mission, but by the 1950s defining the church itself posed a challenge. Its facets included the Havana hierarchy (itself divided on what to do about Batista) and the Catholic Action groups, religious in the prestigious secondary schools, service-oriented projects such as the hospitals and senior citizens' homes and the many Catholic ritual and social justice groups. Nevertheless a composite picture of the church emerges from two surveys published by the Agrupación Católica Universitaria, in 1954 and 1957. The 1954 study supports the thesis of "two churches," for while the church may have wielded a certain influence among the urban bourgeoisie, it did not in rural areas. Although 72.5 percent of the respondents to this survey identified themselves as Catholic, for instance, in rural areas the figure was 52 percent with a further 41 percent of the peasants indifferent concerning reli-

gious affiliation. The receipt of the sacraments also revealed an aston-
ishing lack of consistency: whereas 91 percent of all children were baptized, just 50 percent received first communion, and only 16 percent
of marriages took place in church.[23] There were other differences between the official image of religion and the reality of practice as well.
Many Catholics surveyed accepted the value of divorce, and fully one-
quarter had consulted the *espiritistas* or spiritualists—roughly the
same number (24 percent) that claimed to attend church regularly.[24]

The Agrupación's 1957 survey concentrated on rural conditions. The
figures were even more startling. Approximately 17 percent of marriages had been celebrated in a church service and 34.8 percent in a
civil ceremony. Slightly more than 40 percent surveyed lived in a
common-law arrangement. Moreover, only 52.1 percent of those interviewed declared themselves to be Catholic (41.41 percent did not pro-
fess *any* religion), and among all respondents figures for attendance at
mass were extremely low (see table 2). Even among declared Catholics,
figures for attendance at mass were low: 88.8 percent claimed not to
have attended mass for the entire year, with only 4.3 percent attending
at least three times yearly.[25]

The overwhelming responsibility for unfamiliarity with and disinterest in religion lay with the religious organizations, notoriously
unenthusiastic about working in the countryside. Subjects' responses
concerning their relationship with the parish priest (table 3) tes-
tified further to this neglect. It is little wonder that when asked
"What institution can best improve the situation for the farm
worker?" only 3.4 percent selected the church—approximately 1 percent fewer than chose Freemasonry!

This clearly divided nature of the church at the time of the fidelista
revolution is undoubtedly the most striking facet of the matter, a divi-

Table 2

Attendance at Mass of the Family Head
(farm workers, 1956)

No. of times per year	Respondents (%)
0	93.47
1	2.64
2	1.83
3	1.32
4	0.74

Source: Oscar A. Echevarría Salvat, *La Agricultura Cubana,
1934–1966: Régimen Social, Productividad y nivel de vida del sector agrícola* (Miami: Ediciones Universal, 1971), 15.

Table 3

Relationship of the Family Head with the
Parish Priest (farm workers, 1957)

Relationship	Respondents (%)
Have never seen	53.51
Know by sight	36.74
Have no dealings	1.94
A friend	5.43
A personal friend	2.38

Source: Echevarria Slavat, (cited in table 2).

sion that can be seen even among the hierarchy. Not one variant—class, gender, educational level, political alliance, or others, including the crucial interpretation of the *role* of religion in Cuban society—but all dramatically influenced Cubans' perceptions of the religious issue. Active Catholics critical of the church who were interviewed by the author generally commented on a feeling of promise and potential accompanied by a lack of direction, an inability to harness this energy. The grave dilemma that traditionally has plagued church activities—the sociopolitical responsibilities of religion (or, at times, the lack thereof)—was thus a major determinant in deciding activities for many.

Three basic groups existed within the church in the twilight years of the Batista era. Although in the definite minority, there was an increasingly vocal social reformist group of Catholic laymen, supported vociferously by Archbishop Pérez Serantes (and to a lesser extent by Bishops Evelio Díaz of Pinar del Río and Alberto Martín Villaverde of Matanzas), by social groups such as Catholic Youth (Juventud Católica) and the Young Catholic Workers (Jóvenes Obreros Católicos), and by the majority of secular Cuban clergy.[26] Aware of the repression by Batista's forces, of Cuba's rural poverty and of the need for sweeping social reform, nevertheless this loosely bound group had no unified platform for dealing with these problems.[27] Their fragmented social awareness and varied levels of commitment to the defeat of the Batista regime, along with the wide gamut of their political philosophies, made for a volatile mixture. Nevertheless, their faith led many of them to take a stand against the dictatorship as they attempted to prod the mainstream of the church into a similar course.

At the other end of the political spectrum were the Spanish bishop of Camagüey, Msgr. Carlos Ríu Anglés (another Spaniard), who tried to temper the frustration of Archbishop Pérez Serantes, and Bishop Martínez Dalmau of Cienfuegos, who had to flee Cuba in January

1959, apparently because of his ties with Batista. Other key supporters of traditional Catholicism were leaders of the Agrupación Católica and administrators in the Catholic Villanueva University, which by 1959 had a staff of 150 and an enrollment of about 1,600. Wealthy ranchers and farmers, as well as most of the urban bourgeoisie, also preferred to maintain the status quo, despite the excesses of Batista, and thus to protect their own lucrative interests.

In the middle lay the majority of Cuba's Catholics, a strange combination of people from all walks of life who either believed that politics and religion could not coexist or maintained that they were indifferent to the national situation. Their spokesman was Cardinal Arteaga, who sought fruitlessly a negotiated settlement of the many conflicts facing the nation. "Reconciliation" and "dialogue" became the watchwords of his stance, unrealistic hopes in the volatile political atmosphere of the 1950s. While most Catholics remained indifferent or at least unprepared to act on Cuba's plight, many had respect for what they judged to be the church's official position, defined by Cardinal Arteaga's ineffectual pleas.

Response to the Intensification of the Struggle, 1958

As Batista's power base disintegrated and Fidel Castro's grew, Cuba headed inevitably toward a showdown. The guerrillas exerted relentless pressure in a series of brilliant military campaigns, with Ché Guevara taking Santa Clara in late December and Fidel and Raúl Castro victorious in Oriente. Aided by the establishment of "Radio Rebelde" in February 1958 and a tremendously successful campaign of psychological warfare, the *barbudos* (bearded ones) continually defeated the Batista forces despite overwhelming odds. In this they were also assisted by U.S. press reports that emphasized the brutality and corruption of Batista and by the U.S. military aid embargo introduced in March. Finally, Batista boarded his plane on 31 December and headed for the Dominican Republic.

These dramatic events, and the speed with which they unfolded, brought great tremendous pressure to bear upon the church—hierarchy, religious and laymen alike. All wondered what their role should be.

A surprisingly large percentage of Catholics—although still a most definite minority in the church—participated in the revolutionary insurrection against Batista. The best known symbol of this Catholic participation was Father Guillermo Sardiñas, who, with the permission of his own bishop and of Pérez Serantes and Cardinal Arteaga, left his parish on the Isle of Pines and went to the Sierra Maestra as a chaplain to the rebel army. (For his abnegation and contribution to the revolutionary cause, he was promoted to the rank of *comandante;* after the flight of Batista, he used to dress in an olive-green cassock, complete with his commander's insignia, to the chagrin of his church superiors.)

With differing degrees of commitment and varying political ideologies, many other priests participated in other ways to bring about the overthrow of Batista. There was, then, active church involvement by this progressive minority in the struggle against the dictator. Chaplains were active in the columns of Fidel Castro, Raúl Castro, and Juan Almeida (Fidel also had a Protestant chaplain with his group). Father Madrigal in Havana was the treasurer of the July 26 Movement until he had to seek exile in late 1958. In Oriente active supporters included Father Francisco Beristaín, Father Antonio Rivas, a guerrilla chaplain, and Father Jorge Bez Chabebe, chaplain of the Catholic Youth movement in Santiago. In Manzanillo, Father Antonio Albiza assisted couriers from the Sierra Maestra. In Havana, Father Moisés Arrechea, chaplain of the Colón Cemetery, recruited young Catholics for the Sierra. Also in the capital, Msgr. Eduardo Boza Masvidal and his assistant Father Madrigal hid revolutionaries, as did Father Manuel Rodríguez Rozas. Catholic lay leaders Antonio Fernández, president of the youth wing of Acción Católica, and Enrique Canto, former president of Acción Católica in Santiago, actively opposed Batista.[28] Given their support, and that of many Catholic activists, one can claim with some certainty that more Catholics participated in the struggle against the Batista dictatorship than did militants of the communist party (PSP) at that time.

After the shooting death of the young Catholic student leader José Antonio Echevarría in 1957, certain church sectors became more involved in the opposition to Batista. Catholics who participated in this struggle generally did so as individuals, not as church representatives: they fought against Batista because they despised him and wanted to rid their country of him and because their consciences advised them of the need for such actions, but they fought as Cubans who happened to be Catholics rather than as a result of church pressure. Direct official support from the church hierarchy for these activities was noticeably, and understandably, absent.

Among the estimated 20,000 people killed in the struggle against Batista were a large number of Catholic militants. Increasing public pressure for Batista's resignation in early 1958 (a process that resulted in increased repression by the security forces) forced the church hierarchy to confront and make a statement on the situation. In two years of political tension, even though there had not been an organized Catholic response, large numbers of Catholics had played an important role in opposing Batista. Finally the church was driven to get off the fence, yet even then its fragmented nature resulted in ambiguous messages in the face of revolutionary activity.

An important article in *Bohemia* in mid-January 1959 throws further light on the generally ignored role of church activists. Franciscan priest Julián Bastarrica, for instance, roundly condemned the Batista coup a week after it took place. Lay leaders Andrés Valdespino and Marta Moré, presidents of the men's and women's branches of Juventud Católica, also joined the protest. Members of the Acción Obrera Católica participated actively in strike action against Batista (after which their offices were attacked by government forces), and many Catholics, such as Luis Morales, Juan Fernández Duque, and Ciro Hidalgo, well-known members of the youth section of Acción Católica, were killed. In Oriente, Father Chabebe used his religious radio program on station CMKC to send coded messages to Raúl Castro's column. Outspoken critics of Batista such as Fathers Angel Gaztelu, Rodríguez Rosas, Manuel Colmena, Belarmino García and Ignacio Biaín (editor of the progressive Catholic journal *La Quincena*) also played important roles.[29] In addition, many Christians of all faiths paid the ultimate price fighting against the Batista dictatorship.

When public pressure for Batista's resignation led to even greater repression by Batista's forces in early 1958, church sectors finally had to speak out more boldly, although significantly the hierarchy remained badly divided. Cardinal Arteaga himself set the tone for this ambiguity. The man whose vigorous leadership in the 1930s and 1940s had been largely responsible for the growth in church fortunes was now a sick old man who lacked the vision and energy to take a stand against Batista. Other church leaders simply refused to get involved—despite the energetic prodding of Bishops Pérez Serantes and Martín Villaverde, believing that it was not their business to mix in politics. Father Kelly, the American rector of Villanueva (Catholic) University, also chose noninvolvement, despite the killing of several of the university's students by Batista's forces, refusing requests to close Villanueva as a gesture of opposition to Batista's regime and of solidarity with the state universities, all forcibly closed by Batista. Steeped in its "apolitical" and "neutral" tradition, the church hierarchy offered remarkably little leadership in opposing Batista.

Frustrated by this silence, hoping to animate his fellow bishops to take a stand, Archbishop Pérez Serantes called a meeting of the hierarchy in late February 1958. The incident is important, since it illustrates the amorphous nature of the church, with opposing views held by individuals incapable of reaching a consensus. The archbishop was furious at the oppression in Oriente province and wanted his colleagues to sign a public statement requesting Batista to resign, a move supported by Bishops Martín Villaverde of Matanzas and Evelio Díaz of Pinar del Río but opposed by those of Cienfuegos (Eduardo Martínez Dalmau) and Camagüey (Carlos Ríu Anglés). Cardinal Arteaga, supported by Msgr. Alfredo Müller, then attempted to seek a collaborative tone of harmony, reflected in the wording of the resulting pastoral letter released on 25 February: "We exhort . . . all those fighting in opposing camps to cease the violence and to search for—as soon as possible—an effective solution, one which will again bring to our country the material and moral peace it so badly needs. With this in mind, we do not doubt that those who really love Cuba will know how to prove their worth before God and before history. They will not shun any sacrifice in order to obtain the establishment of a government of national unity, one that could prepare the return of our country to a pacific and normal political life."[30]

Here was one example of the cardinal's unrealistic approach to the civil war in his country, his naive hope for a miraculous solution to a problem that in the Cuban revolutionary context could be resolved only by a political and military victory. In part such a position can be explained by concern over Fidel Castro's youth and inexperience in government, in part by a traditional preference to preserve the status quo. In the face of these factors, from the official church perspective the most attractive role seemed to be that of intermediary, seeking only modest reform—a choice that proved to be too little, too late. No reconciliation was possible between the weltanschauung of Fidel Castro and that of Fulgencio Batista. By preaching harmony and collaboration, Arteaga, wittingly or not, was attempting once again to bury the church's head in the sand. Fully aware of this, Archbishop Pérez Serantes indignantly denounced the cardinal's watered-down document: "I didn't frame my proposal in those confused and ambiguous terms, nor did I mention any 'national unity cabinet', as they're now attempting to do. I asked for a change in government, which includes Batista's departure."[31]

Through their disunity, church leaders in the year before Castro's victory frittered away the opportunity to play a progressive role in the struggle against Batista. Sharing radically different interpretations of the responsibilities of churchmen faced with abuse (and a basic human desire to protect their own interests), church leaders lost the opportunity to build on the support of the many lay Catholics and regular clergy who, faced with these same challenges, had decided upon a course of action. While it is unlikely, given the developments in Cuba's fortunes in 1959 and the early 1960s, that the church would have swayed the nation's future, a unified, courageous stand would have given the hierarchy the credibility it sacrificed through indecision and noninvolvement. Its inability to take a firm moral stand was seen by the populace at large as being sorely lacking.

This failure to act does not diminish the courageous actions of Pérez Serantes, who at this decisive period sought to instill a sense of awareness and responsibility in his fellow bishops, or of the thousands of Catholics who struggled valiantly against the dictator. Yet both within the hierarchy and among the Catholic population at large, these strong divisions drastically reduced whatever role the church as a body was seeking to assume and of course weakened its popular base after Batista fled. Despite the continuing murder and repression in Cuba, church leaders simply sat on the fence, releasing isolated criticisms but refusing to take an active united stand, claiming that they were "above politics." Finally in December 1958, Father Belarmino García said in public what many Catholic activists had been feeling in private: "The Church hierarchy . . . has left the Catholic flock defenseless, and indeed has even insinuated accusations of a lack of discipline, and of defiance, because of the attitude of its very best priests and faithful in the face of the very severe danger facing the nation. The leading Church dignitaries have professed or publicly feigned an inconceivable indifference when faced with the unspeakable deeds undertaken by the forces of repression. These forces, encouraged and rewarded by the supreme power of the de facto ruler, have bragged openly about abuses and cruelties which outrage human dignity, and offend in a sacrilegious manner the Christian spirit and the very core of Christian moral values."[32] Unfortunately, the hierarchy simply was not listening.

At times of great strife and personal danger the normal tendency is to ignore the abuse of human rights suffered by others in the hope that one will be left alone as a reward for this tacit acceptance. In the case of the church prior to the revolution, however, this tendency became deliberate *support* for the status quo, as churchpeople from all religions sought to develop their own base and popularity: through their inaction they both fomented and prolonged its inequities and abuses.[33] "Neutrality" might have initially carried the day in church circles, but in justifying themselves by adhering to this policy churchpeople saw their credibility slowly drain away.

The church in the 1950s clearly felt that both its material conditions (its large number of private schools) and its popular acceptance were improving rapidly and that therefore it had a major role to play in Cuban society. At the same time, having seen its improving fortunes rudely dashed a few decades before, it was understandably wary, and the "official" church took the easy path, ignoring the atrocities of the Batista regime and calling for such nebulous concepts as "harmony," "reconciliation," and "dialogue" at a time when such concepts were clearly inappropriate.

It is important to note, however, that an active church minority spurned the church's official position and criticized the urban-centered policies of church leaders. The private schools might well generate funds and win support for the church among the urban bourgeoisie, but this minority voice believed that a true church mission should seek a more meaningful and widespread social justice in Cuba. Many lay Christians, such as Frank País, a Baptist, or José Antonio Echevarría, a Catholic, transformed this religious philosophy into action, became revolutionary leaders, and were killed by Batista's forces. Many clergy from all faiths actively aided the revolutionary struggle in a secondary capacity, often at great personal risk. In early 1959, Fidel Castro himself would note that "the Catholics of Cuba have given their most resolute cooperation to the cause of freedom."[34] In the next two years, the early promise of this potential would steadily dissipate as the church sank back to its earlier marginal level.

The Protestant Church: From Independence to Machado, 1898–1932

The Protestant church in Cuba followed much the same course as the Catholic church. While there had been token Protestant interest in Cuba before the wars of independence, it was really only upon the outbreak of the 1895 conflict that Protestant missionaries actively considered evangelizing work in Cuba. After the defeat of the Spanish forces in 1898, the floodgates opened behind Teddy Roosevelt and his Rough Riders as ministers from various denominations streamed in, determined to save souls for Christ and wrest the spiritual advantage from their discredited Catholic competition. Their missionary zeal was directed at what one Methodist minister in 1899 termed "an intelligent people, the victims of despotic power, obliged to support as an institution of the State a religion which tended to brutalize them, and the purpose of whose clergy was to vitiate and corrupt them."[35]

Protestant missionaries at this time fulminated against the "Romish influence," in particular against what they saw as a dangerous foreign influence—that of Spain. One notable missionary, Manuel Delofeu, for instance, railed at "the Spanish clergy, of a dominant and intolerant spirit, vicious and corrupt, and so hostile to Cuban ideas."[36] Unfortunately, however, the North American missionaries proved equally "hostile to Cuban ideas," seeking to impress their own cultural, socio-political, and religious values upon the Cubans. If the Spanish through Catholicism stunted political maturity and hindered the development of a Cuban national identity, so did the North Americans, through a Protestantism built largely on models that included U.S. pastors, translations of prayer books and hymns written for an American audience, and massive subsidies from the American Mother Church. Protestant missionaries, then, while apprised of the noxious influence of "Romanism" and of inculcated ideas from Spain, were generally unaware of the double standard they were guilty of practicing. In sum, despite the best intentions, they did not practice what they preached.

This failure was unfortunate, given the promising example of Protestantism among Cuban exiles in Florida prior to the 1895–98 struggle. In Ybor City, Tampa, and Key West, Protestant missionaries had been successful in evangelizing and in employing a practical form of religion. Delofeu, for instance, wrote of his missionary triumphs among the exiles in Key West: 80 marriage ceremonies, 102 burials, 276 baptisms, and 123 members either received in full communion or "on probation." Moreover, he gathered $1,100, distributed "twenty boxes of clothing among the poor, also dispensed great quantities of supplies, consisting of medicines, bandages, lint and clothing to the army of the Liberator and General Máximo Gómez."[37] Together with Henry Someillán and Manuel Domínguez, he worked with the exiles; in Cuba a small nucleus of determined evangelists such as Evaristo Collazo (founder of Presbyterianism in Cuba) and Episcopalian Pedro Duarte joined the mambises in their struggle in 1895. From these promising beginnings, however, the Protestant churches soon became avid defenders of U.S. intervention in 1898 and of the foreign cultural and economic presence that swiftly followed.

For the three decades following the Spanish defeat, Protestantism flourished in Cuba, particularly those forms taught by Methodists, Presbyterians, Baptists, Episcopalians, and Congregationalists. With true missionary zeal, Christians from these denominations took up their crusade to "save" the Cubans from Catholicism and show them the true way. If numbers of converts are the only indicator, they were remarkably successful, as a study of the figures for the growth of Methodism shows (see table 4). As with Catholicism, however, much of this growth was superficial, since it relied heavily on the Protestant school system as a means of generating church members and on extensive subsidies from the Mother Church in the United States (as late as 1941, of the 350 Protestant churches in Cuba, only four had self-supporting congregations).[38] Still, it was felt that the new century favored the introduction of a new power—a role that all Protestant missionaries saw as an appropriate one for the United States to play: "God had exercised an overall guiding hand in first awakening the kindly and enlightened young American nation to the tyranny of Spain. He had then clothed her Christian armies with brilliant success and opened up new territories to be benevolently introduced to American democracy and Protestantism."[39]

The North American influence, accompanied by a determined fervor, a religious zeal, and an almost militaristic campaign plan,[40] was to be a feature of Cuban Protestantism until the early 1960s, in essence because, as Crahan has indicated, "the churches were convinced that salvation lay not simply in accepting religious beliefs dominant in North America, but also in adopting U.S. political and economic institutions and practices."[41]

The first two decades of Protestantism in Cuba represented a period of great expansion, particularly among the bourgeoisie, in much the same way as had occurred in Catholicism. Energetic campaigns to evangelize were accompanied by the inauguration of urban schools, and both proselytizing thrusts were initially successful. One missionary group celebrated the Fourth of July holiday in 1899 by selling religious publications—in all, "1,022 Bibles, Testaments, and portions, mostly the latter."[42] In style there might have been great differences between the eager Protestant missionaries and their rather indifferent Catholic counterparts but not in substance.

The school system was extremely successful in recruiting students to Protestantism, particularly in view of the weakened state of Cathol-

Table 4

The Growth of Methodism in Republican Cuba

Year	No. of Sunday schools	Enroll-ment in Sunday schools	Member-ship	Proba-tioners	School enroll-ment	Teachers in schools	Value of church property	Subscrip-tions to El Evangelista Cubano
1904	19	1,010	986	322	574	24	$110,000	
1907			2,365	1,447				
1909			3,021	1,173			$253,060	
1922			5,151		1,116			1,950
1923							$838,000	
1924		4,000						
1925					1,214		$1,250,000	
1931		5,343	6,492					

Source: Neblett, *Methodism's First Fifty Years in Cuba*. Although incomplete, the general thrust of these figures is a clear and important indication of the growth of Protestantism.

icism in the early years of Cuban "independence." The dearth of
schools in general, the "pro-Spanish" label on many private Catholic
schools, and the value of an education by U.S. instructors (important
given the burgeoning U.S. economic role in Cuba) all proved strong in-
ducements for many parents to enroll their children in Protestant
schools.

Common to the administration of both the Protestant education system and the Protestant church was the lack of Cuban participation—a
characteristic they shared with their Catholic counterparts. School
textbooks were invariably either made in the United States or based
on U.S. culture, promoting U.S. values and mores. In the churches, a
common complaint was the lack of Cuban initiative in devising original hymns for church services (symptomatic, perhaps, of the somewhat superficial nature of the Protestant faith in Cuba). Even the
Methodists were unable to devise original materials, despite their remarkable success in attracting society's best to their schools and
church functions.[43] Their decision in 1938, for instance, to translate
their primer *The Upper Room*—later known as *El Aposento Alto*—
reveals their determination to transplant their North American faith
and practices unchanged into the Cuban context. This paternal view
of Cuban reality would later prove a grave hindrance to the expansion
of Protestantism in Cuba.

One of the most striking features of early Protestant evangelizing
was how much it resembled Catholicism with respect to political activism. Although the Protestants were more emphatic than their Catholic confreres, largely because of their North American prejudices,
both groups urged Cubans to pull themselves up by their bootstraps
and "better themselves." Like the Catholics, the Protestants judged
the status quo to be essentially sound, despite grave social problems,
and condemned all attempts to deviate from it, as in this remarkably
distorted account by a leading Methodist missionary: "In the latter
part of May [1912], Cuba was threatened with a revolution which
might have inaugurated a reign of terror but it turned out to be an abortive uprising. The issue seemed to be between blacks and whites, the
former demanding even larger things than the very large slice of government positions and other good things which have been handed out
to them."[44]

Social change was to come gradually, Protestant accounts concur,
as people improved their station by dint of hard work and self-sacrifice.
Was it not fair to expect that what had succeeded in the United States
would succeed in Cuba? In part, this amalgam of conservatism, nationalism, and religious fervor sprang from the background of the individual evangelizers, for whom "little doubt was felt that the strength of

the U.S. was, to a considerable degree, the consequence of its being a Protestant country."[45] The Protestant pastors encouraged peaceful change, assuring their spiritual charges that they would receive their rewards in the hereafter. In the meantime, they could work to improve their socioeconomic conditions but within the existing political framework. The pastors condemned any kind of political violence, believing from their own experience that reasonable discussion and debate would produce enlightened governing bodies. As a result, when rebellion finally burst forth against the hated dictator Machado, the evangelical churches, according to a leading Methodist missionary, were "less perturbed perhaps than other institutions and groups of society, and forged ahead with their program, calling on all men to seek first the Kingdom of God and His righteousness for then and only then would justice prevail."[46]

Yet the evangelical churches themselves adopted a definite political stance through their courting of the powerful bourgeoisie, their perennial support of U.S. cultural and material values, and their recommendations of piety over activist politics. The parallel with the Spanish model of influence seems self-evident. The Protestant churches also tried in more direct ways to curry favor with the government of the day to improve their own fortunes and to protect themselves from similar maneuvers by the Catholic hierarchy. An entry from Neblett's account gives a good indication of this attitude in regard to the dictatorship of Machado: "On May 20 General Gerardo Machado and Dr. Carlos de la Rosa became president and vice-president, respectively, of Cuba. . . . A cabinet of able men was selected. The task of initiating and enforcing a number of reforms was assigned to Colonel Rogelio Zayas Bazán, Secretary of Government. Colonel Zayas Bazán accepted an invitation to be present and speak to a meeting of the Havana Association of Evangelical ministers held at Central Methodist Church. In presenting the distinguished guest, Dr. José Marcial Dorado, president of the Association, offered the support of Cuban evangelicals to the government in every noble effort toward a moral cleanup, the improvement of customs and the exercise of civic righteousness. Col. Zayas Bazán was visibly moved. As he voiced his thanks, he assured his hearers that the government which he represented was inspired by such high moral ideas."[47]

Their first three decades of missionary work proved a great success for the mainline evangelical churches in Cuba, as statistics on school enrollment and church membership confirm. However, Cuba's move toward nationalism following the overthrow of Machado seemed contradicted by the ever-increasing U.S. presence, raising important questions in Protestant groups about the future role of the church. From the early 1930s to the early 1960s, this concern with establishing a more "Cuban" church would dominate internal discussions of the role and meaning of evangelical groups in Cuban. Like their Catholic counterparts, however, by the time the Protestants had finally decided upon a pertinent evangelical approach, it would be too late.

The Protestant Church: From Machado to Batista, 1933–1958

In Cuba the twenty-five-year period 1933–58 was marked by the rapid growth of Havana, deteriorating rural living conditions, rampant political corruption, increasing U.S. influence and, paradoxically, growing Cuban nationalism. Within the Protestant church during these years the attempt to carve out a separate Cuban identity became a long, drawn-out battle, hampered to a great degree by U.S–based foreign mission societies, which regarded Cuban evangelicals as disorganized and flighty, altogether incapable of maintaining, much less developing, church growth. Accordingly, while autonomy was extended to Protestant churches in Asia and elsewhere in Latin America, Cuba was obliged to remain dependent on the U.S. "parents," much to the displeasure of indigenous evangelicals. Typical of this paternal approach of head offices in the United States was one annual report of the Methodist Episcopal Church South which emphasized the Cuban "tendency to exalt sentiments . . . probably the result of an educational and racial process that traces back through the Latins and Greeks of early times."[48]

The parallel is striking between the Catholic church, which had traditionally staffed its missionary work with Spanish priests, trained many of the Cuban seminarians in Spain, and provided few administrative posts to native-born clergy, and the Protestant church, which was funded largely from the United States, educated Cuban ministers in American seminaries, and exhibited little confidence in Cuban administrative talents. In both cases Cuba was evangelized by a church that imposed its own cultural and religious values on people while in general disregarding their feelings. This overzealous approach created "a Church that is too costly to be carried by the economic power of its membership, and calls for an organization, program, ritual and discipline which is somewhat foreign to the inheritance of the Cuban people."[49]

Further parallels between the churches lie in their educational work and in their neglect of rural areas. Just as Catholic clergy were heavily involved in private schools (usually in urban centers) to generate operating funds, their Protestant counterparts received funds (and widespread prestige) from their flagship schools such as the Candler and Buenavista colleges in Havana, Irene Toland in Matanzas, Pinson in Camagüey, and Eliza Bowman in Cienfuegos.[50] In both cases again, fees were occasionally waived and several schools charged no fees at all; however, the emphasis at these major institutes (as at their Catholic equivalents) was raising funds, winning converts, and developing renown and recognition for their work. In all three goals both churches were successful.

Rural areas were in general disregarded by Catholic and Protestant missionaries alike as they concentrated their limited resources in the more densely populated urban areas. J. Merle Davis pointed out in the early 1940s the widespread "absence of courses [in theological education] for equipping a candidate for the highly specialized problems and needs of the rural environment in which one-half of Cuba's people live."[51] Davis's extremely useful report, prepared partly in hopes that a detailed analysis and resulting new approach might combat a general malaise among evangelical groups, reveals a picture of an urban church; only 3.13 percent of respondents to a widely distributed questionnaire considered themselves as rural workers (table 5).

The evangelical activity reported by Merle Davis was that of church that had progressed as far as it could using traditional missionary activities and strategies. Indeed, in 1942, when the detailed report was published, Protestant church groups had entered a stagnant period, if not a decline. Church membership figures were well padded with as many

Table 5
Occupations of Protestants in the 1940s

Occupations	Percentages
Housewives	28.95
Students	22.96
Unemployed	12.91
Teachers	5.65
Artisans	5.63
Day Laborers	5.22
Clerks	3.60
Merchants, tradesmen	3.58
Farmers	3.13
Officials of the government	2.31
Professions	1.54
Servants	1.43
In commerce	1.36
Retired	.97
Transportation workers	.76

Source: Davis, *The Cuban Church in a Sugar Economy*, 74.

as 30 to 40 percent of listed members absent; only 31 percent of church members actually contributed regularly to support their church; morale among pastors was low; twenty-four of twenty-seven pastors questioned commented on the impossibility of even urban churches supporting a pastor and his family; there was a declining attendance of evangelical youth;[52] church survival depended on U.S. subsidies; and no evangelizing had reached the rural areas. Davis's conclusion, which might have been applied almost as equally to the Catholic church, was that "the Evangelical Church is not yet adjusted in program, upkeep and leadership to the economic and social conditions of Cuba. The Church is a middle-class and expensive institution in a largely lower-class and poverty-stricken constituency. It is an Anglo-Saxon and democratic institution in a Latin and feudal society. It is an urbanized institution seeking to expand in a rural environment."[53]

In the wake of this critical report commissioned by several evangelical denominations, Protestant groups set out to remedy the reported ills and to implement some of the recommendations made. They were largely successful at an organizational level, for instance, with the founding of the Cuban Council of Evangelical Churches and the Association of Evangelical University Students, both in the early 1940s. The societal problems, political crises, and dependency of U.S. mission councils, however, made a more meaningful resolution impossible. Nevertheless, important gains were made. Greater Cuban participation in the decision-making process was encouraged, the inauguration of the Evangelical Seminary at Matanzas in 1948 prompted a more ecumenical approach, attendance and contributions to churches increased throughout the 1940s, and at the same time more emphasis was given to social action projects such as community centers and clinics, schools, dispensaries, and hurricane relief activities, closely paralleling the Catholic Action programs.

This modernizing trend would continue throughout the 1940s and early 1950s: with the rebuilding emphasis that followed World War II, evangelical churches attacked their mission with renewed vigor. It was a time for developing a church with greater social relevance, one that would be appropriate for the modern era. One indication that the message of this revitalized Protestant church was being heard was that, between 1948 and 1953, the American Bible Agency claims to have distributed in Cuba 1.2 million Bibles and tracts.[54] Another result of this aggressive missionary program was the number of evangelical followers—an active 5 percent of the Cuban population by the mid-1950s.[55]

The military coup of Fulgencio Batista in 1952 offered the evangelical church the opportunity to extend its influence, particularly as repression grew and national frustration over Batista's strong-arm tactics increased. True to their fundamental dislike of politics and their weak nationalistic inclinations, however, Protestant groups refused to take sides, in essence accepting the status quo. For its part the National Council of Evangelical Churches adopted as its official position "the task of reconciliation between Batista and the rebel forces," in much the same vein as the stance taken by the Catholic hierarchy.[56]

Another further parallel between Protestants and Catholics can be drawn from the unofficial roles played by individuals in the revolutionary struggle. Among Protestants who were recognized for their commitment to the revolutionary struggle were Frank País (leader of the July 26 Movement in Santiago) and his brother Josué (sons of a Baptist minister), Cecilio Arrastia, Presbyterian staff member of the National Council of Evangelical Churches (who presented Fidel Castro with $10,000 in 1956 to help with the purchase of the "Granma"), Dr. Mario Llerena, a Protestant layman who was Fidel's personal representative in the United States and a leader of Cuba's Civic Resistance Movement, Dr. Faustino Pérez, another Protestant layman, who had participated in the Granma landing and whose home served as the headquarters of the Havana underground, Rev. Rafael Cepeda, Rev. Raúl Fernández Ceballos, Esteban Hernández, and Rev. Mario Fernández.

In early 1959, the Rt. Rev. Alexander Hugo Blankingship, Protestant Episcopal bishop of Cuba, claimed in an interview during the early, heady days of the fidelista triumph that the Protestant church had "worked unremittingly for the success of the revolution."[57] He was of course exaggerating, since the church had worked unremittingly to avoid being seen as overly partisan to either side. As with the Catholic church, however, Protestant individuals had played an invaluable role in the popular struggle, fired by their beliefs in socioeconomic justice and the need to bring it about.

Both churches felt a need for a more pertinent credo and religious style, but ultimately both would struggle fiercely against any type of *aggiornamento*. The challenge to the Protestant church would seem to have been far less severe. It had arrived in Cuba comparatively recently, had an active—if smaller—congregation, possessed more Cuban ministers, and had no long Spanish tradition of hindering social change in Cuba. True, the Protestants were hampered by their dependence on U.S. funds and North American values, yet they were in a far stronger position to build upon their religious base—given their relatively unblemished past—than their Catholic counterparts. Partly because of this position, Protestants played a far more active role in government following the overthrow of Batista than one would expect from their limited numbers.[58] They were, of course, in favor of closing down casinos, cracking down on corruption, and supporting Fidel's severely moralistic approach to his forces. This was no real test of their condition as evangelical representatives, however. As the revolution slowly and inevitably radicalized throughout 1959 and 1960, their support—and indeed that of the larger Catholic constituency—would face a far more profound test. How, then would they reconcile their Christian beliefs with the radical path down which Cuba was heading?

Two

3

From Euphoria to Despair,

1959–1960

In this highly charged atmosphere Fidel Castro and the barbudos traveled from Santiago de Cuba to Havana in early January 1959. The Christian sector was ecstatic, largely because of its extensive individual participation against Batista. Catholics were particularly delighted that one of their own headed the liberating forces, an image that Fidel and his supporters furthered as they traveled to Havana, bedecked with religious medals and visiting religious shrines. Fidel—an alumnus of the well-known Jesuit college Belén—apparently kissed the flag of his alma mater and promised to introduce religious education into the national school system for the first time in Cuba's history. It seemed clear that a new moral influence was to be brought to bear on reforming Cuba. Yet by the end of 1960, less than two years later, a break between church and state seemed inevitable, and the early optimism among church spokesmen was replaced by despair over the rapid progress of social reform and over the development of relations between Cuba and the Soviet Union.

Church-state tensions sprang from three fundamental issues. The first was the far-reaching series of socioeconomic reforms introduced in Cuba shortly after the military victory over Batista. The focus of much discussion and bitter polemic by diverse sectors of the church, these reforms ranged from the Urban Reform Law to widespread educational improvements, from agrarian reform to the appropriation of foreign and national businesses. The second issue was Cuba's decision to reopen diplomatic relations with the USSR. As Washington attempted to undercut the Cuban revolutionary process, the idea of an alternative trading relationship with the Soviets became attractive to Cuba, to the chagrin of the Catholic hierarchy. The "godless communism" personified by the Soviets and their Marxist-Leninist philosophy, particularly in the wake of the McCarthy era, was anathema to most Christian churches, which saw Fidel Castro's radical reforms suddenly transformed from "beneficial" and "Christian" to "communist" and "atheistic." For many influential Christians, horrified by these reforms, the *aggiornamento* of Vatican II would come too late. The third issue dividing church and state was in many ways the natural outcome of this second development: if Castro was offering the *patria* as plunder to the godless hordes in the Soviet Union, the only apparent alternative was an even greater dependence on the most powerful Christian nation of the free world, the United States. Cuban Christians rallied to praise the U.S. system (the same system intent on destroying the Cuban revolutionary process) and to damn atheistic communism. This move first infuriated, then alienated Cuban leaders, who taunted Cuban Christians for following the "Church of Washington." By December 1960 the lines dividing church and state had been drawn, and the early promise and hope had vanished: bitterness and mistrust became the order of the day.

Socioeconomic Reform

The deterioration in church-state relations can be appreciated better if some attention has been paid to the flowery praise and mutual backpatting that characterized the church's initial support of Fidel Castro and his plans for sweeping reform in Cuba. Speaking in Santiago de Cuba on 3 January 1959 in his usual ornate style, Archbishop Pérez Serantes summarized the popular victory: "The tenacious determination of a man of exceptional talents, supported with enthusiasm by almost all his fellow Oriente citizens, as well as by a very considerable part of the Cuban population . . . have been the letters with which Divine Providence has traced in the Cuban sky the word *triumph*. Due to this process, the Maximum Leader of the movement has been able to bear from East to West the laurel of this victory, of such extraordinary resonance."[1] Pérez Serantes welcomed the guerrilla victory with enthusiasm and urged the new government, in words that must have pleased the fidelistas enormously, to reshape the fabric of contemporary Cuba, concluding: "In sum, let the Head of State ensure that social justice be rigorously practiced, according to the norms of the Gospel."[2] The archbishop was specific in his requests for a new Cuba, inviting the insurgents to share his aspirations: "We want that, just as every morning at dawn the sun shines for all, so too that nobody will ever be lacking their daily bread; that there never be a scarcity of food, clothing, housing and the appropriate kind of education, of such a nature that it will qualify people to improve their situation, so that they can climb the steps of the social scale—something which should be the privilege of all."[3]

These words must have sounded tremendously encouraging to Fidel Castro and his followers, for they echo the goals outlined in Fidel's defense speech "History Will Absolve Me" following the 26 July 1953 attack on the Moncada garrison, and reflected in several programs drawn up in the Sierra Maestra struggle. Castro could therefore be excused for believing that he had the church's backing to undertake sweeping social change in Cuba. For their part, church leaders must have taken heart from the goals of reform espoused by the fidelistas, as well as from the discipline and self-control of the rebel troops and their apparent religiosity, for many guerrilla fighters wore religious medals and scapulars.

Catholic and Protestant churches bestowed official support upon the young revolutionary government. Known Christians were appointed to important positions, open government prevailed, and all seemed pleased with the initial moves, among them the abolition of gambling and prostitution and a widely publicized campaign against corruption. The first difficult matter to be evaluated by church representatives came toward the end of January 1959 with the execution of an estimated four hundred war criminals. Pérez Serantes in a pastoral of 29 January indicates the church's reaction. The archbishop pleaded for clemency toward the prisoners yet went to some length to show that (1) these measures "were not more numerous, nor more harsh, than those applied in other places in similar circumstances by exceptionally responsible men";[4] (2) the state, of course, possessed the right to decree the death penalty; (3) the context of Batista's brutality had to be taken into account, a level of repression that had led to the deaths of some twenty thousand Cubans ("With a viciousness, unsuspected in the minds and hearts of Cubans, many of our youth have been tortured and vilely mutilated");[5] and (4) many critics of the unchristian execution of war criminals had been conspicuously silent during the Batista excesses. Pérez Serantes thus officially requested clemency but understood why the executions had been decreed.

Typical of the Protestant churches' reaction was a cable sent to President Eisenhower by faculty members at the Matanzas Theological Seminary in the wake of critical U.S. press coverage of the executions: "Urge withhold criticism of Cuban Government which has overwhelming popular support including civic, church and other democratic organizations. American silence on countless crimes of Batista Government makes present criticism of executions offensive and dangerous to Cuban-American relations. Press reports overlook the model reform, order and renewed faith in government created by the new regime."[6] After a month in power, then, the revolutionary government had solid church support, on even as sensitive an issue as political execution. It was not to last. Within another month, their own interests threatened, the churches would voice their strong opposition to Castro's government.

Educational Reform

At issue was the government's wide-ranging plans for reform, which threatened to reduce the autonomy of the churches' schools and programs as well as their social influence. Consequently they resisted and criticized the reforms, determined to use their political connections to remind the government of the active role Christians played in the struggle against Batista. In most Latin American countries this favor-for-favor approach would have worked, but not in Cuba in the midst of an emotional and determined campaign to bring about a genuine social revolution. Given the Catholic church's improved fortunes since World War II, Catholic participation in the insurrection, and Fidel, a Belén alumnus and friend of Archbishop Pérez Serantes, the church believed that it could win protection for its own educational institutions, which in 1959 had about 65,000 students. The Protestant churches, with a number of members in influential government posts, believed they too held a strong position, if not to lobby the favors for themselves, at least to neutralize Catholic request for preferential treatment.

While Catholic and Protestant representatives sought to defend their own largely private and lucrative schools, nobody could deny that Cuba needed far-ranging educational reform. Nearly a quarter of the population was illiterate. Despite the stipulation in the 1940 Constitution that all children between the ages of six and fourteen attend school, 44 percent in 1953 did not—in Oriente, 60 percent. The question was how the revolutionary government, with limited funds at its disposal, could meet nationwide expectations of educational reform and still allow the religious schools to maintain their privileged education.

By February 1959 the debate over educational reform had become heated. There were two issues, as far as the Catholic hierarchy was concerned—the teaching of religion in public schools and the right of

Christians to private education. Together they would offer the government its first major internal challenge, and when the problems had ultimately been resolved—in both cases to the detriment of the church—they would be seen in influential church circles as proof of the pro-communist slant that the government was rapidly taking on. The glitter surrounding the Belén alumnus quickly began to fade.

Pastoral letters were issued by church representatives on 13 February—"La Enseñanza Privada" ("On Private Education") by Archbishop Pérez Serantes—and on 18 February—a collective pastoral, "Al pueblo de Cuba: Circular del Episcopado Cubano" ("To the Cuban People: Communiqué of the Cuban Bishops"). The first came a month after the government had published Law II, which invalidated courses and degrees given by all private colleges (including Villanueva, the Catholic University) after 30 November 1956, when the public universities had been closed by Batista in retaliation for their opposition to his dictatorship. Insults were hurled at Father Kelly, the Villanueva president, and his fifteen fellow North American Augustinians. Villanueva was accused of consistently subordinating Cuban to U.S. values. The issue threatened to plague church-state relations, especially when it moved from a discussion of private versus state education to the broader debate of freedom versus communism, a harbinger of the bitter problems to come. Enrique Pérez Serantes, followed within a week by his fellow bishops, added substantially to this argument with their own interventions, thereby speeding up the growing polarization.

In his 13 February letter, Pérez Serantes used the Villanueva University incident to criticize the government for not allowing parents freedom of choice regarding their children's education. More particularly, he claimed that parents wanted religious education within the public school system, a point he supported with a reference to Fidel Castro himself:

> The war is, then, against religious education in the public schools; the war is against all Catholic schools, even the most prestigious, which is Villanueva University. Catholicism—that's the enemy.
>
> Can they say that being a student at a Catholic school automatically constitutes a danger for society?
>
> Perhaps they're afraid that, after studying at public school, there's a possibility that our youth will be less educated or less manly.
>
> Let a response be made on our behalf by Dr. Fidel Castro, a former student at the [Catholic] schools of Dolores and Belén.[7]

The indication of the church's future position came in the shape of a strongly worded reference to communism, since Pérez Serantes went out of his way to show how "masons and communists and these people in favor of laicism" were uniform in denying people freedom of educational choice. According to Pérez Serantes, all three groups saw religious education as the means to their own undoing and so resisted it tenaciously: "Let's put things clearly: the enemy that they're fighting is just one, the only one in the world that communism fears."[8]

This injection of "the communist threat" into the archbishop's pastoral was symptomatic of the preoccupation of the entire Catholic hierarchy. It found itself in a great dilemma, for whereas it approved of the humanitarian thrust of Cuba's new revolutionary laws it was unprepared to make concessions when these reforms impinged on its own rights. The hierarchy's resulting strategy was to associate any reforms too radical for its liking with communism, a concept that in Cuba in the 1950s caused widespread concern.

In their joint pastoral of 18 February 1959, the bishops began on a bullish note, stressing that their position was upheld by a majority of Cubans "since recent statistics, undertaken with complete scientific vigor, have shown that in Cuba 95 percent of the population is Catholic, with 5 percent Protestants and their followers."[9] The hierarchy then continued the basic theme of the earlier letter by Pérez Serantes, indicating the need for parents to educate their children as they saw fit (in private or public schools), as well as to have access to religious education in all schools: "95 percent of Cubans are Catholics; 95 percent of Cubans demand their freedom: they refuse to continue to be condemned to ignorance in religious matters."[10]

As in the case of Pérez Serantes's pastoral, this circular then widened its scope, injecting the communism vs. Free World polarity into the discussion. Several countries—largely in Europe and the Americas—were cited to show how widely respected was the concept of religious education, after which the example of the Soviet bloc was given by way of contrast and a provocative challenge thrown out:

> On the other hand, the government of Janos Kadar in Hungary annulled the law which allowed religious education in public schools. That's the tendency of communist governments.
>
> And now we ask the government and the people of Cuba: on whose side will Cuba line up at this moment?[11]

The debate surrounding educational reform in many ways rang hollow and in the long run served to show the church's insecurity with its newfound social status. Since the republic's founding, all public schools had been required by law to be of a lay nature, with religious instruction expressly forbidden. Therefore, the implication of the joint pastoral ("That's the tendency of communist governments") in reality had no bearing on the Cuban case, where schooling had been of a lay nature for nearly six decades. What the hierarchy was demanding for Cuba's alleged "95 percent of the population" was thus unprecedented and a risky gamble of their prestige, a gamble that they would lose.

The heavy-handed references to the dangers of communism so soon after the revolutionary victory uncovered a more deeply rooted problem for church-state relations. True, the government was expected to mobilize all resources at its disposal to resolve the glaring socioeconomic inequities noted by Enrique Pérez Serantes in his 3 January pastoral, but the line between an energetic policy of social reform and "the threats of excessive State control" was fine indeed. Adding to the confusion, particularly for the majority of Spanish clergy, was a dread of any facet of communism. Shortly after the Korean War, and in the grip of the Cold War, Cuba under Batista had received generous U.S. funding to fight communism. Later, as the revolutionary process advanced, opponents of the government would look back on Batista and his notorious anticommunist agency, BRAC, and feel that, despite his excesses, Batista had at least fought communism. The bishops' fears, shared by many Cubans, thus served to widen the gap between the revolutionary process and the church hierarchy—less than two months after the flight of Batista.

Agrarian Reform

Perhaps none of the early reforms undertaken by the revolutionary government revealed the badly divided nature of the Christian churches, most clearly of the Catholic church, as did agrarian reform. On 17 May 1959 the official Agrarian Reform Law was promulgated, dissipating any remaining church-state unity. By the end of 1959, while many grass-roots Christian sectors supported the thrust of the reform, the entire hierarchy had come out against it, including early supporters Bishop Martín Villaverde of Matanzas, Auxiliary Bishop Evelio Díaz of Havana, and, to a lesser extent, Archbishop Pérez Serantes of Santiago. Their objections were many, but their central fear was that unless the church could rally support to prevent it, Cuba was heading inexorably toward communism.

The specifics of agrarian reform were straightforward: a limit of 1,000 acres was placed on all estates, with highly productive plantations exempted to a maximum of 3,333 acres, and compensation for all expropriated property was to be paid in the form of twenty-year bonds yielding an annual interest of 4.5 percent. Owners of large plantations and cattle ranches opposed the reforms, while the rural work force supported them. As had the issue of educational reform, these changes in the agrarian sector polarized Cuban society, leaving the church as arbiter caught in the middle. It was an impossible situation for the church to resolve; it culminated in a churchwide rift, followed by government scorn and growing mistrust at the church's attitude.

The two most outspoken church representatives to defend the Agrarian Reform Law, Bishops Evelio Díaz and Alberto Martín Villaverde, gave guarded praise to the legislation in mid-1959. Evelio Díaz spoke prophetically about the need for a new sensitivity to Cuba's poor: "It's time to wake up to a dramatically new Cuba, especially for the majority of our population who until now have lived, or rather survived, in the most precarious and disgraceful conditions." From his many years of experience in a poor rural diocese in Pinar del Río, Díaz was sensitive to the need for a radically new model of land tenure in Cuba and therefore enthusiastic in his support for the reform: "We cannot help praising and blessing all those who contribute to the development of that necessary and magnificent objective into a happy reality. Indeed let us hope, with our confidence placed in God, that the new Agrarian Law (on which to a large extent the future prosperity of our nation depends) will prove the fundamental pillar of our common well-being."[12] Perhaps in an attempt to win over more conservative factions in the hierarchy, Bishop Díaz sought legitimacy for this reform in various papal encyclicals—Leo XII's "Rerum Novarum," Pius XI's "Cuadragessimo Anno," and Pius XII's "Optatissima Pax." The thrust of his pastoral was the need for national reconciliation, for greater social cooperation, and for a just redistribution of resources—particularly at the expense of the wealthy, whom he urged to show understanding and fraternal compassion. His conclusion, both dramatic and forceful, must have raised false expectations on the part of the government: "The Agrarian Reform, in its just intentions and its necessary introduction into our country basically conforms with the church's thought in regard to the principle of Social Justice. The realization of this project should engage the awareness of all Christians who, as such, after laying aside all personal and selfish interests, should contribute to the interest of the common good in a generous and peaceful manner, as befits a good Cuban and a better Christian."[13]

As the summer of 1959 passed, church representatives met on several occasions to analyze both the intent and the practice of agrarian reform. Within Cuba, the many changes and new pieces of legislation, the continuing criticism from the U.S. media, and the bickering among the citizenry all contributed to concern about where the country

was heading. As social improvements and nationalistic fervor continued and support for Fidel Castro remained high the "communist
threat" loomed ever more ominously over the middle and upper
classes and little joy was spared the government that had brought in
urban reform and agrarian reform laws.

This concern, accompanied by the increasing criticism of the United
States, led church representatives to temper their praise of agrarian reform. *Bohemia*, for instance, published an article by Bishop Alberto
Martín Villaverde on 5 July which, along with a "preferential option"
for the *campesinos*, quoted from Pius XII ("The Church defends the
right to hold private property, a right which it considers fundamentally unbreachable") and noted that the renting of land to sharecrop-
pers was not in itself unjust. Finally, while supporting the concept of
the reform ("We should rejoice as Catholics that there is an Agrarian
Reform, and we should ask God to enlighten those whose duty it is
to undertake it"), the bishop then warned readers against the communist influence of the reform, a warning soon to be taken up by other
members of the hierarchy.[14]

This reorientation among liberal churchmen is most clear in the
case of Archbishop Pérez Serantes. Not one to engage in subterfuge,
the elderly churchman was direct in his assessment of agrarian reform,
which he supported totally in theory since "it tends to redeem the
peasants from the deplorable state in which they presently are, a state
not just of poverty, but really of veritable misery in many cases. And
this in such a privileged country in which nobody should really experience the blow of hunger."[15] Although the archbishop reserved judgment on the practice of the reform, claiming not to have access to suffi-
cient elements on which to base an opinion, he had a word of caution
for Fidel Castro: "In this particular case, experts versed in communist
doctrine (which has been circulated in Cuba for the benefit of the
Cuban people) have found in the above-mentioned Agrarian Reform so
many similarities, or affinities as some claim, with the thought of
Moscow's faithful and disciplined followers, that they've begun to suspect that the latter—together with the architects of the Agrarian
Reform—have drunk from the same fountain. It is only right that Dr.
Castro, certainly far distant from the directions emanating in Moscow,
should know perfectly well that this course of action will in no way
favor the success of the Revolution."[16]

This swing from enthusiastic support to direct warning typified the
changes in mood of the church hierarchy between 1959 and 1960. The
polarity becoming evident in Cuban society was to a certain extent reflected by the lower church, where many church representatives (notably the Franciscans, as well as influential Catholic lay groups) encour-

aged the hierarchy to take a more balanced view of the revolutionary process. In this they were unsuccessful, coming up against "a sort of rationalistic Christian unrealism which made [the hierarchy] tend to have greater concern for rights to property, for instance, than for its just distribution."[17] On the other hand the Spanish clergy were in general extremely conservative and used their majority voice effectively to bolster the bishops' increasingly rigid views. As with the educational and house reforms, larger, more universal considerations overshadowed the inherent value of the agrarian program (and of all the reforms per se)—the fear that members of the revolutionary government might have "drunk from the same fountain" as the "moscovitas." This concern became the overriding factor in every subsequent church position. In such a climate, an unbiased evaluation of the ensuing societal changes was as difficult for church spokesmen as for other members of the bourgeoisie. For everyone, history was moving too quickly, and their response, particularly in the context of the pre–Vatican II era, was quite predictable.

The Cold War Climate

The years 1959–60, a dramatic turning point, completely altered the course of Cuba's history. The earliest months of the revolution brought rapid social reform to the most impoverished sectors of Cuban society, largely at the expense of the bourgeoisie and the small upper class. In addition to Fidel Castro's unquestionable charisma, most Cubans soon appreciated that important changes had been obtained to their benefit. The reforms that acted as a catalyst to this social restructuring, together with the intangible but important pride in Cuba as a focus of worldwide interest, combined to strengthen the fidelista position. These changes produced societal pressure and tension as bitter struggles evolved among pressure groups seeking to dominate the political process.

By the spring of 1959 the battle lines were drawn. The reductions in rents and telephone rates, the condemnation of racism, the intent to nationalize educational and medical services, and the steep tariffs on imported luxury items indicated to many middle-class Cubans that the revolution could only bring them misfortune. Many left for Florida. Others remained in Cuba to fight the leftward tilt of the revolutionary government by democratic means (the tack taken by the popular media), by the traditional Cuban system of graft (as in the Cattlemen Association's $500,000 fund to bribe newspapers),[18] and by force of arms.

The armed resistance to the revolutionary government increased throughout 1959 and 1960 and culminated in the CIA-sponsored Bay of Pigs invasion of April 1961. On 13 June 1959, for instance, three bombs exploded during one of Castro's speeches condemning critics of the agrarian reform. Two months later came the discovery of a plot by some Las Villas farmers to overthrow Fidel Castro. Flights originating in Florida for the purposes of dropping leaflets and incendiary bombs on sugar plantations were commonplace. In October when an aircraft bombed a sugar mill in Pinar del Río, among the twenty people captured were two American pilots.[19] This campaign of subversion, which helped create a climate of concern and fear, left the government with two alternatives—to relax radicalization or to harden fidelista resolve. It chose the latter course.

Another factor in the equation was the reaction of the United States. The early agrarian reform hit U.S. investment hard, generating much frustration among large landholding companies used to government bribery and unfettered control of their vast properties. By June 1959, U.S. spokesmen had expressed concern over the nature of agrarian reform and, while granting that the process aided social reform, demanded prompt and fair compensation for all titleholders.

U.S. Ambassador Philip Bonsal's diplomacy and the polite tone of official correspondence bore no resemblance to the reaction in North American political and military circles to the increasingly militant tone of the Cuban reforms. The course of this spiraling atmosphere of mistrust and eventual loathing was set by Fidel Castro's visit to the United States in April 1959, in particular by his meeting with Vice-President Richard Nixon. By the summer of that year the popular media in the United States reflected the Eisenhower administration's attitude toward Cuba, hinting rather clumsily at the increasingly Communist tilt of the revolution. For example, the *Wall Street Journal* of 24 June 1959 suggested that, like a watermelon, "the more the Revolution is sliced, the redder it gets."[20]

By that summer, Richard Nixon's relentless lobbying and the CIA's analysis of Cuba's reform programs had persuaded Washington to view Castro as procommunist, if not already entirely communist. Rumors flew about Soviet designs on the Caribbean, and it was reported that submarines had been sighted in those waters. A general climate of uncertainly prevailed. It was time to reassert U.S. hegemony over its own backyard with a renewed Monroe Doctrine, to make Fidel Castro toe Washington's line.

In Havana, meanwhile, the revolutionary government did little to accommodate Washington's wishes, instead introducing new laws designed to lead to the takeover of foreign investments. For U.S. investors it was time to withdraw from Cuba and cut their losses. Their action would lead to a rapid exodus of foreign technicians, which in turn would cause drastic production cuts and accentuated social tension as even the most basic goods became scarce.

At the end of the first year of the revolutionary process a confrontation of gigantic proportions loomed, involving not only polarized social groups within Cuba but also the United States, which could hardly be expected to sit still with its political and economic hegemony seemingly threatened. The increasingly disturbed tone of Washington diplomacy, counterrevolutionary activities, internal political crises (most notably Fidel Castro's resignation of 17 July, leading the same day to that of President Urrutia), growing economic problems, and social polarization all contributed—depending on one's position—to elation or despondency, nationalistic pride or despair.

The second year of this radical restructuring proved much the same, with one major exception: the Soviet connection. Cuba, under increasing pressure by Washington, turned toward Moscow for economic assistance and a market for her sugar. In Havana, Fidel Castro continued to lambast the recalcitrant Eisenhower policy toward Cuba. In Washington, pressure mounted on the president—in the year before an election campaign—to break relations with Cuba, or at least to reduce Cuba to obedience by cutting the sugar quota on which the economy depended. March 1960 was perhaps the point at which the course was set for U.S.–Cuban relations for the next quarter-century. Two incidents deserve particular attention—the destruction on 4 March of a French freighter, the *Coubre* and, on 13 March, President Eisenhower's decision to accept a CIA recommendation to arm and train Cuban exiles and to plan an invasion of Cuba. This decision marked the beginning of a new phase in aggression against Cuba, with the president himself taking a role in what had been a covert war headed by the intelligence service. For Cuba the impact of the *Coubre*'s sinking lay not only in the extent of the casualties (seventy-five longshoremen killed and two hundred injured) but also in the symbolism of the explosion (in 1895 the destruction by a mysterious explosion of the U.S. warship *Maine* in Havana harbor had help push the United States into war against Spain). Fidel Castro condemned the Eisenhower administration for its stance against Cuba, blamed the explosion on them, and warned the U.S. government, "You will reduce us neither by war or famine."[21]

Cuba and the Soviet Union began to develop cordial relations in the spring of 1960, confirming the church hierarchy's worst fears about the direction of the revolutionary government. First came the announcement on 31 January that Anastas Mikoyan (at that time first deputy chairman of the USSR's Council of Ministers) was to visit Cuba after meeting with U.S. diplomats in Washington. The church's reaction to this announcement was negative, and when Mikoyan arrived there were several demonstrations condemning the Soviet Union. In one highly publicized incident, Catholic students from the Villanueva University removed a wreath placed by the Soviet politician at the statue of Martí in Havana's central square—a major diplomatic affront. An air of confrontation dominated the visit, as the church loudly voiced its displeasure and encouraged dissent at the Soviet delegation's visit.

A major agreement was signed as a result of Mikoyan's stay in Cuba, one which could only have infuriated both Washington and church leaders. The Soviet Union agreed to buy 425,000 tons of sugar for 1960 and a million tons each year for the following four years. In addition, the USSR agreed to lend approximately $200 million to Cuba at an interest rate of 2.5 percent—approximately the same amount that Cuba had unsuccessfully sought to borrow from European banks only a few months earlier. These moves by the Soviet Union signaled strong support for the Cuban Revolution, and while liberals in Washington urged the Eisenhower administration to curb its opposition to the fidelistas and its threats to cut all sugar imports from Cuba, hotter heads prevailed. The U.S. government increased its pressure, giving presidential approval to the plan to arm and train Cuban exiles and to invade Cuba.

Thus far the United States had been attempting to force Cuba back into line, threatening the revolutionary government with economic blackmail as well as its political overthrow. In contrast, the Soviet Union had been the epitome of patience and understanding, supporting the revolutionary process and its basic goals. Cuba's relationship with each country had been strictly bilateral, as it dealt separately with each over specific issues. Thus, while the Cold War climate obviously permeated both relationships, Cuba until the summer of 1960 was able to maintain a discrete policy with each superpower. In June these bilateral relationships shifted dramatically to a trilateral one, a U.S.–Soviet–Cuban triangle. The Eisenhower administration's policies of confrontation on the one hand and the Khrushchev line of support on the other swept Cuba into the vortex of superpower politics.

The months of June and July represent a microcosm of this dynamic, as both the United States and the Soviet Union sought to imprint their seals on the revolutionary process. On the heels of Cuba's officially reopening diplomatic relations with the Soviet Union in May, Raúl Castro traveled to Czechoslovakia in June, perhaps to discuss the supply of arms to Cuba. Two U.S. diplomats were expelled as counterrevolutionaries, and the United States built a 50-kilowatt radio station on

Swan Island to attack Cuban policy. In late June the major U.S. refineries in Cuba were expropriated after they refused to process imported Soviet crude oil. On 6 July, Eisenhower reduced the sugar quota by 700,000 tons; that same day Khrushchev offered not only to buy that amount of sugar but also to defend Cuba.[22] As the struggle for influence in Cuba continued, it became obvious to all—including a despairing Catholic hierarchy—that Moscow, the center of atheistic communism, was winning the battle for hearts and minds.

One final round remained in this trilateral struggle. Arms continued to flow to Cuba from the Soviet bloc, and in September, Fidel Castro accepted the Soviets' offer of rockets to defend Cuba from an impending invasion. That fall, presidential aspirants John Kennedy and Richard Nixon both supported the overthrow of the revolutionary government by "freedom fighters." At the time perhaps 1,000 counterrevolutionaries were based in the Escambray mountains and a further 1,500 were receiving substantial aid through the CIA. (Nixon, one of the prime instigators of war against Castro since the spring of 1959, had to remain silent on the plans to invade Cuba in April.)

In summary, the urban bourgeoisie (the church's most powerful supporters) was devastated by the revolutionary reforms and the increasing communist influence on their government. The expropriation of the large U.S. chain stores and factories meant a drastic shortage of consumer items for this group, made worse by high tariffs on the imports that trickled in until Eisenhower's ban on 13 October 1960 on U.S. exports to Cuba. The agrarian reform had significantly reduced free enterprise in rural areas, and the Urban Reform Law badly undercut the bourgeoisie's privileges, particularly its second phase beginning in October 1960 which gave the government the right to expropriate all property in excess of the owner's primary dwelling.

The church was also adversely affected by these changes, forced to give up property and buildings as a result of the educational and urban reforms. More serious was the blow to its status and influence, based to a great extent on its many prestigious schools—all of which were "intervened" by the state. The church, which felt that it played a valuable role in Cuban society, bitterly resented these takeovers. Moreover, since church fortunes had improved sharply just before the revolutionary victory, large sectors of the church understandably opposed the revolutionary process.

Washington, long used to having its own way with Latin American countries, continued its short-sighted policies which combined with Moscow's long-term aspirations for the island to fuel the fire in revolutionary Cuba. The badly disaffected bourgeoisie latched on to the villain indicated by the church, international communism. In the aftermath of World War II, the partition of Europe, the development of the Cold War mystique, and events in Hungary and Korea, as well as the earlier Spanish Civil War, conspired to present a one-dimensional picture of communist society. The reaction among Cuban bourgeoisie against "atheistic communism" (Moscow) and in favor of the "Free (Christian) World" (Washington) was predictable.

Most church members came from a class with a set of traditional spiritual and social values. Church leaders, too, were not unnaturally influenced by factors such as world circumstances, their fear of an opposing belief system, and the loss of prestige which they had slowly and painfully established, as well as their rather limited property. Their initial relief at the fidelista victory vanished as the import of the reforms dawned on them. With the injection of the "East-West struggle," the church hierarchy descended into despair, expressed through outspoken opposition and denunciation. However, the church had again lost touch with the majority of Cubans. Even though large numbers of Cubans (not just Catholics) were indeed alarmed at the evolution of the U.S.–Soviet–Cuban triangle, and the success of a national Catholic convention in November 1959 with a million people present clearly indicated the level of opposition, a large majority of Cubans were reaping the benefits of the revolution's social reforms. The more the church insisted on the unhealthiness of the link with the Soviets, the weaker its position became with many impoverished Cubans who wondered why the church had not been as free to criticize the excesses of capitalism. The church's denunciations of the Soviet Union in 1960, then, proved self-destructive not only because they angered the revolutionary government but also because they reconfirmed the church's traditional disregard for socioeconomic conditions.

The Church's Response to the U.S.–Soviet–Cuban Triangle

Throughout the first year of the revolutionary process the official line among both Catholic and Protestant groups was that, however troubling recent social reforms might be, in the last analysis reason would prevail. Revolutionary rhetoric and reforms had to be introduced, ran this line of argument, but under pressure from traditionally influential sectors the government would moderate its program. This was the time-honored way in Cuba, and indeed throughout Latin America. Undoubtedly the "socializing" trend apparent in the early reforms was troubling, but this was, after all, Cuba, where accommodation to pressure from business groups and from the United States was a widespread tradition. Surely Fidel Castro was too smart to get carried away by nationalistic excesses.

To convince the government of the strength of their lobby, Catholic groups organized several protests and marches culminating in a successful mass rally in late 1959 with an estimated million participants, a figure far in excess of the actual number of practicing Catholics. The Protestant churches, a more homogeneous but far smaller group,[23] chose a different avenue, one aided by their comparatively recent arrival in Cuba, well-publicized emphasis on a modern approach (using dispensaries, clinics, and schools to emphasize their value to Cuban society), a high percentage of native-born ministers, and their rejection of celibacy as requisite for ministerial life.

In contrast to the Catholic church, the Protestant church supported the revolutionary government's reform programs as both necessary and long overdue. Writing as late as December 1960, one Protestant observer who voiced concern at the increasing state role nevertheless praised the nature of the reforms: "What Castro said he would do, he is doing, and this part of his program has elicited the Evangelicals' Yes. Even a blind man traveling from one end of the island to the other would be convinced by the noise alone that social redevelopment is under way in Cuba. The construction of new public buildings, and schools, of homes and roads and hospitals, makes a pleasant sound in Cuban ears."[24]

While approving this central thrust, many Protestants were concerned at the leftward tilt of the revolution. Unlike the Catholics, however, they rarely spoke out, perhaps believing that a policy of tacit support would aid their case in government dealings. As one church representative, Rev. Cecilio Arrastia, explained in April 1966, "We were simply theologically unprepared for what happened. We Protestants had no program. We just wanted to help Fidel get rid of Batista. And then we went back to our regular work."[25]

Traditionally critical of their Catholic archrivals (and of the influence they exercised), Protestants continued to react more favorably to the new government until international political repercussions forced them to take sides. The much-discussed visit of Mikoyan in February 1960 hastened the social polarization and brought a skeptical comment from the conservative newspaper *Diario de la Marina* in the wake of the Soviet visit: "Thank you. . . . your visit has . . . defined the camps."[26] It had, and church-state relations slipped into the currents of the Cold War.

The debate on Cuba's role vis-à-vis the United States and the Soviet Union boiled down to this issue: if Cuba continued to jeopardize its traditional relationship with the United States, it could well find itself allied with the Soviets, purveyors of official atheism. Given this potential danger, the church hierarchy preferred to ignore U.S. pressure on the revolutionary government and to urge Fidel Castro to settle with Washington at all costs. Anything was preferable to an alliance with the Soviets. In view of the large Spanish presence in the Catholic church, this was not a slavish identification with U.S. values. Rather it was the growing alliance with the Soviet Union that disturbed the clergy, a position also feared by Cuban Catholics from the bourgeoisie and the upper class, those closely attuned to North American cultural values. Unfortunately this view clearly clashed with the Cuban government's national sociopolitical aspirations, and with both sides so adamantly pursuing their distinctive goals, a rupture between church and state was inevitable. On the one hand, church leaders, buoyed by the successful Congreso Católico Nacional of November 1959, pressed ahead with confidence, apparently holding an inflated view of the strength of their position.[27] On the other hand, the revolutionary government, certain that it still held wide popular support (a poll taken by the Cuban journal *Bohemia* in June 1960 showed that Fidel Castro still had the support of 80 percent of the population), was equally determined to buckle under neither to pressure from Washington nor to the continued raids by counterrevolutionary groups.

Elated after the Congreso and its estimated audience of one million (previously 10,000 people had attended the event), Catholics were once again reminded of the communist threat in December with the defection of two priests, Fathers Eduardo Aguirre and Ramón O'Farrill, both outspoken opponents of Batista. Charging that the revolutionary government was a communist dictatorship that persecuted the clergy and planned to found a national church, the two priests received extensive media coverage in the United States. December also saw the sentencing of Huber Matos to thirty years' imprisonment, following his accusations of increasing communist influence in the government. Then, on 20 January 1960, the government expelled Spanish ambassador Juan Pablo de Lojendio.[28] These events fed Catholic fears over the leftward drift of the revolutionary process, fears kept alive by Cuba's bishops. The introduction of the U.S.–USSR element into the debate in early 1960 clarified matters substantially, and confrontation became inevitable.

Mikoyan's visit to Cuba in early February 1960 only intensified fear among Catholics, who refused to accept the presence of a representative of an "atheistic" country. The protest campaign was led by the Catholic hierarchy, in particular by Archbishop Pérez Serantes assisted by Msgr. Eduardo Boza Masvidal (appointed auxiliary bishop in February 1960), another fierce anticommunist. (It has been suggested that the students who removed the wreath placed by Mikoyan at the José Martí memorial, many of whom were from Villanueva University, acted at the urging of Boza Masvidal.) Together they lambasted the revolutionary government, and the pastoral letters of Archbishop Pérez Serantes whipped up a frenzy of Catholic opposition to the radical direction Cuba was taking. Perhaps more than anything else, then, it was the incipient Cuban-Soviet relationship that scared the hierarchy, which seemed to ignore continued U.S. pressure on Cuba and the Castro government's limited options.

In May 1960, a week after the government announced the restoration of Cuban-Soviet diplomatic relations and the arrival of Ambassador Kudriatsev, the archbishop of Santiago delivered a fiery broadside, "Por Dios y Por Cuba." A long and impassioned document and the first official pastoral on this matter, it stirred considerable controversy among Cuban Catholics. "We can't say now that the enemy is at the door," Pérez Serantes wrote, "because in reality it is already inside our home, speaking loudly, like some one located in their own estate."[29] Citing Pius XI's encyclical *Divini Redemptoris* ("Communism . . . is intrinsically perverse"), the archbishop went to great lengths to illustrate to his flock the nature and the dangers of communism. Based on a philosophy of dialectical materialism ("although hidden beneath appearances which are at times enticing"), communism was atheistic, stripping mankind of its necessary spiritual base, and was in short "the denial of all human values" (563). Since man was reduced to merely organic matter, "he lacks freedom and any kind of moral curbs to withstand the attack of the basest passions, emotions which cannot be calmed by any simple human consideration." Pérez Serantes apparently found family ties, property rights, and social harmony only in Western Christian capitalist society, for he wrote that communist society "denies the existence of the matrimonial link, and its indissoluble nature, and denies the right to hold property and so many other things—indeed it goes so far as to attempt to subvert the entire social order from its very foundations, all the time claiming to form a new unity, without God and his holy law, yet it is submerged in a sea of hate and rancor" (563).

The remainder of the pastoral letter was concerned with two issues, the correct Catholic response to communism and the appropriate Catholic solution to social discord. On the first, Catholics were to have to do "with communism, nothing, absolutely nothing" (564), to steer clear of "this implacable and powerful enemy of Christianity," and to be wary of alluring promises. The remainder of the pastoral laid out a society restructured along new Christian lines based on Catholic social doctrines and spiritual renovation through catechism and "the best weapon, the Decalogue prayers" (566).

While only one-quarter of the pastoral concerned the communist threat to Cuban society, its timing and tone sent a stern warning to the revolutionary government. The increasing U.S.–Cuban tension as well as aid pouring in from Moscow must have alerted Pérez Serantes to the few avenues open to Cuba should the revolution continue. From his perspective, Cuba must be "saved" from the atheistic Soviets. This important speech laid the groundwork for future church attacks on the revolutionary government's ties with the Soviet Union, attacks that were to increase dramatically as U.S.–Cuban relations continued to deteriorate.

By the summer of 1960, church-state polarization was complete. Masses were said for the "victims of religious persecution" in communist societies and to celebrate the anniversary of General Franco's victory in Spain over communism. After mass, supporters and opponents of the revolutionary government met in bloody confrontations. Bombs were planted at some churches, among them Msgr. Boza's and Fr. Germán Lence's. [30] At this point the church hierarchy intervened. It released on 7 August its first collective pastoral letter on the dangers facing Cuba and threw the collective weight of the church behind Pérez Serantes. The letter began by acknowledging several successes of the revolutionary process including agrarian reform, industrialization projects, income redistribution to the advantage of the poor, the construction of schools and hospitals, the opening of beaches and sports centers to all Cubans, and the sensitive approach to the rural problems. It then concentrated on the bishops' gravest concern, the continuing advance of communism, which had to be avoided at all costs. The bishops studied the question of Cuba's developing relationship with Soviet-bloc countries, claiming that they had nothing against commercial ties with the Soviet Union (although in fact, several of them opposed ties of any kind). They were concerned more with government leaders, trade unionists, and journalists who had praised the system in Eastern Europe and drawn parallels between the social revolutions of those countries and Cuba. This view was impossible to tolerate, since "Catholicism and communism correspond to two understandings of man and of the world that are totally opposed to each other, and which it will never be possible to reconcile." [31]

The bishops moved from the general to the specific, condemning the fabric of Soviet society and its materialistic, atheist policy. For Cuba's bishops, "those governments that are guided by such a belief are among the worst enemies known by the church and humanity,

throughout all history." In a section of the pastoral significantly entitled "We condemn communism," the hierarchy criticized the "dictato-
rial regime" of countries that sacrifice the well-being of the people to
the "ambitions and convenience of the ruling group," turning citizens
into "veritable slaves"; that deny people alternative sources of media
information; that play havoc with family life, "driving women to leave
their home in order to undertake, away from their house, the harshest
tasks," while ignoring parents' wishes for their children's education.
Communism, the bishops wrote," is a system which brutally denies
the most fundamental rights of the human person."[32] The gloves were
clearly off as the church hierarchy not only expressed their opposition
to the changes that were taking place in Cuba but also encouraged
Cuba's Catholics to oppose the changes. It was a challenge that the revolutionary goverment had been expecting and to which Fidel Castro
soon responded.

When this collective pastoral letter was read, trouble broke out in
some churches as Catholic supporters of the revolutionary process denounced their bishops' provocative statements. There is also evidence
that revolutionary militants deliberately disrupted church services.
Thus days later Msgr. Evelio Díaz, who earlier had been the prelate
most supportive of the revolution, angrily ordered that unless clergy
and churches received protection, all churches would remain closed.
Three days after the letter's release came the government's reaction:
President Dorticós condemned those who wished to use religion as
a weapon against the revolution and vowed, despite church provocation, to continue respecting all religious faiths. That same day, 10 August 1960, in a speech to agricultural workers, Fidel Castro himself issued a blistering attack on the hierarchy.

Castro began by pointing out that the revolution had been made not
against the priests but against the large landowners. Its goals were
being challenged by persons with the most to lose, who were using religion to rouse popular anger against the revolution, a campaign aided
by outside forces. The church was turning an essentially political
issue—the search for a more just socioeconomic order—into an emotional one by claiming a threat to religious freedom. Fidel Castro reflected on this confusion and on what he saw as the selfishness of the
hierarchy.[33] Until this speech, he had made a point of remaining outside the church-state debate. Now that the lines were being drawn so
clearly and the religious controversy was flaring again, he had no alternative but to speak out. His words enraged the Catholic hierarchy, all
the more bitter that such words could come from an alumnus of Belén.

By now, the discussion over the "religious question" had been completely taken over by the debate between Free World–Washington–

Christian values and their Communist-Moscow-atheist counterparts. The government, of course, increasingly pressured by the United States politically, economically, and militarily, was pleased to receive aid from the Soviet Union. In addition it was rapidly running out of patience with what government leaders saw as an increasingly recalcitrant and dogmatic hierarchy that was willingly shielding the organizing efforts of counterrevolutionary groups. For their part, the bishops found themselves increasingly disturbed at the Soviet role in their country's affairs and at the growing support for the Soviets shown by government leaders. In this ideological tussle, the real issues were lost sight of as Cold War rhetoric got the better of many participants.

Drawing upon a remarkably selective memory, Archbishop Pérez Serantes raised this spiraling tension a notch in his emotional pastoral of 10 September significantly entitled "Ni traidores ni parias" ("Neither Traitors nor Pariahs") His ostensible point—that Catholics who criticized Marxism were precisely not traitors nor pariahs—soon gave way to an analysis of the United States versus the Soviet Union, condemning the latter unequivocally. He began with a disclaimer: "We are not linked to the North Americans by any ties of blood, language, traditions, coexistence, or training. Nor had North American officials "or Falangists or the Franco supporters" influenced him. However, he wrote, "We don't feel embarrassed to admit, and indeed it would be cowardly not to admit it, that we have no hesitation in choosing between North Americans and Soviets."[34]

For the first time, a Catholic spokesman had explicitly reduced the debate over revolutionary reforms and the Marxist-Christian dialectic to this simple geographical dichotomy. Many Cuban Christians also found this to be precisely the central issue, and whatever other opinions they held were subordinated to it. The Cuban hierarchy, then, and many Catholics at odds with the revolutionary process agreed with Pérez Serantes's simple choice: "Cuba yes, communism no. We shall always repeat: Cuba yes, slaves never!"[35] In this debate there was no middle ground.

Pérez Serantes released one more major pastoral letter on this issue two months later, significantly on the day of the feast of Christ the King. He appeared to sense that the church's advantage was slipping, in view of a large middle-class exodus to the United States (at times accompanied by their priest), increasing social polarization, greater government control, and vocal popular support for the reforms introduced. The archbishop of Santiago attempted to regain the unity of the Catholic Congress of a year earlier by writing of what he saw as the two alternatives facing Cuba: "Roma o Moscú" ("Rome or Moscow").

The pastoral was an outpouring of frustration and bitterness warning Catholics about the dangers of communism. Pérez Serantes developed two central themes. First, he suggested that the essential struggle was not between Washington and Moscow but between Rome (the seat of Christianity) and Moscow (the center of atheism). Urging Catholics to oppose the onslaught of communist atheism ("We are soldiers of Christ, members of the invincible Armada, the Church"), he presented examples of "the most illustrious and exemplary representatives of humanity during these last twenty centuries," contrasting these with representatives of "socialism and communism, philosophies which, more than arid, are totally sterile and reduced to ashes."[36] Second, he developed a central theme of an earlier letter, the Washington-Moscow confrontation. He began by citing Leo XIII's teachings that communism was "a moral virus which wriggles like a snake throughout the innermost entrails of human society and brings it to danger and ruin."[37] After denouncing the brutality of communist invasions ("driving their horses over millions of victims from all classes, leaving behind rivers of blood"), he praised the Christian bulwark raised by the United States ("Never has any single nation, let us finally state, been more devoted to this objective").[38] That support for the U.S. position on Cuba should have constituted a central concern in two such important episcopal documents reveals a great deal about the church's attitudes at that moment. Views expressed by such an influential figure posed a direct threat to the revolutionary government. It was particularly galling to the government's supporters to see the most outspoken churchman in the country praise the foreign power bent on subverting reforms.

The final curve in this spiral of invective and emotion came in December 1960, although it was already clear that coexistence between the church and the revolutionary government was now impossible, so distant were their respective positions on almost everything. On 4 December another collective document was issued by the hierarchy in the form of an open letter to Prime Minister Castro. In a tone far more subdued than anything produced by Pérez Serantes, it complained only about "national" concerns shared by the bishops, specifically the use of Marxist analysis in textbooks and various pressures applied against the church following upon their criticisms of the government. Priests had been insulted, access to the media had been curtailed, and agents provocateurs had disturbed religious ceremonies, while the government had consistently accused the church of operating schools for the privileged. Moreover, the document continued, government spokesmen had declared that "to be opposed to communism was the equivalent of being counterrevolutionary," a view the bishops refused to accept. The letter concluded with the bishops assuring Castro of their "continued prayers for the Lord to enlighten him."[39]

Speaking on television twelve days later, Fidel Castro delivered the coup de gr‹alt›ĉce to the moribund church–revolutionary government relationship. Upset by the paternalistic approach of the hierarchy, the prime minister took issue with the church's long and biased campaign of criticism and berated the bishops' phobia with communism: "In the first place, we must say that the government does not have to render an account of its conduct to the bishops: the revolutionary government does not have to render an account of its political activity to the *falangista* clergy. . . . One of the refrains that the bishops like to repeat is that the government officials have said that to be anti-Communist is to be counterrevolutionary and that the government has not [denied it]. . . . Do they want us to clarify the matter? Do they want an answer? Well, then, we do believe that to be anti-Communist is to be counter-revolutionary, just as it is counterrevolutionary to be anti-Catholic, anti-Protestant and anti-anything that tends to divide Cubans."[40] This position was one that the church could not support; the standoff between church and government only got worse, and it was becoming increasingly clear that only one winner could emerge. The church, true to its Spanish nature and influenced by the historical context of the "Cold War" and pre–Vatican II conservatism, gambled by staking its credibility on this frontal attack on the revolutionary government—a battle it could not hope to win.

The story of relations between the church and the revolutionary government for the first two years of the fidelista process, while complex, can be reduced to a simple summary: "The Church, fragmented, unsure, too closely linked with the foreigners and the rich, challenged a popular government and was resoundingly and humiliatingly defeated. The bishops have sounded the call to battle. The faithful did not respond."[41]

During this period, the church in Cuba passed from its early unrealistic expectations (which Fidel Castro chose not to dash, perhaps believing that he could realize his reforms without alienating the church) to its demise as a political force by the end of 1960. The initial enthusiasm to a certain extent was an example of gracious self-deceit. The "peaks" had been so few in comparison with the many "valleys" during the church's centuries-long existence in Cuba that church leaders understandably clung tenaciously to any promising opportunity. In the late 1950s, that avenue seemed to have presented itself. Not only had there been a renaissance of Catholic hopes and prestige in the forties and fifties, but the hierarchy had carved a distinct place for itself through its positions against the dictator Batista. These positions were not solid and were often self-contradictory, but they showed that the church was finally coming to grips with its historical context and, however tardily, was realizing the need for fundamental social change in Cuba—a dramatic new position for the Cuban Church, notwithstanding a few earlier isolated pastorals of outspoken individuals.[42]

The church had thus pursued a far more progressive policy in the 1950s—despite a divided hierarchy—calling for dialogue, reconciliation, and social reform. After the revolutionary victory, the church at first continued calling for reform. The problem became what to do when these reforms impinged upon church territory, in either spiritual or earthly matters.

When the reforms to be introduced in Cuba proved far more radical than originally envisaged, the church sought to strengthen its position by organizing demonstrations, including the November 1959 Congreso Católico, an admirable index, the church thought, of Catholic support as well as a subtle muscle-flexing to remind the revolutionary government of Cuba's "Catholic nature." The church's conclusions were false, however, false since the congreso's turnout of a million people, despite inclement weather, was due less to the religious fervor of Cuba's population than to a political opposition that channeled popular frustrations into this powerful show of force. The congreso may even have contributed directly to the church's undoing since, emboldened by the massive turnout, the church judged its influence to be far stronger than it was and adopted a more confrontational stance toward the government.

Even this fragile power base began to disintegrate in early 1960, when large numbers of middle-class Cubans chose the path to Miami, just over ninety miles away. Since they represented the backbone of the church as well as of the internal opposition movement, their loss was critical. A far smaller but still influential number of progressive Catholic intellectuals and lay leaders continued to support the revolutionary process and to feel a corresponding frustration at their hierarchy's intransigence and apparent desire for confrontation. In his 21 November 1960 pastoral, Pérez Serantes, protesting against this pro-government stance (which had led some Catholics to interrupt anti-Castro sermons by singing the national anthem), urged prorevolutionists to take advantage of "the important resource of retiring from church as calmly as they had entered," and that is precisely what they did.[43]

An extraordinarily complex combination of factors confronted the church in Cuba. In addition to division within the church, a false estimate of religious strength, and an identity crisis affecting the entire church structure, the clergy had to deal with the thorny issue of sweeping social reform, the emotional issue of communism and its influence on Cuba, and the roles and policies of the two superpowers toward Cuba. The influential Spanish clergy, approximately two-thirds of all the priests on the island, had been trained under the Franco dictatorship, and believed in the rather dated view of communism presented in an earlier encyclical, *Divini Redemptoris*, which in turn based its views largely upon the Spanish Civil War, as well as the Russian and Mexican Revolutions. These outdated views were bound to create havoc—and did.

Not only clergy but all Cubans were forced to question their political, social, ideological and philosophical values and to accept or to reject the government package, complete with its ideological compromises and tenets. It was a divisive process, particularly among the bourgeoisie whose interests were most directly challenged by government-sponsored reforms. When the middle class left in large numbers, the church's support system quickly collapsed.

Seeking to turn back the revolutionary tide, the church made the issue of communist influence the central one. Within Cuba, the radical socioeconomic reforms, the rise in prominence by mid-1960 of communist representatives, and the superpowers' relations with the government, convinced the church that "the enemy was within." The church rejected dialogue with communists, holding the view that Catholicism and communism were mutually exclusive. This rejection meant that inevitably the Church would throw its collective weight behind any project to diminish the threat of "godless communism," a position Fidel Castro encountered in April 1959 when he traveled to the United States: "The constant and obsessive concern of North Americans, public and private, with the single question of Communism irritated Castro and indeed others in his entourage: it was as if the U.S. did not care what Cuba was, provided it was not Communist."[44]

With great gusto the church entered the debate over the U.S.–USSR relationship with Cuba, another costly strategic blunder. The conservative *Diario de la Marina* stated in September 1959 that "Catholicism . . . is the only force capable of opposing the advance of theories propagated by Soviet propaganda,"[45] and many Catholics fervently believed that. Unfortunately for the church the injection of the Washington-Moscow debate proved another costly strategic blunder. For while the vast majority of Cubans, without any doubt at all, were not communist, they were anti-interventionists. In addition to their newfound patriotism resulting from the extensive international interest in their country, they increasingly came to see the United States as the perpetrator of sabotage and counterrevolution, directed at destroying popular government reforms.

Given Cuba's history and the traditional U.S. political and economic influence there, the church's strategy in supporting the United States as the defender of Western Christian ideals of freedom was the most promising. Unfortunately for the church it backfired badly. The animosity and distrust emanating from Washington and Havana, compounded by the Soviets' generous economic aid, military support, and apparent understanding did little to win Cubans over to the church's position. "Roma o Moscú" (which for every practical reason was in reality "Washington o Moscú") might well have been a burning issue for many Catholics but not for the vast majority of Cubans. Rome and its spiritual influence meant little to them; Washington seemed determined to wrest from them the few social advantages they had recently acquired; Moscow—for whatever reasons—was showing them a warmth and understanding that Washington never had. The concern of Cubans about communism and totalitarianism was overshadowed at this moment by their revolutionary process, which meant accepting aid from whoever would provide it. It was a policy that the church simply could not follow, and it made alienation between the church and the Cuban population inevitable. The official severing of diplomatic relations between the United States and Cuba implemented by Washington on 3 January 1961 only reconfirmed the errors made by the church hierarchy: like Pérez Serantes, they had chosen Washington over Moscow and in doing so had severely damaged what limited credibility remained to them.

4

Confrontation, 1961

Throughout 1961, and to a lesser extent in 1962, the fundamental issues of 1959–60 continued to dominate church-state relations. The difference between these periods lay in the intensity of passions in 1961–62 as fidelistas and Catholics moved from words to action to support their political-religious beliefs. Finally, militant churchpeople faced a choice—exile or confrontation. While each path drew many followers, those choosing confrontation most profoundly marked church-state relations and made a more rational rapprochement first unthinkable, then impossible.

Even after 3 January 1961, when Washington broke of diplomatic relations with Cuba, many members of the bourgeoisie refused to believe that the revolutionary process could last much longer without toning down its rhetoric and reining in its socioeconomic reforms. A similar delusion existed—that the bishops, despite their bluster, must realize that many of the reforms enacted by the revolutionary government had been necessary. In this scenario, the rupture of diplomatic relations was merely another move on the diplomatic chessboard to bring Cuba's government back into line. Was not this in the Latin American tradition? And while the fidelistas, with ever greater support from pro-Soviet PSP members, were determined to continue the radical restructuring of Cuban society, the same line of thought assumed that the Soviet Union was only flirting with the revolutionary government and would never assume the international political risks (much less the economic costs) of courting the fidelistas seriously. Accordingly, many Cubans left for Miami to wait things out, confident that the revolution

91

would be brought to heel, that cooler heads would prevail, and that they would then be able to return to the patria. They would wait in vain.

The U.S.–Soviet–Cuban Triangle

In 1960, and even more in 1961, the religious question in Cuba came to be influenced less by the acts of Cubans themselves than by international considerations, as both superpowers sought to chart Cuba's destiny. Assistance from Moscow and Peking continued to flow in during this time—tens of millions of dollars in armaments, large-scale grants and credits for equipment and technical assistance, and generous contracts to purchase Cuban sugar. "At the end of November, Cuba and China concluded an agreement whereby the Chinese would buy a million tons of sugar in 1961, and grant a credit of $M60 for equipment and technical aid. . . . In mid-December a new Russo-Cuban agreement was also signed. Russia would buy 2.7 million tons of sugar at 4 cents a pound. . . . Russia expressed her willingness to defend Cuba 'against unprovoked aggressions,' but made no mention of missiles. . . . Thereafter vessels sailed regularly to Cuba from the Communist ports of the old Hanse, and articles describing the beauties of East Europe appeared frequently in Cuban magazines. . . . In January Castro announced that 1,000 young Cubans would study agrarian collectives in Russia."[1] This tremendous amount of multifaceted aid designed to win the hearts and minds of Cubans caused church representatives to suspect that their worst fears were about to be realized. Many still believed, however, that the U.S. government, long used to getting its way in Cuban matters, would once again intervene. Could the United States afford to have a Soviet satellite just ninety miles away? Many opponents of the Castro regime thought it was simply a matter of time before Cuba would be "liberated."

Relations between Cuba and the United States were suffering from mutual hostility and accusations hurled by both sides. Having always considered Cuba a poor relation, a country that exported cheap raw materials to and imported refined goods from the United States, Washington had difficulty understanding the Cuban position or even considering the revolutionary government an equal negotiating power.[2] Like Cuba's bourgeoisie, U.S. policymakers found incongruous the idea that Cuba would dare to question the countries' traditional relationship. And, as Soviet aid to Cuba grew, so did Washington's ire—as well as its resolve to bring Cuba to her knees. Yet, the U.S. economic blockade was bound to fail as long as the Soviet Union was prepared to take up the slack.

Cuba's effrontery was widely expected to backfire and to lead eventually to the overthrow of Fidel Castro. To accelerate this process, Cuban exile groups received assistance, largely through murky U.S. government intelligence channels. The results, in late 1960 and early 1961, were a systematic terrorist campaign and economic sabotage designed to encourage the Cuban population to seek the overthrow of the Cuban government. As in Batista's time, the Catholic hierarchy remained conspicuously silent, neither praising the government's educational and medical reforms nor criticizing terrorist aggression such as occurred in Havana in the winter of 1960–61.

> All through the winter there had been small infiltrations, by the CIA and the exiles, rumours of invasion, emergencies, conspiracies and acts of violence. . . .
>
> Many bombs were laid, letter boxes blown up, water mains destroyed, sugar and tobacco plantations set aflame. . . . The Havana-Santiago express was derailed. . . . There was occasional hi-jackings of aeroplanes, bomb attacks on crowds, while big fires were lit, and the big Havana store of El Encanto was destroyed in April.[3]

The government, understandably, would take notice of their actions and clear opposition.

In part because of the church hierarchy's refusal to condemn such acts of terrorism, in part because of the bishops' campaign against priests who supported the revolutionary process, there followed a media campaign critical of the church. Contributing factors included the general lack of interest among Catholics in the remarkably successful 1961 literacy campaign, the continued "estate of death" ("latifundio de la muerte") resulting from the church's ownership of Havana's Colón Cemetery,[4] and a series of highly critical comments on the church's attitude by Fidel Castro. This official displeasure shows up most clearly in the cartoons in "The Week in Caricature" section of *Bohemia* for 19 March 1961, less than a month before the Bay of Pigs invasion. One cartoon, titled "Falangist Clergy," shows a monk intoning, "And Jesus said: 'Love your neighbor as yourself'" while behind his back he lights a bomb. Another, "The Requirement," shows a person entering heaven being chastised: "You forgot to pay your entry fee!"[5]

This ham-fisted campaign to wrest prestige from the clergy, as well as the encouragement given to develop a nationalist church directed by Father Germán Lence, sprang from a deep frustration shared by many revolutionaries astonished at the church's ability to pretend that nothing had changed. Particularly galling was the hierarchy's refusal to condemn terrorist acts, only confirming for many that the hierarchy really did belong to the "Church of Washington" and was therefore at the very least a potential enemy.

The spiral of tension between revolutionary government and church hierarchy continued throughout the spring of 1961 against a background of the looming superpower confrontation. Lines had been drawn by the bishops' collective pastoral of December and Fidel Castro's increasingly derisive criticisms of the hierarchy, and while relations between church and government remained taut, they still functioned. The invasion at the Bay of Pigs would rapidly lay all doubts to rest; the confrontation became inevitable.

The Bay of Pigs and Its Impact on Church-State Relations

By the fall of 1960 it was common knowledge that a CIA-sponsored invasion of Cuba was in the offing, a combined strategic operation of several exile groups, as opposed to the earlier smaller, isolated sabotage and infiltration missions. The Cuban government on several occasions denounced this role of the United States and mobilized for war (by April 1961, many Cubans had had basic military training). The United States, lending its support to Cuban exile groups, was masterminding the invasion, and several ships bringing the invasion force were reported heading toward Cuba. A state of national alert had been declared, and all suspicious or potentially counterrevolutionary citizens—including many clergy—were being closely observed and sometimes rounded up and forcibly detained; guns had been distributed and members of the militia were being dispatched throughout the island. Tension was high and the great uncertainty disturbing. The Bay of Pigs would be a strong formative influence on Cuba's national psyche, causing many Cubans to leave, radicalizing many others.

With the country in this state of high tension and anxiety over the fate of the revolution, a new wave of bombing raids took place on 15 April. Damage to military targets was limited, but seven people were killed and these attacks were clearly only the harbinger of a more serious invasion. On 16 April at the funeral celebrations for the victims, Fidel Castro for the first time publicly declared the socialist nature of the revolution, understandably causing tremendous concern among conservative church circles:

That's what they can't forgive us for, the fact that we're here right in front of them, that we've made a revolution right under the very nose of the United States! . . .

And we'll defend this socialist revolution with our guns! . . . We'll defend it with the valor shown yesterday by our antiaircraft gunners who riddled with bullets the planes of our aggressors! . . . Fellow workers and peasants, comrades all, this is the democratic, socialist revolution of the poor. . . . And, in order to defend this revolution of the poor and for their benefit, we're prepared to give our lives.[6]

For the church hierarchy, caught up in the Cold War hysteria and without the benefit of the liberalization of Vatican II, their worst fears were confirmed: the revolution was "going communist," and Fidel Castro had finally had the effrontery to admit it. Mindful of the numerous atrocities committed in the Spanish Civil War and of traditional church teachings concerning the communist threat and, in some cases, fearing directly for their lives, more and more churchmen chose one of two options, fight or flight.

The historical facts of the Bays of Pigs landing on 17 April are relatively straightforward: the invasion lasted only two days, during which 1,180 men of the 1,297 who landed were taken prisoner. In spite of the CIA's claims that a popular uprising would overthrow Castro, the invasion had the opposite effect on many Cubans, strengthening their loyalty to the fidelista cause. Moreover, while many were perturbed at the declaration of the socialist revolution, the majority were prepared to follow Fidel Castro in whatever course he chose. For many formerly undecided, the invasion helped define the position they wanted to take.

Church consternation grew as the revolutionary government outlined the role specific Catholics had played in the abortive invasion. Headed by Manuel Artime, a former leading member of the Agrupación Católica Universitaria, Brigade 2506 (as the invasion force was called) had been named after the serial number of another member of the ACU, Carlos Rodríguez Santana, killed accidentally while training in Guatemala. (Other members of the Agrupación continued to participate in the resistance.) More damaging was the presence of three Spanish priests, Tomás Macho, Segundo Las Heras, and Ismael de Lugo, and a Protestant minister. The stylized cross prominently featured in the center of the invaders' shoulder patches was another reminder of the religious aspects of the invasion. Contributing to this air of a modern-day religious crusade against the communist infidel was the grandiose proclamation of Father Ismael de Lugo, which was to be read to the Cuban people after the landing and the invading force's "victory over communism":

> The liberating forces have disembarked on Cuba's beaches. We have come in the name of God, justice and democracy, with the goal of reestablishing the rights which have been restricted, the freedom which has been trampled on, and the religion which has been taken over and maligned. . . . The assault brigade is made up of thousands of Cubans who are all Christians and Catholics. Our struggle is that of those who believe in God against the atheists, the struggle of democracy against communism. . . .
>
> Catholics of Cuba: our military power is overwhelming and invincible, and greater still is our moral strength and our faith in God, in his protection and his help. Catholics of Cuba: I embrace you on behalf of the soldiers of the liberation army. Families, relatives, friends: you will soon be reunited. Have faith, since the victory is ours, because God is with us and the Virgin of Charity cannot abandon her children. Catholics: long live a free Cuba, one that is democratic and Catholic! Long live Christ the King! Long live our glorious Patron Saint![7]

The revolutionary government interpreted this proclamation as proof of a Catholic conspiracy against the government, and its policy toward the church changed noticeably as it sought to stifle the activities of a potential fifth column. Before the invasion, security forces had rounded up all suspected counterrevolutionaries or their supporters, among them many Catholics. Now, all bishops and most priests were placed under house arrest. Archbishop Evelio Díaz and Auxiliary Bishop Boza Masvidal were detained by security forces, and Cardinal Arteaga, who had apparently lost his mental faculties, sought diplomatic asylum in the Argentine embassy. As tension between church and government leaders continued unabated and harassment of Catholics increased, many church leaders realized that their religious mission could now be fulfilled only in extremely trying circumstances. Their dilemma was made all the more distasteful by the memory of their relatively privileged position a few years earlier. The ranks of those leaving Cuba understandably swelled. Speaking with the benefit of hindsight nine years later, Father Carlos Manuel de Céspedes, then rector of Havana's San Carlos and San Ambrosio seminary and in 1988 secretary-general of the Cuban Episcopal Conference, summarized the situation at that time:

> The climate was very different then. . . . Everything came to a head when many well-off individuals who were feeling the pinch

of the Revolution tried to use the Church as the standard-bearer for their anticommunism. I wasn't in Cuba at the time, but I have no doubt that many priests actively supported the counterrevolutionary movements that arose, especially after the summer of 1960, and that culminated in the Bay of Pigs invasion in April 1961. I don't know how much, but I am certain that counterrevolutionary meetings were held on church property, and that some priests urged Catholics to take part in counterrevolutionary activities and to go into exile.[8]

After the invasion, one priority stood out in government representatives' statements on the "church problem": that the way to diminish church influence was to take control of the schools run by religious groups. In 1955, there were 212 Catholic schools on the island educating 61,960 students and about 50 Protestant schools. Most Catholic schools were private and largely run by priests and nuns, accounting for 1,167 of the 1,872 religious on the island. Only 556 were Cuban.[9] The need to use all educational resources fairly had been clear to organizers of the 1961 literacy campaign, many of whom had been incensed when church officials rejected the campaign and continued to operate their own excellent private schools. In Cuba's revolutionary situation, many found incongruous a twin-track educational system, with one increasingly radical lay state system coexisting alongside an extremely conservative religious private system that also catered to the social class that had exploited Cuba's poor. On what can be termed educational grounds, then, many had been chafing to take over the facilities and resources of all private schools, Protestant as well as Catholic.

The main incentive for nationalizing the educational system, though, was based on more direct political needs, since such an action promised not only to cut church revenues but also to dilute church influence over the tens of thousands of youngsters attending its schools. If the government simultaneously became the sole teacher-accrediting body, the raison d'être of the church's educators in Cuba would be destroyed and the church severely hampered.

The May Day parade two weeks later offered the leadership an opportune occasion to explain its position and to solicit the masses' cooperation. One of the pantomimes presented in the celebrations showed two priests bearing signs saying "Falangist clergy" and carrying bombs, while nearby a costumed Uncle Sam angrily cracked his whip.[10] Even with the stage thus set, many Cubans were unsure just how the prime minister would deal with the religious question, for, despite widespread opposition to the revolutionary process by churchpeople, traditional Cuban apathy to religion rendered their influence far from threatening. Whatever doubts they might have entertained were quickly dispelled. For Fidel Castro, the Lugo proclamation had proved the last straw: "Three priests accompanied the brigade of invaders. Were they three Cuban priests? No, not a single one of them was Cuban. They were just three Spanish priests, three Falangist priests. . . . So, what happened? The fascist and Spanish Falangist priests came to wage war against the revolution? Very well, then: we'll inform people here that in the next few days the revolutionary government will pass a law declaring null and void any permits held by foreign priests in Cuba to remain here. . . . And that law will have only one exception—do you know for whom that will be? Well, any foreign priest can stay, with a special permit, providing that the government considers him suitable, and that he hasn't been fighting against the Cuban Revolution."[11]

The second part of the government's package of reprisals concerned the private school system. Prime Minister Castro announced that the schools would be nationalized and all facilities would pass to the state—which also reserved the right to name and appoint teachers. A final stern warning was issued to practicing Christians, advising them to steer clear of counterrevolutionary activity and to avoid using their religious beliefs as a cover for political opposition.[12] This, however, was an extremely tardy response to a fait accompli, while the damage done to relations between the church and the revolutionary government would take many years to undo.

The Aftermath of Playa Girón: Exile and Polarization

After the Bay of Pigs invasion, nothing was ever the same: political lines were now firmly drawn, military victory had strengthened the revolutionary process, and Fidel Castro's May Day speech had resolved any remaining ambiguity in church-state relations. For many Cubans the only possible choice was voluntary exile, and a new wave of emigration began.

The church in Cuba has been criticized for capitulating unceremoniously to the revolutionary government and encouraging Catholics—including hundreds of priests and religious—to leave Cuba. In the post-Girón political climate, however, the decision to leave was understandable, albeit perhaps mistaken. Fearful of reprisals by the government and mindful of the massacres of the Spanish Civil War, the most prudent choice seemed to be to move abroad. This choice, comprehensible in theory, robbed the church of its power base, leaving those who remained with little support. The church hierarchy blazed the trail by closing the Havana seminary and sending the older students to seminaries abroad. They were joined there by many religious and priests without teaching positions after the government nationalized the school system and others who were simply scared or perhaps alienated by the rapid social changes of the revolutionary process.[13] Aided by church organizations in the United States and by the U.S. government itself, church leaders still in Cuba counseled exile to their flocks. The latter responded by flooding the U.S. Immigration and Naturalization Service with visa applications.

The more liberal Catholics criticized this policy, claiming that the church's mission was to serve the needs of its faithful, not to preach escapism. By seeking to "save" Cuban Catholics from socialism, many church leaders were simply confirming Fidel Castro's criticisms concerning the "Church of Washington" and its lack of interest in the people's social needs. The church had begun to "have its feet in Cuba, but its mind and heart in Miami and Madrid."[14] Disregarding such criticisms, the church continued to encourage exile with remarkable success. Most felt that the wiser course was to shun the revolutionary process and retire abroad, then return to Cuba "in happier times" to rebuild the church. A minority decided to stay and see what the future held. It was this small nucleus who, despite tremendous pressure, would keep the candle of church interests alight in increasingly difficult times.

Among this stubborn and articulate minority who stayed, two different interpretations of the church's role developed, a soul-searching process that polarized church members. Although perhaps a healthy exercise in itself, it scarred the Christians who chose to remain in Cuba. So profound was the impact of this division that it can still be sensed more than a quarter of a century later.

The standard-bearer of the conservative Catholic cause had been the *Diario de la Marina*, but since its interdiction in May 1960 and growing government control of the media, the responsibility for rallying the faithful had again fallen on church leaders. Archbishop Pérez Serantes's pastoral letter of March 1961, "¡Vamos bien!" ("We're Doing Fine!"), although lacking his earlier impassioned rhetoric, proved that not all the bishops had been intimidated. Indeed, while acknowledging the growing clamor against "the enemy here in Cuba, the Church" and the demand for "the extermination of those who are unconditionally with the Church, the only bastion to impede the revolution," Pérez Serantes claimed, with his natural optimism, that the church was not only resisting well but was indeed becoming more "Christian" because of its current difficulties.[15]

More belligerent in his frequent condemnation of the government was the auxiliary bishop of Havana, the parish priest of Nuestra Señora de la Caridad (scene of a violent confrontation between Catholics and revolutionary supporters in September 1961), Msgr. Eduardo Boza Masvidal. As the church's fortunes waned in 1961, Boza Masvidal, an outspoken anticommunist and president of the Catholic Villanueva University, became increasingly aggressive. His parish bulletins revealed the extent of his traditional views, and in his February 1961 pastoral, "La patria que soñó Martí" ("The Fatherland that Martí Dreamed Of"), he suggested that even the revered patriot-revolutionary would be opposed to the fidelista process. It thus became clear that further problems between church and the revolutionary government were inevitable.

Less than three months after the Bay of Pigs invasion, Boza Masvidal's weekly bulletin of 2 July, "Fuertes en la fe" ("Strong in Our Faith"), encouraged Cuban Catholics to "vitalize their faith, to live it in a full, virile fashion, to manifest it publicly and to view it as an ideal for which it is worth struggling, making sacrifices and even dying, and to irradiate it around us." He then drew a historical parallel to support his call to action: "It is necessary for us Christians to realize that we constitute the militant Church, that we are soldiers of Christ, and for us to feel our vocation of apostolate and conquest, to be 'dangerous' for today's paganism and atheism—just as Christians in the first century were dangerous for Roman paganism."[16] This highly combative and energetic clergyman continued to use the pulpit to call down the government and was taken into protective custody at the time of Playa Girón. Widely supported by the nucleus of Catholics opposed to Fidel Castro, Boza was the center of controversy until the September 1961 demonstration outside his church, after which the conservative remnants of a once-powerful church lobby would lose their chief spokesman, and the church would enter a period of what may be called "internal exile."

A radically different interpretation of the church's role was held by another segment of the Catholics who chose to stay in Cuba. Driven by an urge to radicalize their faith and by a desire to break free of the traditional religious teaching, this minority within a minority urged their bishops to come to terms with the revolutionary reality of Cuba and to work constructively within the new process. The tragedy of this radical Christian lobby (a similar division was also occurring within the Protestant churches) was that its members not only became marginalized within their own church but also were lumped by many revolutionaries with the troublesome "counterrevolutionary church group." (It is a situation that still exists in Cuba, although popular uneasiness about them has greatly diminished.)

Perhaps the most outstanding example of these *cristianos revolucionarios* was Father Guillermo Sardiñas, a parish priest on the Isle of Pines who had joined the guerrillas in the Sierra Maestra as a chaplain. Subsequently promoted to the rank of comandante, Sardiñas angered his ecclesiastical superiors by supporting wholeheartedly the thrust of the revolutionary government's reforms. At an open-air mass on Mothers' Day in 1961, Sardiñas expressed his own frustration at the intransigence of many of his clerical colleagues: "More than sixty years ago, Pope Leo XIII issued the encyclical *Rerum Novarum.* . . . What is the Church waiting for? Until there happens in every country what happened in Cuba?"[17] Among his church colleagues, however, his voice was one of a small minority: Sardiñas was—unfortunately—a generation ahead of his time.

Other representatives of this revolutionary grouping within the mainline churches sought to continue the call for modernization but largely to no avail. Among the most eloquent spokespersons of the cristianos revolucionarios was the Franciscan Father Ignacio Biaín, who, while definitely not an uncritical fidelista, supported many of the social changes realized by the revolution. When repeated criticism of his editorial positions in the progressive Catholic journal *La Quincena* went unheeded, the church hierarchy finally handed over the editorship to a more traditional colleague. "I accept the revolution, I sympathize with it, and want it to triumph," Father Biaín wrote in 1961, "because I see in it the definitive solutions of very old and very deeply rooted social ills, and because in addition I don't see any basic conflict between my convictions and the new system."[18] He also dared to criticize his colleagues for their reluctance to view the revolution unselfishly: "To stand aggressively in front of the present system, especially when we know that we cultivated so carefully (too much!) a concept of coexistence with the prerevolutionary status quo, so unjust in its structures and permanent deeds, seems to me a grave error for anyone to make—but is even more grave for a Christian. . . . Those Christians of tomorrow who are not completely mad will judge us harshly if this process culminates without our cooperation or what would be worse, with our opposition to it."[19] Father Biaín's removal from *La Quincena* and his isolation afterwards pointed out the impossibility of change from within the church at this time. With church leaders unwilling to brook any dissent, the traditional perspective dominated once again.

An even sharper confrontation within the church occurred in the case of a short-lived group, Con la Cruz y por la Patria ("With the Cross and on Behalf of the Fatherland"), instituted in July 1960, whose major advocate was the outspoken older priest Germán Lence. Throughout 1960 and early 1961 the Con la Cruz organized religious activities and ceremonies in which they showed their support of the revolution. Other minor associations including the Unión de Católicos Universitarios ("Union of Catholic University Students") and the Avanzada Radical Cristiana ("Radical Christian Advance Guard") were composed of similar dissident Catholics pursuing like objectives. Among most Cuban Catholics, though, the pleas of such groups were largely ignored.

Eventually Father Lence was forbidden by church leaders to exercise his priestly functions, provoking a barrage of criticism from the government media. Lence contributed to the debate by bitterly criticizing his fellow priests who, he claimed, were blinded by their own selfishness: "And when we've come in from the countryside and traveled along Havana's Fifth Avenue, where there seems to be a kind of rivalry to see who can build the most sumptuous temple, we know that they're not doing this to spread the Christian message, but rather to store up foreign exchange and export it."[20] His good intentions did not prove sufficiently strong to rally the few revolutionaries of Catholic persuasion to his cause, possibly because of the divisive nature of his goals for the church but more importantly because events at Playa Girón and then at the Virgen de la Caridad celebrations made such debate irrelevant. Time had simply run out for a debate on the issue, and the church was clearly in no position to respond to the government.

The Church at Its Nadir

The church in Cuba was tottering, and the coup de grace came in September 1961, on the feast day of Cuba's *patrona*, the Virgen de la Caridad del Cobre.

Although it is not clear exactly what took place concerning arrangements for the processions, what is certain is that the religious ceremony was intended by many as a show of force in political as well as religious terms. Approximately 4,000 people participated at this celebration held at the parish of the Virgen de la Caridad in Havana, where Msgr. Boza Masvidal was parish priest. Popular, extroverted and headstrong, the auxiliary bishop had long seemed determined to stave off the communist threat almost single-handedly and to make up for the traumatized silence in which other prelates apparently found themselves. As the afternoon progressed, tension grew, especially when the participants headed toward the presidential palace shouting slogans against the revolutionary government and the Soviet Union. Some spectators later claimed that a U.S. flag was waved. Apparently, many of the crowd surrounded the demonstrators, and a melee resulted. Shots were fired, and a passing seventeen-year-old was killed.

Boza Masvidal has since claimed that he attempted to calm parishioners' anger at the government and to comply with government requests. He said he obtained permission for the procession but that government officials canceled it on the eve of the festivities. He advised people to go home afterwards, he said, "but if the people didn't agree with their rights being trampled on, what could I do?"[21] The government claimed that Boza Masvidal deliberately manipulated the ceremony in an attempt to whip up counterrevolutionary sentiment. Minister of the Interior Ramiro Valdés said that an official permit was granted the priest for a local celebration but that he had invited clergy from all over the island. Afterwards Boza "stated falsely that the permit had been denied, and indeed attempted to convert it into a counterrevolutionary demonstration."[22] This incident, combined with reported disturbances on the same feast day in Camagüey, Colón, and Sancti Spiritus, proved to be the last straw for the revolutionary government, and reprisals swiftly followed. Two days later an operation was undertaken to round up clergy suspected of harboring counterrevolutionary sentiments, including Msgr. Boza Masvidal. On 17 September the government expelled 130 priests and religious, sending them on the steamer *Covadonga* to Spain.[23] The church was devastated: its principal source of income, its schools, were cut off, the number of priests had declined from eight hundred to two hundred in just three years, most of the faithful had left, and relations between church and government leaders bordered on hostility. (Many sincere Christians who were also sincere revolutionaries buried their religious feelings to avoid queries about their political loyalty.) The church in Cuba had reached its nadir in the modern period.

The government went to great lengths to show that its policies were not directed at Christian churches per se but rather at groups who used religion as a shield behind which to plan counterrevolutionary strategies. Government officials claimed that the problem was political, not one of faith or theology. Few practicing Christians believed this position, though; indeed it was widely rumored in October 1961 that the government was "about to enforce a new law forbidding priests to hold services in the presence of persons between the ages of 3 and 20."[24]

There is no evidence to support the argument that the revolutionary government set out to destroy organized religions, although it clearly tried to inhibit and limit religious activities. After the Virgen de la

Caridad procession, religious processions were banned, and sports and cultural activities were scheduled by the national sports and recreation institute, INDER, usually on Sundays to compete with church services and to inhibit young Cubans from attending catechism classes. But these moves in themselves, as well as the discrimination against practicing Christians in some places of employment or study, did not represent a government policy to directly destroy religion. Rather they reflected a widespread resentment against religious activists who had conspired against the revolution. The government's goal was to influence and intimidate but not to destroy. Encouragement was still extended to priests and religious who supported the social reforms of the revolutionary process. Clearly, then, the government sought to differentiate (in an overly simplistic fashion) between "good" and "bad" religious practices—with itself as the ultimate arbiter of what was acceptable.

The portrayal of the church in the government-controlled print media provides insight into how the revolutionary leadership interpreted the role of the church and what kind of church the government hoped for. In late 1960 and in 1961, negative media views supporting the official government line were expected. In fact, the media's approach to the church was more complex, indicating, by extension, that the revolutionary government held a less one-dimensional view than is widely thought.[25] Thus, while seeking to undermine the political influence of the church, the government was prepared to leave strictly spiritual practices alone.

Positive references occurred in the media especially where church activities helped those in need.[26] Indeed, the cover of the 22 January 1961 issue of *Bohemia* featured the full-sized portrait of a Catholic volunteer in the literacy campaign, with a prominently displayed crucifix. The Christian aspects of the Sierra Maestra (site of the guerrilla war against Batista), such as the collective baptisms,[27] are occasionally referred to in glowing terms. The media's basic message, according to the director of the Salesian college at Guanabacoa, was that "you don't betray your Catholic conscience if you collaborate with socialism."[28] This message would be repeated by other clergy supporting the revolutionary process as the government sought a compromise with the church, hoping to see more priests and religious like the two nuns who threw themselves wholeheartedly into the 1961 literacy campaign. For them, "'to serve the poor [was] to serve Christ' and they realized that the Redeemer was not within the cloisters, but rather walked along the roads of Cuba.'"[29] It was a view shared by few of Cuba's clergy, increasingly wary of the government's leftist trajectory.

Predictably, the media ran articles on the progressive church in other countries along with interviews with foreign religious talking of the need for a constructive dialogue between Christianity and Marxism; all were designed to remind Cuban Catholics that their church was hopelessly behind the times and that they needed to revitalize their religious leaders and encourage them to cooperate with the revolutionary government. Even after the September 1961 demonstration, the government was prepared to welcome the support of the church—provided that the church was prepared to embark on a radically new course.[30] It was a naive hope, as virtually everybody knew. As Father Carlos Manuel de Céspedes, then director of the Seminario San Carlos, later pointed out: "Fidel had admitted that our Revolution was a Marxist one, and I imagine that, generally speaking, those who solidly backed the Revolution looked on Catholics as their sworn enemies. For their part, Catholics felt the same: it was a Communist Revolution, hence intrinsically bad. You had to fight it or flee. Only the perceptive and tranquil minority could imagine themselves joining it."[31] One person who did not see it necessarily as a case of fight or flight—on a philosophical level at least—was Fidel Castro. With a consistency in his observations concerning the religious question that has not been appreciated, he sought both to encourage and to cajole, explaining the essence of true Christianity as he saw it, pressing Cuba's Christians to radicalize their faith. It was, however, a campaign that would win few converts.

Fidel Castro on Religion

Writing in the conservative *Diario de la Marina* on 1 February 1959, Father Enrique Méndez, S.D.B., concluded that the moral fiber in Fidel Castro's social reform program meant that "Fidel Castro is a product of Christian education in our time. In the robust composition of his thought one can see the traces of a form of logic, a morality, and a conception of life that are characteristics of Catholic philosophy."[32] Such views were popular during the six-month honeymoon between church and revolutionary government leaders, after which they were hastily discarded by a somewhat embarrassed church hierarchy. Given the radical shift in perception, this begs the obvious question: which had changed, Fidel Castro's thought or the church's perception of it?

Given the importance of Fidel Castro in the Cuban revolutionary process, ignoring his views on the religious question would produce, at best, a distorted and unidimensional study of the confrontation of church and revolutionary government. The appearance in Havana in late 1985 of the book *Fidel y la religión (Fidel and Religion)* shows the significance—even when the church's role is so minor—of the religious question for Castro.

Fidel Castro made few observations on religious matters during the revolution's first year. He attended several religious ceremonies—including the massive November 1959 Catholic Congress, various thanksgiving ceremonies, baptisms, weddings, and the like—but in general he took pains to steer clear of controversial matters concerning the church. Indeed, in words that would come back to haunt him, Fidel Castro commented on television in June 1959: "Nobody can call into question the position of these leaders of the Catholic Church whose firm conduct at difficult moments is well known. . . . The Cuban Church has adopted a position which is truly revolutionary."[33] Devoting his energy to the reforms then sweeping the country, the Cuban leader sought to create a spirit of cooperation and reconciliation, and for the first year, particularly the first six months of 1959, aided by the enlightened views of some of Cuba's bishops, he succeeded. When the inherent and inevitable contradictions between the revolutionary program and the status quo became more manifest, however, this harmony began to disintegrate.

The January 1960 incident in which the Marquis of Lojendio, Franco's ambassador to Cuba, summoned Spanish church leaders and supporters well-known for their criticism of the government, marked a turning point in Castro's stance on organized religion, and revealed to conservative church leaders the danger of his "leftist militance." Throughout 1960, tension slowly mounted with each new pastoral letter and communiqué. The first collective pastoral letter of 7 August 1960, emphasizing the danger of the communist advance in Cuba, and a remarkably strong ultimatum delivered by Msgr. Evelio Díaz were answered in a blistering attack by Fidel Castro: "I would like to see a pastoral letter condemning the crimes of imperialism, the horrors of imperialism. . . . And then we would see that those who condemn a Revolution which is with the poor and the humble, which preaches love for one's neighbor and fraternity among men, which preaches equality, which practices love, generosity and the common good; those who condemn a Revolution like this, are betraying Christ, and at the same time they'd be capable of crucifying him again."[34]

In October and November, Archbishop Pérez Serantes issued two further attacks on the revolutionary government's continuing leftward drift, followed in December by the final joint document, a critical open letter to Fidel Castro, urging him to reject communism. That same month, Fidel Castro responded angrily on several occasions to what he saw as unnecessary meddling by the church leaders. He based his outspoken response on three premises: the church traditionally had supported military dictatorship, while ignoring the miserable plight of the masses; the church's anticommunist fixation was counterrevolutionary ("as it is to be anti-Catholic, anti-Protestant, or anti-anything which tends to divide Cubans");[35] and some church spokesmen were deliberately spreading lies about alleged government harassment, while at the same time the sacraments were being denied *milicianas* (women members of the militia) by conservative clergy. For Fidel Castro, it all sprang from the inherently superficial view of Christianity held by the church in Cuba—a view that was simply incompatible with the dramatic revolutionary process on which the country had embarked and a view that would not be allowed: "A true Christian is one who loves his neighbor, who makes sacrifices for others, who obeys the doctrines of Christ and gives what he has in order to go and serve his fellow human beings. Let these 'Christians' leave their temples and go out to the fields to help the sick, plant trees, build houses, assist the Agrarian Reform, sew smocks for the children who have no clothes. That's what being Christian means! On the other hand, going to church to conspire against our fatherland is the action of a Pharisee— never of a Christian."[36]

In 1961, Fidel Castro would take up these themes again and again in his public speeches. He seemed especially disturbed by the church's sudden interest in social concerns, in light of its traditional acquiescence to the status quo and refusal to speak out on manifest social injustices. To Fidel Castro this interest smacked of political opportunism, as he suggested somewhat ironically on national television in March 1961.[37] As an example of what the church could do, he cited the admirable work and abnegation of several religious orders in Cuba, praising "those institutions which we have to recognize, since they have been devoutly dedicated to serving the sick and the blind. This is also true of those religious bodies which have helped in our hospitals, the nuns who have worked in the leprosariums and hospitals. All those who undertake work to help humanity deserve our respect. Indeed anybody who makes personal sacrifices to help others deserves our respect."[38]

This personal view of a practical Christianity, of practicing what one preaches, represented the essence of Fidel Castro's interpretation of the role of the church. For him, faith without works was selfishness, while, conversely, religious leanings compounded by the determination to work toward a practical form of justice seemed to represent a more honest form of Christianity. In the context of a church obsessed with the Cold War, and prior to the Second Vatican Council, it was a view that simply did not fit in with the thinking of Cuba's hierarchy.

The Bay of Pigs invasion convinced church and government leaders that dialogue was impossible at that time, thereby preparing the ground for both the demonstration at Boza Masvidal's church and the subsequent deportation by the government of 130 clergy. It finally convinced the Cuban prime minister that the church as a body was not prepared to contribute to revolutionary reform programs. (Indeed, two months earlier he attacked church leaders for seeking to sabotage the literacy crusade.)[39] In the light of the continuing politicization of religion, the Castro government declared, religious education henceforth was to be restricted to the churches themselves. In this same speech of 1 May 1961, Castro explained his concept of religion, once again taunting the established church for its distorted perspective: "To our mind it is true that [religion and the revolution] can coexist perfectly, and that the revolution is not in the least opposed to religion, that it is they who have used religion as a pretext to fight justice, to fight the workers and the peasants, to fight the lowly; it is they who, forgetting Christ's saying that it is easier for a camel to pass through the eye of a needle than for the rich to enter the Kingdom of Heaven, landed here with the *latifundistas*, with the sugar mill owners, with the bankers, to murder lowly children of the people, to murder workers and peasants, to murder negroes and humble Cubans."[40]

Although the prime minister was not the only factor in determining the government's position vis-à-vis the church, Fidel Castro's outspoken denunciations of what he saw as "unchristian conduct" by church authorities was an important catalyst in establishing collective opinion. It is also worth noting that the opinions Fidel Castro expressed in 1960 and 1961 on religious matters were remarkably consistent with views he expressed later—to Chilean Christians in 1971; to Jamaican clergy in 1977; to visitors such as Mexican Archbishop Méndez Arceo and Jesse Jackson and (in January 1985) three U.S. Catholic bishops, including the head of the U.S. Episcopal Conference; and most clearly in *Fidel y la religión* (1985). His position on a justice- or action-oriented religion is much the same as it was more than two decades ago. Unfortunately for church-state relations in the early 1960s—yet to encounter the formative experiences of Oscar Romero's assassination or the major conferences of Medellín (1968) and Puebla (1979), much less of the religious "base communities," Nicaragua's Christian-Marxist revolution, and the impact of a score of articulate defenders of the theology of liberation—these views were simply unacceptable to the church.

The Church at a Crossroads

With the deportation of a sizable proportion of Cuba's remaining clergy after the demonstration outside Boza Masvidal's church, church and revolutionary government alike recognized that to continue along this path of confrontation and mutual recrimination was futile and counterproductive. The government was embarrassed to have the foreign media citing the deportations as an example of official "repression" and "brutality," whereas the church, with much more to lose and barely two hundred priests left on the island, feared that a repetition would lead to the virtual extinction of church activity. The need for a long period of introspection and self-evaluation thus became apparent—one that would last for six years of official silence by the church, unbroken until April 1969.

In September 1961, the clergy had been denounced by the prime minister as "the fifth column of the counterrevolution, here within our country."[41] With the loss of the hundreds of private Catholic schools, most of Cuba's clergy and religious suddenly found themselves without a raison d'être. The corresponding widespread loss of prestige, accompanied by much overt suspicion and harassment, hurt. Virtually all the church's middle-class support had either left the country or was planning to; polarization threatened to destroy their ever-thinning ranks. Aided by papal envoy Msgr. Cesare Zacchi and a spirit of renewal emanating from the Vatican under Pope John XXIII, church leaders began the gradual and painful process of self-examination.

The question most frequently asked by church leaders during the next six years of introspection was why their fortunes had fallen so dramatically during 1961. More important, the bluster of some fiery pastorals had been easily deflected by the government, which retaliated swiftly, condemning the obvious pro–U.S. feelings of the "Church of Washington." The church had clearly sought to take on the revolutionary leadership; it had lost badly and now retreated to assess its parlous condition. Many theories could be put forward, built around the church's advice for the faithful to leave, its excessive identification with U.S. policy, its response to government harassment, the Cold War climate, the Spanish factor, or the Cuban church's distance from the reinvigorated theology being developed elsewhere in Latin America. Perhaps the last word should be left to the most important figure in the church at that time, Archbishop Pérez Serantes. As he confided to a foreign religious shortly before his death, "All that is happening to us is providential. . . . We believed more in our schools than in Jesus Christ."[42]

5

"De profundis . . . ,"

1962–1969

The sad state of church morale at the end of 1961 forced the Catholic hierarchy to listen to the urgent appeals of Pope John XXIII that the church abandon its impractical strategy of confrontation along with its short-sighted policy of counseling Catholics to leave Cuba and adopt a more modern approach. Slowly and reluctantly church leaders took stock of their weaknesses:

> The theological and ethical tenor of the [Cuban] Church was, at best, of 1950s vintage, while the transnational Church had moved briskly into a new world. The political tenor of the [Cuban] Church was of tough "Cold War" vintage, while the transnational Church had entered into an entirely different set of relations with Communists and Communist countries. . . .
>
> Although the Cuban Catholic Church had expressed frequently, and consistently, its concern for the poor, the sick, the weak and infirm, it had failed to articulate the concerns about development which flowered in the international Church during the 1960s. Its people were theological orphans in a rapidly changing Church.[1]

As 1962 dawned, the church found itself widely excoriated, reduced to a fraction of its former membership and the ranks of its religious decimated. It was clearly the time to pursue a drastically different tack.

The seven-year hiatus that followed was a period of silence and reflection that ultimately led to the church's reconstruction. During this time, with considerable difficulty due in no small part to internal divisions, the church sought the beginnings of a diplomatic rapprochement with the government. It is to the credit of a nucleus of enlightened church leaders that, despite continuing friction with government officials, the church held firm to this goal.

Other important factors contributed to this fence-mending process. The revolutionary government, increasingly supported by the Soviet Union and confident in the wake of the Bay of Pigs fiasco, no longer felt threatened by the church—particularly since so many opponents of the regime were now in exile. Moreover, the churches no longer constituted "refuges for reactionaries"[2] and thus posed a limited political challenge. Finally, with little to lose, government leaders looked with more tolerance on church initiatives. The tension around the religious question slowly dissipated, leaving a breathing space during which an accommodation could be reached.

Strains in the Modus Vivendi

Such an accommodation evolved slowly and at an uneven pace and was fraught with obstacles emanating from both church and government circles. The revolutionary government, confident that no further counterrevolutionary offensive was likely from the church, and deeply concerned over severe economic problems and shortages, left the church to itself; thus began its long, and often painful, phase of introspection.

Two troublesome issues threatened to destroy this arrangement: the development of the Unidades Militares de Ayuda a la Producción (Military Units to Aid Production), or UMAP's and the Father Loredo case in 1966, which resulted in the arrest of the charismatic young Franciscan, an episode that has still not been satisfactorily explained. It is significant that neither issue in fact resulted in any noticeable deterioration of the nascent accommodation, when just a few years earlier these issues would have exploded into well-publicized incidents. That this did not happen indicates the desire by both sides to pursue a policy of damage control.

The case of the UMAP's should be understood in the context of international pressures to which Cuba was subjected after the Bay of Pigs invasion, culminating in the October 1962 missile crisis. Frequently harassed by Cuban exile groups based in Florida, the Cuban government introduced legislation in late 1963 obligating all Cuban males between the ages of seventeen and forty-five to military service. Yet understandable though the context might have been, it is clear with the value of hindsight that the UMAP's were unjustifiable and were a poor policy. They were set up at the same time to accept all "anti-social elements," homosexuals, deviants, criminals, and others not trusted for incorporation into the regular armed forces. These work camps clearly were intended as detention centers for undesirables. In 1966, three young priests (among them Monsignor Jaime Ortega Alamino, current archbishop of Havana) were called up and transferred to the UMAP's, an action that reflected the government's jaundiced view of churchmen. Although the priests' time in the camps was reduced by the government, the fact of their inclusion remained a bone of contention between church and government officials. (The UMAP camps, it was subsequently conceded by members of the revolutionary government, including Fidel Castro, had been a serious error in judgment, and they were closed down in 1968. Among many Catholics, though, they remained a symbolic reminder of a heavy-handed government policy.)

The second development with a potential to rock church-government relations during this period took place over a two-week period starting in late March 1966. Two people had been killed in a frustrated attempt by a Cubana de Aviación engineer, Angel María Betancourt, to hijack to Miami a plane flying on the Santiago de Cuba–Havana route. The pilot deceived Betancourt, convincing him that they had landed at Miami when in fact he had brought the plane back to Cuba, and in the ensuing fracas Betancourt shot and killed both the pilot and a guard before escaping. The story captured press attention for several weeks,[3] culminating in Betancourt's arrest in the San Francisco church in Havana two weeks later.

Opposing testimony was put forward concerning the role of a young Franciscan, Father Miguel Loredo, accused of harboring the criminal, so that many unanswered questions remain about the events leading to the arrest.[4] What was undeniable was that Betancourt had sought refuge in the church. The media attacked Father Loredo and his superior, the parish priest at San Francisco, Father Serafín Ajuria, and reminded people of the church's erstwhile opposition to the revolutionary process: "Once again the enemies of the people could count upon support from the altars in order to protect themselves after having violated the Fifth Commandment: 'Thou Shalt Not Kill.'"[5] Perhaps the most significant aspect of the whole episode, however, was what did *not* happen. (By comparison one has only to recall the emotion-laden sequel to Boza Masvidal's September 1961 procession.) Because of the negligible opposition from Christian groups and the commitment by church and government leaders to avoid capitalizing on the incident (the role of the papal nuncio in this process should not be underestimated), the government chose to dampen any anti-Catholic sentiment that might have resulted from the episode. Media coverage of the priest's alleged role was conspicuously muffled, an extraordinary development in the relations between church and revolutionary government that revealed clearly how both sides had entered a new phase in their relationship.

The Accommodation: Signs of Accord

Several indicators suggest that this new trend in church-state relations had become reasonably well established by the mid-1960s. Individually, they may appear unimportant, yet when viewed collectively, their concrete and symbolic significance implies a major advance in the resulting accommodation.

Besides nationalizing all private media (including church media), until late 1961 the government had encouraged a primarily negative portrayal of the church in its media. The one-dimensional caricature presented showed the clergy to be grasping, egotistical, dishonest, and immoral persons, receiving money from the United States to foment discord and actively engaging in espionage and sabotage. Stripped of their own newspapers and radio programs, church leaders were of course unable to respond to these charges. Occasional articles highlighted positive advances, usually in relation to outreach or social action programs, such as dispensaries and work in homes for senior citizens, to illustrate Fidel Castro's suggestion that the church pursue a more practical path.

Government-controlled media appeared to have set a more positive course overall during 1962, reflected in such pieces as "Salomón Bolo Hidalgo, El Cura Revolucionario del Perú" and a subsequent interview with the priest in question,[6] a study of some Buddhist monks who supported the Cuban revolution,[7] and several on Félix Varela.[8] In mid-1963, three more balanced pieces replaced the usual harsh criticisms of the Vatican, traditionally a target for the Cuban media for its political meddling, power, and enormous wealth (in the face of widespread world poverty, it was often pointed out).[9] This is not to say, of course, that in the official media criticism of organized religion disappeared,[10] but rather that it was moderated. One example of the new government direction appeared in an issue of the traditional communist newspaper *Hoy*, at the time perhaps the organ most strident and dogmatic in its denouncement of religion. While *Hoy*'s official line was that religion, as the "opiate of the masses," would lose its raison d'être in a truly communist nation,[11] its approach was deliberately subtle. In an article "Saints on the Wall and Study Circles in the Home" ("Santos en las paredes y círculos de estudio en la casa"), a reader asked about the appropriate reaction of party militants at a study circle held in a house decorated with religious pictures. The editorial advised him to live and let live: "In that case, the animator [orientador] of the study circle, who lives in that house, supposing that he doesn't share those religious beliefs, would proceed correctly by respecting the religious sentiments of his family members by allowing them to keep the religious pictures on the walls, since they are cooperating by allowing him to use the house for the revolutionary task of spreading Marxist-Leninist principles and ideas. Pictures of saints on the wall won't harm the revolution."[12]

Just as the church hierarchy had toned down its denunciations of government policy, so now government officials in general abandoned their criticisms of organized religion. As a result, by 1969, as one North American visitor noted, there was "no propaganda against the church or against religion, either in the press or on radio or television . . . [but] rather a general neglect."[13] While this might not seem to represent a particularly sympathetic government policy, in the context of recent years of strife and mutual recrimination it constituted an important gain.

Accompanying the media's mixture of benign neglect and encouragement of a more active form of Christianity was a variety of minor but symbolically significant gestures. Marking a new beginning was the release in March 1963, on the day of the burial of Cuban-born Cardinal Arteaga, of the only four priests in prison for counterrevolutionary activities, Cuban Reinerio Lebroc and Spanish priests Franciso López Blásquez, Ramón Fidalgo, and Luis Rojo. In 1964 an occasion for an exchange of views between church and the government came with the death of Father Guillermo Sardiñas, epitome of the "guerrilla priest" ethic. (In his last years Sardiñas had been badly neglected by the church hierarchy, who were greatly displeased with his habit of saying mass in his olive-green cassock emblazoned with the star indicating his rank as a comandante in the rebel army.) Another government gesture was the dedication of a new school in January 1969 to the memory of another revolutionary priest, the Colombian Camilo Torres, whose mother was a friend of Fidel Castro. The death of Archbishop Pérez Serantes in April 1968 provided a similar opportunity for dialogue. As archbishop of Santiago de Cuba, Pérez Serantes had personally intervened to stop the slaughter of the 26th of July Movement revolutionaries in 1953 (and had therefore, indirectly at least, saved Fidel Castro's life). A resident of Cuba for several decades, aware of the appalling conditions in which the peasants lived, the archbishop had always been an outspoken critic of government policy, including the socialist program of Fidel Castro. Yet Pérez Serantes, despite violent objections to the policies of the revolutionary government, had maintained an excellent personal relationship with the Castro family: "It was not surprising, then, that the first wreaths to arrive for the funeral at the cathedral in Santiago de Cuba were those of Fidel Castro, with another from his brother Raúl."[14]

Although perhaps not of an earth-shattering nature, several practical steps were taken by the revolutionary government to ameliorate conditions for the church. Fidel Castro visited the nunciate on the occasion of Pope's Day in 1963 and again in 1967 when the papal nuncio was appointed bishop. More tangible was the permission to allow more priests to come and work in Cuba, including several who had earlier been deported. Perhaps the most striking symbol of the government's moderated attitude was Monsignor Francisco Oves, who had been deported in 1961. Having returned in 1964, he was appointed archbishop in Havana and pursued an extremely progressive political line until he stepped down because of poor health. Both the government and the church were enjoying "the benefits of mutual toleration. In early 1968, 210 churches, 31 religious communities, and numerous religious bookstores and Catholic hospitals operated on a regular basis in Cuba, while the Castro government put up no opposition to the three new bishops named to Cuban sees late in 1967 and even allowed the duty-free import of forty Volkswagens for the use of the clergy."[15]

Another noteworthy development during this period (and one that continued into the 1970s) was the establishment of stronger ties between church leaders in Cuba and their colleagues elsewhere in the world. The impetus for this new policy came from Rome in the midst of the major reforms emanating from the Second Vatican Council of 1962–65, but the Cuban church readily accepted the idea, having realized its own need for an aggiornamento. The reunion of Latin American bishops (CELAM) in Medellín, Colombia, in 1968, attended by several representatives of the Cuban church, would cement this desire for reform and support the Cuban bishops' major push for change which they would express most eloquently in their two collective documents of 1969.

During this period several well-known church figures visited Cuba, their missions to strengthen the nascent innovations and to report to Rome. Among them were Belgian sociologist François Houtart, Argentinian Aldo Büntig, and Msgr. Sales de Araujo of the Social Action Department of CELAM. Msgr. Eduardo Pironio, the newly elected president of CELAM, visited Cuba in September 1969, returning to the island four months later. Later there were visits from Pedro Arrupe, superior general of the Jesuits; the powerful Cardinal Agostino

Casaroli of the Vatican Secretariat of State; Archbishop Antonio Quarracino, president of the Lay Department of CELAM; Msgr. Maximino Romero de Lema, secretary of the Sacred Congregation for the Clergy; Msgr. López Trujillo, secretary general of CELAM; Cardinal Bernard Gantin, president of the Pontifical Commission for Justice and Peace; and Msgr. Manuel Vieira, bishop of Mapula, Mozambique. Fidel Castro met personally with Cardinals Gantin and Casaroli and Bishop Vieira. The influx of prestigious church visitors from abroad, encouragement from Rome stemming from the magisterium of Vatican II, the arrival of more clergy, a new, dynamic, and wholly Cuban church leadership, and visits abroad by Cuban church representatives (three bishops attended the Vatican Council sessions) all helped to move the Cuban Catholic community along the road to modernity.

The period 1960–73 saw also a remarkable shift in the composition of the Cuban Episcopal Conference, following the deaths of Bishop Alberto Martín Villaverde (Matanzas) in November 1960 and of Cardinal Arteaga (the first native-born cardinal in more than four centuries) in 1963. Arteaga, severely limited in the public eye by his frequent dealings with Batista and his excellent relationship with the dictator's wife, was of the typical "pre-Conciliar" mold, sadly out of touch with the reality of revolutionary Cuba. Hampered both by perspective and by failing health, the cardinal was ineffectual as a church leader in his final years and did little to promote a modernizing influence in his church. The death of Pérez Serantes in 1968 and the resignation of Msgr. Evelio Díaz (Havana) in 1970 and of Msgr. Alfredo Müller (Cienfuegos) in 1971 provided opportunities for the Cuban church to replace the old guard with a new generation of younger clergy, more attuned to the needs of the church in Cuba's revolutionary context. The emergence of an all-Cuban hierarchy in particular nullified the earlier criticism that Franco's Falangist priests ran the Cuban church and helped to establish the credibility of the "new" church.

The Vatican responded well to the revolutionary government's initiatives toward the church, well reflected in skillful diplomatic representation by Ambassador Luis Amado Blanco, a Catholic, at the Holy See. As a result special attention was accorded Cuba by high-placed Vatican officials.[16] Profoundly influenced by John XXIII's imaginative vision, the Vatican made an exception of Fidel Castro (in contrast to Argentine president Juan Perón) by not publicly or formally excommunicating him when Cuban officials broke canon law by their treatment of church property and of Cuban bishops such as Boza Masvidal.[17] Indeed, to show how relations between church and goverment leaders were improving, Pope John XXIII sent President Dorticós a medal in early

1963. A dramatic new course was being urged by the pontiff, one that Cuba gradually began to acknowledge.

Nuncio Zacchi's Tenure: "Servilismo más Abjecto" or Sensitive Diplomacy?

Little arouses more passion among exiled Cuban Catholics of this time than the name Cesare Zacchi, the Vatican's emissary in Cuba during this crucial period and for several years afterwards.[18] In 1962 he was officially appointed chargé d'affaires by the Holy See, replacing Monsignor Centoz, and he wasted little time in explaining the nature of his role as troubleshooter. "Here, my principal task is to reduce the distrust between the Cuban clergy and the government," he said in an atypically straightforward fashion.[19] Such an aim, while much to be desired, could only place the papal nuncio on a collision course with many traditional Catholics in this extremely conservative church.

Fifty years ago, Pope Pius XI described communism as "intrinsically evil." For many Catholics, any attempt at cooperating with the communist enemy was therefore tantamount to treason. Zacchi's greatest failing in their eyes was that he tried to apply the progressive teachings of Vatican II in Cuba before most of Cuba's clergy, and indeed the majority of the faithful, were ready even to consider them. The complaints about the nuncio remitted to the Holy See by disgruntled churchpeople testify not only to Zacchi's dedication to his mission but also to the shortcomings of many of Cuba's Catholics at that time. At the same time, as some of his most acerbic critics have grudgingly admitted, his pragmatic attitude did lessen tension between political and religious leaders and brought them to an accommodation that has manifestly benefited the church.

There are many anecdotes about the progressive (some would say socialist) nature of Zacchi's thought. To a large extent these derived from his excellent working relationship with Fidel Castro, a union that of course was anathema to most Cuban Catholics. Writing in 1970, for instance, Irish Parliamentarian John Horgan captured the range of Zacchi's talents: "In all this, the role of Msgr. Zacchi is of major importance. He is a tall, slim, quite un-Italian figure, who speaks Spanish, English, and French with considerable fluency: his comfortable house in the Vedado suburb of Havana is, in its own way, as important as the Russian or Chinese embassies. For several years he was probably on better terms with the government than with the hierarchy. History was created at one reception when Castro, in a moment of levity, tried

Msgr. Zacchi's skullcap for size. His gifts of patience, diplomacy, and tact have been responsible not only for the continuing good relationship between the Cuban government and the Holy See, but for the process of growth and maturity which is becoming evident in the Cuban hierarchy as a whole."[20]

Msgr. Zacchi's earlier diplomatic experience in Austria and Yugoslavia (from which he was expelled) had provided the young diplomat a useful framework within which to judge the potential role of the church in this socialist society. His style, vitality, and ideas, so different from those of his predecessor, Msgr. Centoz (seventy-two years old when relieved of his posting), clearly paralleled the dynamic spirit of Vatican II. They also constituted grave barriers to his acceptance by traditional Catholics in Cuba, who were further alienated by his penchant for the dramatic gesture. Yet this same flair helped convince the government of the pontiff's sincerity and of the council's reforms. Cuban Foreign Minister Raúl Roa praised Zacchi for going "beyond the demands of diplomacy. . . . At the time of Girón [the Bay of Pigs invasion], he sent a telegram to Fidel congratulating him on his victory over the invaders whom he called traitors to the Fatherland—and don't forget that there were four priests among the invaders."[21]

Zacchi's fourteen years in revolutionary Cuba represented a controversial stimulus for the church. He rankled many members of the "old guard" (within both church and government), but it is undeniable that his intelligent diplomacy was of paramount importance in initiating the enormously difficult task of restoring credibility to church activities.

Zacchi's approach to diplomacy, and to the role of religion, remained constant during his tenure in Cuba. The church, he felt, "should adapt to all regimes, since its imperative is the care of souls, and as a result the flock should not be abandoned."[22] His first mission in Cuba was to stem the panic among clergy that had led to the voluntary exile of most priests and religious and to remind them that their primary responsibility was to stay and minister to their flocks. In this task Zacchi had help from a special emissary sent by the Vatican.[23] Thereafter he maintained that his mission was to exact the best possible conditions for Catholics and for the development of Catholicism in general: "Msgr. Zacchi attempts to remain on good terms with the civil authorities, the objective being to obtain as much as possible for the Church's benefit. He doesn't hide his game, and acts openly, and honestly. Not a few people have reproached him for having too much contact with the regime, to which he responds that the Church's mission is to continue evangelizing the people, in whatever circumstances it may be, and for all the time that may prove necessary, but without committing itself too evidently."[24]

What credibility the church gained during this critical time came largely through the nuncio's diplomatic initiatives. Zacchi worked within the system, described by Ivan Vallier as one in which "nuncios are oriented to officials in sovereign states. . . . Relations between the Holy See and sovereign states are critical for regular religious work in the field. Without the proper 'working conditions' at the national level, the Church cannot proselytize and cannot make contact with residential bishops, and through them, with the faithful."[25]

The point raised consistently by Zacchi's detractors, however, was precisely that he committed himself too wholeheartedly to establishing "working conditions on the national level," encouraging Cuban Catholics to join the mainstream of Cuban revolutionary society. Having established that the problem between church and revolutionary government was not religious but political in nature, he criticized the "deformed" vision of Cuban exiles. Much to the chagrin of the latter, he employed the derogatory term "gusanos" (worms) when attributing these views, thereby angering them even more.[26] He urged Cuban Catholics to recognize that the Cuban Revolution was solidly established because, he stated, "I consider the Church to be aware of the change of political system in this country; it is an incontrovertible fact which is now irreversible. As a result, the Church should adapt to these changes, as it has shown in Europe, and adhere firmly to its obligations as mother and spiritual guide."[27]

For members of the church who opposed Fidel Castro's revolutionary government, this pragmatic invitation to cooperate with the socialist experiment—to collaborate with the enemy—represented a major setback. Here, in their beleaguered country, was the papal representative, the highest ecclesiastical authority in Cuba, informing them, presumably with the blessing of the Pope, that their opposition was based on a fundamental misreading of the Cuban context. What was worse was to hear Msgr. Zacchi criticize the prerevolutionary situation and praise the positive aspects of the socialist experiment: "The people have obtained a radical change in their material well-being. One cannot deny that now there exist conditions which were necessary before; there has been a redistribution of the wealth and of the social product. Now there is social justice—something which was not prevalent before."[28]

Conservative Catholics disliked Msgr. Zacchi's applauding the redistribution of wealth in revolutionary Cuba, his good personal relations with Castro, his criticism of Catholics (and especially priests and religious) for abandoning their patria, and his insistence that they come to terms with post–Vatican II reality. But what really infuriated Msgr. Zacchi's detractors was his advice on how they should demonstrate their faith in revolutionary Cuba.

The nuncio's advice on the kind of contribution, or prophetic witness, that the role of Catholics should consider within the contemporary Cuban context was again based on his view that one had to make the best of any given situation, working with that reality and seeking to obtain from it whatever benefits were possible for the church. For him this meant, specifically, that Catholics should work within the revolutionary process, thereby raising their collective profile and developing their credibility as a group whose views warranted consideration by government and society. If they undertook such activities, he maintained, they would be taken seriously within Cuban society. Conversely, continuing to ignore the new social process would turn them into social outcasts. Catholics must become integrated (*integrarse*) into the mainstream of Cuban society: "I'm saying that all the time. Catholics should join the mass organizations in the society where they live. They should collaborate in voluntary labor, and join the militia; they should become members of sporting and cultural organizations and, in an active way, should join the student movement and professional institutions. In this way, naturally, a mutual influence will be produced. Moreover, in this exchange, certain ideals of Catholic thought, certain conceptions about life, can be introduced into views held by the revolution. In this way the revolution would be truly representative of all forms of national perceptions."[29]

Concerning the desired form of political participation by young Catholics, Msgr. Zacchi cited both the right for all people to participate actively in the political decision-making process of their country and the limits resulting from the one-party system in Cuba. In light of this reality, far from objecting to Catholics' participating in this process, he in fact enthusiastically encouraged them to do so.[30]

Msgr. Cesare Zacchi's term in Cuba ranks as one of the major formative experiences in the contemporary church there. Compared to Eastern Europe, where he had indeed witnessed persecution of the church, he found in Cuba that "nothing like that happened. The Castro government has been very tolerant."[31] The nuncio believed that cooperation and credibility building, rather than the confrontational path urged upon him by exiled Cubans, would best serve Catholic interests and that the church in Cuba could be coaxed to accept the Vatican II spirit. While his critics fiercely denounced him, Zacchi remained confident of the validity of his approach and of the need for the Cuban church to come to terms both with contemporary church social teaching and with the revolutionary process. With some satisfaction, he was able in 1966 to cite major advances in church-government relations: "Cuba is the first socialist country in which peaceful coexistence between the State and the Catholic Church can be classified in more precise and correct terms, since what there really is here is joint activity in all work which can be directed to benefit the people."[32]

The Continuing Role of Fidel Castro

When asked in an interview if he considered Fidel Castro a Christian, Msgr. Zacchi gave a response which ever since has been repeated with much bitterness by exiled Catholics: "Of course . . . from an ideological perspective, he is not, since he has declared himself to be a Marxist-Leninist. However, I consider him to be, ethically, a Christian."[33] Opponents of the revolutionary government found this interpretation treasonous. Their response, while understandable, fails to take into account how Fidel Castro sought better relations with the church and tried to divert demands from within revolutionary circles that the government take even stronger measures against the church. Much of Fidel Castro's work has been to develop, consciously and carefully, a policy of détente, simultaneously urging church leaders to pursue a practical, service-oriented Christianity. Without his work, the initiatives of Msgr. Zacchi would probably have failed, a circumstance the nuncio appreciated: "The existing relations between the government and the Church are very cordial. No kind of government persecution has been unleashed against the priests; neither have churches been closed, or religious services interrupted. . . . I remember how in Yugoslavia, where I had been appointed the Pope's representative, the churches were closed, there was an implacable campaign of religious persecution, and I myself was expelled from the country. Here in socialist Cuba, however, nothing like that has happened. The Castro government has been very consistent."[34]

During this period of constructive engagement, a time of relative stability for the government with more Soviet aid and growing national confidence in Cuba's ability both to defend itself and to play a larger international role, Fidel Castro's views on religion remained in essence the same: the church had to serve the interests of the masses first, to forgo its erstwhile privileges, and to avoid serving as a facade for the counterrevolutionary struggle. If the church pursued such policies, the revolutionary government would be pleased to cooperate. Unlike the years 1959 to 1961, however, when Cuba faced extensive opposition from counterrevolutionaries,[35] Castro's observations on the church during the period of Msgr. Zacchi's tenure consistently called for cooperation rather than confrontation.

Fidel Castro's analysis of the roots of the conflict between the church and the revolutionary government also remained consistent, focusing on the falangista Spanish clergy, who catered to the powerful upper class and urban bourgeoisie while ignoring the appalling conditions of Cuba's poor, especially the rural sector: "Many of our peasants didn't know what a church or a priest was—except when he came by every two or three months to perform baptisms in that area, and to charge two or three pesos for each baptism."[36] Moreover he maintained that the role of religion, because it had opposed the revolutionary government during the period 1959 to 1961, could be reduced to a class issue since the bourgeoisie used religion to defend their earthly, not their spiritual interests.

Some of Fidel Castro's views concerning the religious phenomenon did, however, clearly develop during this period. Chief among the factors behind the changes were the relationship developed by Zacchi, the emergence in Latin America of clergy with clear socialist and in some cases revolutionary orientations (notably Camilo Torres), and developments within the church, especially Vatican II and Medellín (in which Fidel Castro took a particular interest). These principles, in many ways the logical extension of his earlier views, clashed with those of more orthodox Marxists: Dr. José Felipe Carneado, for example, the Central Committee member who acted as liaison for the church's dealings with the revolutionary government, clearly exasperated the Nicaraguan priest Ernesto Cardenal by stating, "In Cuba one can not be a Christian and a revolutionary, because here the Revolution defined itself as Marxist-Leninist and therefore atheistic because Marxism is atheistic." Fidel Castro himself struck a different note when speaking with Cardenal, declaring that "all the qualities that make a priest are the qualities needed in a good revolutionary."[37]

The idea of a union between revolutionaries and Catholics was officially propounded by Fidel Castro during this period, angering orthodox church and government leaders. He was influenced by the example of Camilo Torres, in whose honor he dedicated a school in January 1969 with the words "The revolutionary change in Latin American societies is a task and an undertaking in which all men of good will and Christians will get together."[38] During this period Castro seemed to grasp the value of such a strategic unity more clearly than before— perhaps influenced by the nuncio but largely because of the major changes taking place within church circles throughout Latin America. He began to appreciate that, with Vatican II, fundamental structural changes were to be realized within the church, that a distinctive model had of necessity to spring from the church's "preferential option for the poor." His closing speech at the Intercultural Congress in Havana in June 1968 gives some indication of this appreciation: "Without a doubt we are now faced with new data, new facts. We revolutionaries, especially we who pride ourselves so much on being revolutionaries, on our Marxism-Leninism, we simply have to analyze these new facts. Because there can be nothing more anti-Marxist than the petrification of ideas, still there are ideas that are bandied about as Marxist, yet are veritable fossils. . . . Marxism has to keep growing. It mustn't succumb to hardening of the arteries; it must constantly reinterpret, with a frank, scientific objectivity, the realities of today; it must behave like a revolutionary force and not like some pseudo-revolutionary church. These are the paradoxes of history. How, when we find some of the clergy becoming revolutionary forces, can we resign ourselves to lapsing into ecclesiastical forces?"[39]

This plea to avoid the petrification of ideas and, in passing, to recognize the revolutionary nature of true Christianity has been a constant feature of Fidel Castro's observations. At all times, he has defended the practical application of such religious sentiment and lambasted the exploitation of religion by people seeking to defend their own interests at the expense of the majority. He has also been consistent in chiding his fellow revolutionaries to be less dogmatic about organized religion, but in this he has been less successful. Perhaps nowhere are these ideas more articulately expressed than in his intervention at the 13 March 1962 ceremony to mark the anniversary of the death of student leader (and Catholic militant) José Antonio Echevarría. The master of ceremonies read Echevarría's "political will," deliberately omitting these lines: "We believe that the moment for fulfillment has come, we believe that the purity of our intentions will bring us the favor of God to bring about the reign of justice in our Fatherland." At this point Fidel Castro took the microphone and asked, "Can we, comrades, be so cowardly and such mental cripples that we come here to read José Antonio's will and we have the cowardice, the moral misery, to suppress three lines?" He went on: "The true revolutionary does not commit such stupidity. . . . Using these criteria we would have to begin by suppressing all the writings of the forerunner of independence, Carlos Manuel de Céspedes as well as those of Maceo, Máximo Gómez, and Bolívar. We would have to suppress the writings of Martí. We would have to suppress the whole revolutionary concept from Spartacus to Martí. When he invokes religious feelings José Antonio loses nothing of his heroism and his glory. . . . The counterrevolutionaries have used that phrase of José Antonio to fight the Revolution. With the hypocrisy and moral duplicity that characterize them, it's easy to explain why they would do it. But it is hard to explain why revolutionaries would suppress those lines. . . . We know that a revolutionary can have a faith, that he *can* have one."[40]

Clearly the Cuban leader has more sensitivity to the religious question than he is usually credited with. Perhaps this awareness of the Christian ethic, combined with the diplomatic initiative of the papal nuncio, made possible the period of constructive silence—a tremendous feat if one considers the acrimonious relationship of the period 1959–61. Msgr. Zacchi was apparently aware of the church's debilities, and his energetic endeavors to remedy these in the light of Vatican II touched a respondent chord in the Cuban leader. The end result was the beginning of the procession out of the catacombs.

Modus Vivendi or Modus Moriendi?

Former Acción Católica executive Manuel Fernández describes the church's posture during this period as "a modus vivendi which, let's not fool ourselves, consists in our adapting to suit the communist regime. In return," he writes, "all we receive is a very reduced level of tolerance on the part of the civilian authorities."[41] This view implies that here was a piece of diplomatic negotiation rather than any meaningful accord, a sop to the liberal Vatican at the expense of the mainstream of Cuban Catholicism.

While there is something to this argument, one cannot help but hear in it tinges of envy and perhaps of the frustration felt by Cuba's exiled Catholic community, the reaction of any political exile group that no longer exercises any influence on the patria. Perhaps, too, there is an element of guilt at the kind of Catholicism practiced in prerevolutionary Cuba, in contrast to changes sweeping the rest of the Catholic world—although it is unlikely that many exiles would agree. Certainly the changes resulting from Vatican II would have encountered tremendous resistance in the Cuban church, with or without the fidelista revolution, given the innate conservatism of the institution.

An alternative interpretation would dispute the validity of the "modus moriendi" claims and would indicate great benefits for the church on both spiritual and social levels. Perhaps the least visible is the growth in the spiritual nature of the church, in part the logical result of its seeking to develop within a surrounding, theologically critical, Marxist society. During this time, church representatives were forced to confront the traditional role of their work and compare it with the reality of socialist Cuba. These religious were forced by poor material living conditions to appreciate a reality that was new to many of them. Bolstered by the Cubanization of the clergy, the church experienced spiritual growth from the severing of the church's traditionally close ties with the United States, a factor most notably true for the Protestant church.

The need to fend for itself in difficult material conditions, especially when faced with suspicion and occasional discrimination by the government, thus had a beneficial, purifying effect on the Cuban church. More important, it strengthened the message being conveyed by Rome through Zacchi, that the church in revolutionary Cuba had to come to terms with its new context and turn away from the religion of the good old days. As one observer noted at the time, "The Church begins to understand that its historical location is Cuba, its mission is to serve, and its structure is to be a communal one."[42]

On a more public level, particularly after the mid-1960s, the church saw fairly substantial improvements in its condition. Responding to the liberalizing impact of Vatican II and the 1968 CELAM meeting in Medellín, the government of Fidel Castro sought to make tangible concessions to various churches in Cuba. John A. MacKay, Presbyterian minister and president emeritus of Princeton Theological Seminary, wrote: "I found no evidence of religious persecution. As a matter of fact, members of the clergy are given special consideration." Five years later, Rabbi Everett E. Gendler echoed McKay's words: "Except for the Jehovah's Witnesses—whose antigovernmental stance seems as unacceptable to Cubans as to us in the U.S.A.—the practicing denominations are at the least tolerated, perhaps respected, and always treated with consideration by the government. Evidence of this is everywhere."[43] The government's concessions seem to have been beneficial in strengthening progressive gestures by churchpeople.[44] Lacking the exiles' emotional ties with the Cuban *patria*, and not having made their sacrifices—loss of livelihood, material goods, indeed an entire identity and way of life—these clergy are able to view the Cuban experience more dispassionately. Moreover, unfettered by the pre–Vatican II traditions so deeply rooted in Cuba, they can perhaps comprehend more readily the broad sweep of social change in revolutionary Cuba— and the role of the church in that context.

This crucial stage in the church's development can be reduced to a struggle toward modernization. The prime mover in this coming to terms with reality was Msgr. Zacchi, who fostered a climate of benevolent negotiation, aided by Fidel Castro who was himself eager to reduce tension between church and government leaders within the context of contemporary revolutionary Cuba. The result was a meaningful "modus vivendi" from which the church benefited spiritually as well as materially—unfortunately with some pronounced internal divisions. Although aided by the nuncio's skillful diplomacy as he prodded the church to come to terms with the magisterium of Vatican II and Medellín, eventually it was the core of the Cuban church itself that realized that the time had come to emerge from the catacombs. The result of these diverse influences was, to answer the question posed earlier, a meaningful "modus vivendi," one from which the church benefited spiritually as well as materially—but unfortunately with some pronounced internal divisions. As lay Catholic leader Raúl Gómez Treto suggested in 1969, the church recognized that its mission of "bringing the Gospel of Peace, love and salvation to *all* men—which is the essential apostolate of the Church—cannot be carried out properly within our doors, in a religious ghetto. Of necessity it requires a *secular* projection outwards, toward our *century* [hacia el siglo], in other words, toward the world of human beings and their present structures onto which we have been inescapably grafted by God's design."[45]

The fundamental question was whether the church would be able to rid itself of what Catholic thinker Andrés Valdespino called "the Christianity of the whited sepulchers."[46] In the spring of 1969, following a seven-year period of introspection and evaluation, the Cuban episcopal conference emerged from its silence ("de profundis" or "out of the depths") to face this question.

6

Emerging from the

Catacombs, 1969–1978

Some Cuban Catholics called it as the "most scandalous fallacious document, the most audacious and one-sided, on the difficult moment that we are living."[1] For others it smacked of betrayal and falsification,[2] clearly the result of some such Communist pressure as "You people sign this document—the pastoral letter—or else you all get out of here."[3] Most of Cuba's clergy, according to one foreign priest, simply refused to read it,[4] while a number of Cuba's Catholics denounced their church leaders for producing this apparent heresy. What generated these heated reactions was the first of two pastoral letters published in 1969 which together would catapult the church into the modern era.

Under the guidance of the papal nuncio, the church adopted the Vatican Ostpolitik to obtain from the revolutionary government "at whatever costs, the guarantee (endorsed by the State) to respect Church structures of control, the validity of canon law, and protection of the right to worship."[5] For the traditionalists in the church this general direction was bad enough. When the Cuban hierarchy took the initiative with their 1969 pastorals, their action was tantamount to treason. The furor surrounding the documents unfortunately distracted attention from their essence. That the bishops were even thinking in such directions was distasteful to traditionalists, for whom the modernizing trend of Vatican II would always be a problem. In fact, after the self-imposed seven-year silence of the Episcopal Conference, many Catholics had become quite used to their bishops simply saying nothing.

In light of the dramatic reception accorded the pastoral letters, their contents are somewhat anticlimactic. Indeed a case can be made that the church hierarchy was finally stating the obvious, leaving one to ask only why it had taken them so long. Nevertheless, these documents—in particular the first, coming after so many years of silence—have greatly influenced the development of the modern church in Cuba. The April 1969 collective pastoral, read during the week of the eighth anniversary of the Bay of Pigs invasion, has been called the "second coming of the Cuban Church."[6]

In the April document,[7] the Cuban bishops tried to come to terms with the issue of Cuban–U.S. relations, seeking to bring about a humanitarian resolution to the continuing standoff. In particular they condemned the blockade imposed by the United States because of its adverse effect on the Cuban population at large. Influenced by the teachings of Medellín, the bishops wrote, "Our pastoral mission is essentially a service of inspiration and education of the conscience of the believers, in order to help them to understand the responsibilities of their faith, both in their personal life and in their social living" (289). Drawing upon Paul VI's encyclical *Popolorum Progressio,* they offered "a reexamination of our social morality in the light of the responsibilities we face regarding the problem of development" (290). Couched in these seemingly innocuous observations, however, were some rather pointed recommendations that constituted a clear contrast with the earlier silence of the church.

The bishops were disturbed, they wrote, by the lack of economic development, the result in large part of "internal difficulties, due to the fact that these problems are new and involve complex technical demands, although they are also a product of the deficiencies and sins of men." The hierarchy then turned to the impact of the U.S. blockade and "the concrete condition of isolation [in] which we have been living for so many years" (293), ending with a crescendo condemning the results of the blockade:

> Is this not the case of the economic blockade to which our country has been subjected, and whose automatic continuation multiplies grave inconveniences for our country? Such inconveniences mainly burden our workers in the cities and in the fields, our housewives, our growing youth and children and our sick. Lastly, to cut this narration short, they burden so many families afflicted by the separation of their dear ones.
>
> In seeking the common good of our people and of our faithful, in serving the poorer among them, according to the command of Jesus and the commitment at Medellín, we denounce the unjust conditions of the blockade, which is contributing to unnecessary sufferings, and to making all efforts at development more difficult. Therefore, we are appealing to the conscience of all those

in the position to solve this problem, to initiate decided and efficient action aiming at the lifting of the measure. (293)

Cuban Catholics reared on bland admonishments, pre–Vatican II teachings, an "apolitical" stance, and identification with the Christian West were scandalized by this fiery language.

The second collective pastoral letter, "On Contemporary Atheism,"[8] was released by the Cuban bishops on 3 September. Concerned like the first with a politically volatile topic, it nevertheless had less impact, largely because Cuban Catholics had been somewhat prepared by its predecessor but also because this letter did not directly criticize U.S. government policy. The essential theme of the document was faith and, more specifically, how to guide and develop faith in Cuba's revolutionary context.

Once again the document relied heavily on the influence of Paul VI and on the teachings of Medellín, the general thrust of these being to urge a modernization and an openness in the way Cuban Catholics practiced their faith. Divided into two sections ("The problem of faith" and "Growth in the faith"), the pastoral urged upon laymen and clergy a spirit of renewal in the church through liturgical revitalization, a more serious interest in Bible studies, and an updating of the catechesis. "We encourage our priests, our religious and our laymen to continue on this new path which the Council opened to us and which has been amply ratified in Medellín" (304).

"Fear not!" the pastoral letter admonished. "For the Church, this is an hour of courage and of trust in the Lord." Over and over the bishops stressed the need to modernize the church's interpretation of religious life: "We exhort the priests and catechists according to these principles enunciated, to know how to integrate the most authentic of our tradition with the present dynamism of the post-conciliar Church into the Christian education of children and adults; to help the integral evolution of man in today's world, subject to rapid and profound social changes; to orient, with fidelity, the insertion of our Christians in that new pluralistic world which is being constructed to the spirit of the gospel, so that they can give a true testimony as such to all their brothers. That they know how to admit with serene objectivity the healthy elements of criticism of religion that can operate as a purifier of the faith" (306). Indeed, they pointed to the limitations of traditional religious practices, expressions "which can be deformed and mixed in some measure with an ancestral religious patrimony, where tradition exercises an almost tyrannical power. There is the chance that these expressions can be easily influenced by magical practices and superstitions that reveal a rather utilitarian character and a certain fear of the divine" (302). The basic goal, then, was to steer away from "traditional-ist" practices, seeking to provide a daily witness of a practical and in-herently relevant Catholic life-style within the revolutionary process. The bishops described their own contribution to the church as one that should be "adequate for the administering of the sacraments which may lead our faithful to a vital experience of unity between faith, the liturgy and daily life, by virtue of which Christians may reach the wit-ness of Christ" (304).

This modernizing trend included accepting the reality of Cuba's unique revolutionary situation, evaluating the positive aspects of that reality and of the challenge for the church, and then embracing the challenge of applying the message of Medellín to that reality. This ulti-mately meant adapting to a socialist society with little apparent room for the church spiritually, politically, or socially, a society directed by a Communist party whose dogma was radically opposed to that of the church. It was a difficult step for the church to take—particularly since just eight years before church leaders had denounced the revolutionary government in no uncertain terms. Nevertheless, the bishops forged ahead, urging their own *aggiornamento* of the church and reminding Catholics of the essential Christian message, "to look at all men—because they are men—as our brother" (300).

Many Catholics, accustomed to viewing Communists as the enemy, reacted to the bishops' post-Medellín approach to communism with suspicion and rejection. Anticipating such a reaction, the September pastoral emphasized the challenge facing Cuban Catholics living in this historical moment and warned them against withdrawing behind a veil of self-pity and rejection: "We should be able to discern the posi-tive aspects of the crisis through which our world is passing in this turn of its history. *It is a crisis of maturity and of growth and in no way simply a crisis of agony*" (307, emphasis added). The church was attempting a difficult balancing act, with the continuing exodus of Cuban Catholics and government skepticism concerning the church on the one hand, the recent stormy history of the revolutionary gov-ernment and the Catholic hierarchy on the other, and now the teach-ings of Vatican II and Medellín tossed in along with the determination of many Catholics to remain apart from the mainstream of revolution-ary society.

This thorny issue of integration within the revolutionary process was frequently referred to in the collective pastoral, the bishops sug-gesting that Catholics must deal openly and fairly with the commu-nists: "We have to approach the atheistic man with all the respect and fraternal charity which the human person deserves by the mere fact of being a human. We should not exclude his honesty in taking a position, which can be very sincere, nor should we avoid collaboration in the practical order of our terrestrial realizations. For example, in the undertaking of development, in the promotion of all men, and all of man, there is an enormous area of common perseverance among all people of good will, be they atheists or believers" (301).

While lacking the drama of the April pastoral, the September document had an extraordinary value in seeking the fundamental modernization of the Cuban church. Its pragmatic suggestions urged Cubans to ignore certain old-fashioned practices, instead living out their faith by participating in the revolutionary process. It challenged believers to seek a dialogue, an *apertura*, with nonbelievers. The bishops wanted both to break with the past and to establish a new relationship with the country's political leaders and with a revolution that was by now firmly entrenched. Their pastoral undercut the martyrdom complex of many Cuban Catholics and revealed to the revolutionary government at the very least a desire to cooperate within the process. It was a seminal document for the church in Cuba.

The Government's Reaction to the New Church

Contrary to the image projected by North American media, Fidel Castro does not wield total power: Despite the Cuban president's many responsibilities and a propensity to get involved in a variety of matters often only marginally connected to his mandate, he neither directs all facets of government nor sets official policy, as we are sometimes led to believe, on everything from new strains of alfalfa sprouts to medical training, the fishing industry to foreign policy.

To understand the government's position on the religious question requires a sensitivity to the different attitudes toward religion held by the traditional Marxist-Leninists in the government, both the original followers of the prerevolutionary Communist Party, the PSP, and members of the new party, the Partido Comunista de Cuba, or PCC. While Fidel Castro generally maintained his earlier position on the role of religion, the party pursued a very different line. Receiving these apparently contradictory signals, the bishops can be forgiven for wondering if they had indeed chosen the right track.

Fidel Castro's role in the church-government debate remained much the same as before: Less skeptical of the church's goals than many of his colleagues, more open to the hierarchy's observations and methods, he continued to favor what has become known as the Christian-Marxist dialogue. The best statements of Castro's views of religion came during his lengthy tour of Chile in 1971 and were repeated in their essence in his address to Jamaican church representatives when he visited that country in October 1977.[9] Together they help to fill out the image of the president's interpretation of religion and are a useful comparision for his observations in Frei Betto's 1985 interviews, published as *Fidel y la religión*.

During his Chilean tour, in the course of which he met with many church representatives, including the impressive Cardinal Silva, Fidel Castro struck several key themes. He remained extremely skeptical of the kind of dogmatic religious life practiced by the middle class: "There were religious practices which had become mere rituals. . . . What was happening in Cuba? It was all exceptionally weak and lax, something merely formal, which had no value and no future."[10] He developed this point in a press conference in Iquique, the most interesting point being his consciousness of the evolution of the Latin American church as a whole, and in particular its social awareness developed after Vatican II. "At the time when the Cuban Revolution was produced, there didn't exist either in the Church or in Christianity the movement for change which exists today. Indeed in our country religion was not something followed by many people. It was the religion of one single class, for the benefit of that single class. . . . It was a situation that was completely different from the picture we see in many places in Latin America, where religion is the religion of the people" (19).

By 1971, Fidel Castro had also become more articulate in defining the similarities between the Marxist and Christian ethics, a new development in his understanding of the religious question. As had been the case a decade earlier, the fundamental concern of religion, as indeed of politics, was its relationship with the people. Religion for the sake of religion was thus to be rejected, while conversely religion at the service of the people, religion as a means of improving social conditions, was to be encouraged. As a result, he not only supported the general post–Vatican II thrust but drew parallels between its goals and those of communism: "Religion is intended for mankind, who represents the center of its objectives. All these factors, I claim, are ten thousand times more developed in socialism and communism. As a result, there is more coincidence between communism and Christianity than there can ever be between capitalism and Christianity" (11).

In his farewell speech in Santiago's Estadio Nacional, the Cuban President dwelt upon the similarities between Christianity and Marxism and the potential for effective joint action, limitless in the Latin American context:

> When people examine the similarities between the objectives of Marxism and the most beautiful precepts of Christianity, they

will see how many points of agreement there are, and will understand why a humble priest has experienced hunger—because he
sees it in his flock—sickness and death, a man who has experience with human suffering; or like some of those priests who
work in mines or with humble peasant families, and can identify
with their situation, and struggle next to them; or selfless individuals who sacrifice their life to tend the sick, suffering the worst
diseases. . . . When people look for similarities, they will see that
the strategic alliance between revolutionary Marxists and revolutionary Christians is indeed a real possibility.

The ones interested in preventing such alliances are the imper-
ialists, who are of course reactionary. (22)

This major development in Castro's appreciation of the new church
conciencia social, the possibilities of church and revolutionary government cooperation, was reinforced by the dialogue between Chile's Cardinal Silva and (Marxist) President Salvador Allende, a productive
working alliance which appears to have surprised him. While the
Cuban situation, for obvious historical reasons, was vastly different,
nevertheless it seemed to Castro that the possibility of such a strategy
could be at least considered.

Fidel Castro extended this concept to a possible strategic alliance between Marxists and Christians throughout Latin America. Through
his much publicized meeting with a group of revolutionary clergy, the
"Ochenta Sacerdotes" (Eighty Priests), and in talks with many other
representatives of the clergy, the Cuban president saw how this alliance could work and referred on several occasions to its potential benefits. In particular he emphasized Che Guevara's influence on his thinking: "It was Che who said that on the day that Christians become
conscious of revolutionary matters, this development would be deci-
sively important" (10). Taking great pains to show that it was a "strategic alliance" and not a "tactical alliance" (the difference between the
two not being, however, overly clear), he emphasized the need for such
cooperation in the struggle for Latin American liberation. In a speech
at Concepción University, Fidel Castro urged the realization of Che
Guevara's dream:

We should know how to appreciate the tremendous importance
and value engendered by that development of political consciousness, shown by the Christian masses in this continent, because
. . . the concept of revolution is based on the art of uniting forces,
of bringing together forces which will then participate in the decisive battles against imperialism. . . .

In Latin America we have to develop a policy of broad union
with all forces that have become aware of the basic situation of

exploitation suffered by our continent. . . . From that perspective
we welcome with all our support, indeed we appreciate it tremendously, the movement which has developed within the Christian
sector in recent years. (20–21)

The visit to Chile—in the midst of a Marxist experiment—convinced
Castro that a union of the progressive Christian sector was not only
desirable but also, in certain contexts, viable. What had been isolated
and small-scale experiments in Cuba, both before and during the revolution, were now replaced by concrete examples in the Latin American
context of this Marxist-Christian alliance. The change significantly influenced Castro's way of thinking.

Some of the president's more candid observations underscore these
developments, revealing too his limitations in assessing the church.
Speaking with the Ochenta Sacerdotes, Castro was able to poke fun
at his own resistance to change in the church in an exchange with a
priest in the audience:

> Fidel: All this has changed so much since I was a student in the
>   religious schools. Now I don't see you wearing any cassocks.
> Priest: The priest isn't made just by the habit he wears. . . .
> Fidel: No, but I still have the habit of seeing the habit. (9)

It was in Chile, then, that Fidel Castro realized, based on the changes
stemming from Medellín and Vatican II, on the recent phenomenon
of worker-priests and guerrilla priests, on the role of revolutionary
Christians, and on his own Christian training, that a union of Marxists
and progressive Christians was indeed desirable and, in some cases,
practicable and that this model could apply to the Cuban context.
"There was no attempt made at reconciliation [in Cuba]. It couldn't
be done because the precedents for such a development didn't exist.
The precedents have been given by the leftist movement of priests in
Latin America. It's curious that you are the ones who will help us to
develop this policy and seek rapprochement. . . . This kind of movement originated outside Cuba—in Latin America. It has had a certain
influence, but *we should have encouraged it more. It's necessary for
us to take the initiative so that this movement will develop also in
Cuba. That's my opinion*" (13, emphasis added).

Church progressives in Cuba can be forgiven for finding in Fidel
Castro's words the hope of a new, more productive relationship between the church and the revolutionary government—for taking Castro at his word. The same churchpeople can also be excused for their
concern over the discrepancy between Fidel's expansive words of encouragement and the role of religion described in official publications
of the Partido Comunista de Cuba.

Although Cuba's constitution (1975) establishes that the state bases its view of religious activity on "the scientific materialist conception of the universe,"[11] it also guarantees freedom of conscience and the right to practice any religion. While this guarantee is honored to a far greater extent than skeptical westerners might imagine, it is true that the party has traditionally been extremely rigid and notoriously dated in its portrayal of religious life. Indeed, its accusations against the church of dogma and of being closed to new ideas could also be laid at its own doorstep. At the very least the official party line, with its benignly negative view of the religious phenomenon, hardly encourages progressive Christian circles. If in the 1970s Fidel Castro wanted to develop a strategic alliance with the Christian sector, he first needed to persuade party ideologues to modernize their position.

The "Theses and Resolutions" prepared by the PCC Central Committee's Department of Revolutionary Orientation, for instance, define religious beliefs as having their roots "not only in ignorance but also, and principally, in the material conditions of social existence. . . . The development in the construction of a new society, the subsequent improvement in the standard of living—in cultural and material spheres—of the masses, together with scientific materialist propaganda, will lead gradually to our surpassing religious beliefs" (4–5). This view that religious faith is based on ignorance and is bound to disappear is hardly the basis for establishing a strategic alliance with the church, as outlined by Fidel Castro.

Other official documents of this time, such as the resolutions of the PCC's first congress in 1975, seem to have been written by persons with ideological blinkers on in regard to the church. Religious leaders, the party claimed, have assumed "sociopolitical positions which were scarcely conceivable twenty years ago," not because of the influence of Vatican II or Medellín or the radicalized faith of millions of Christians but rather because of "the profound crisis—in political and economic as well as social and moral matters with which the capitalist system is struggling" (41). The church has become, PCC documents claim, more accepting of the revolutionary process for one reason, "the general crisis of imperialist capitalism and the contradictions inherent in it" (28). To support the idea of an opportunistic church that is still essentially conservative, Fidel's condemnations of the Cuban hierarchy in 1960 and 1961 are cited, but no reference is made, for example, to his words of encouragement in 1971 to revolutionary Catholics in Allende's Chile (23, 26). The implication of this is that nothing had changed in the Cuban Church—a dubious assertion. Such shallow treatment of a worldwide phenomenon, and a deliberately selective approach to the question, was bound to disturb progressive Christians in

Latin America, for whom in so many other areas Cuba provides an excellent role model. It has taken the PCC a full generation to realize the dangers inherent in this outdated position and to begin to come to terms with its limitations.

Contradictory signals have come not only from Fidel and the central committee but also from the very *orientaciones,* or guidelines, of the latter. Party cadres, for instance, were advised that "a serene, respectful tone, that will not hurt the feelings or the individual nature of the believer" was to be used in dealing with Cuban Christians (24), a policy perhaps difficult to act upon given the official view of the essence of religion: "Religion—according to Marxism-Leninism—is . . . a reflection of man's awareness, and of exterior reality. Its origin stems from earthly considerations and not celestial ones. In regard to other forms of awareness, what is special about it is that in essence it constitutes a fanciful, distorted reflection, a false one too, of a reality which is determined fundamentally by conditions of man's material life" (18).

Equally disturbing to Christians influenced by the Vatican II spirit was the reappearance of an outdated interpretation of the political role of the church: "The social role of religion is determined by its conservative content, its rejection of struggle, and its submission to so-called supernatural powers, which are nothing other, for the religious consciousness, than the explanation of natural phenomena and the oppressive forces of the exploiting classes. Their preaching that the social process is predetermined by some supposed providence or divinity, their insistence on the need to conform, and on the meekness of the exploited and the oppressed in return for a supposed life without end after death; their denial of the right to violence while they justify the violence and cruelty of the exploiters, etc., all make of religion a helpful ideological element for the dominant classes in societies where exploitation is common" (18–19). The duty of the party, given this set of assumptions, was "to act in such a way that, in the active struggle to build a new society, the masses will gradually liberate themselves from religious beliefs" (20). This was hardly the basis for the "strategic alliance" favored by Fidel Castro: somewhere along the chain of command, the signals were becoming confused.

For many Christians this one-dimensional view of religion by party ideologues confirmed their worst fears about the revolution. There was no room for accommodation with a doctrine that claimed that their own beliefs were based on ignorance, "a fanciful, distorted reflection, a false one too, of reality."[12] For Christians actively supporting the revolution and seeking more meaninful cooperation within it—a minority within a minority—it must also have been not just a severe blow but a confusing one. Who, they must have wondered, was setting offi-

cial policy on religion—the party bureaucrats loyally toeing the traditional line or President Castro with his expansive and encouraging invitation to cooperate? Throughout this period, ambiguity would
plague church circles concerning the official view of the government
toward religion, the same ambiguity that party cadres felt with respect to the new line of the church hierarchy.

The Church Takes the Initiative

"Catholics and Communists have entered into many kinds of dialogues and relations throughout the world. Cuba has been left behind,"[13] wrote Jorge Domínguez in 1972, a neat summary of the
church's dilemma during its first decade under the revolutionary government. Launched by the 1969 pastoral letters and emboldened by the
olive branch extended by Fidel Castro (although discouraged by the
continued hard line of some party ideologues), Catholic and Protestant
church leaders decided to take the initiative. They would show the revolutionary government that theirs was not a fleeting stance, that they
were determined to prove their value to the revolutionary structure.

At this juncture, church leaders and the Christian populace were not
in agreement with such a venture, especially Catholics and, to a lesser
extent, Protestants. The great majority of Cuban Christians were
confused by this new social activism of their hierarchy and in general
opposed it. Nevertheless, their leaders remained dedicated to constructive engagement, hoping to wear down their congregations' conservatism, a strategy that has met with some success.

Observations on religious life by visitors at this time point out the
considerable obstacles church leaders faced. The most bitter visitor
was Ernesto Cardenal, who, when saying mass in Cuba, had "the feeling of celebrating a false rite in a sect, and that true Christianity is
outside. Seeing the small attendance, the mournful faces, I think: the
Cuban Church is crushed, no question."[14] Similar conclusions were
drawn by a visiting Spaniard, Celso Montero Rodríguez. While his support for the enlightened hierarchy was evident, so too was his concern
for the adaptability of church members: "Without any doubt, the difficulty seems to stem from the fact that a large proportion of Christians
have still not learned how to live as Christians in this new society.
As a result, they will have difficulty inculcating this need with hope
in their children."[15] A visiting North American delegation from various mainline U.S. churches spoke with the priest and parishioners at
an exclusive church in the fashionable Miramar section of Havana.
The fact that they were an interfaith group "brought a frown to the

priest's face and the incredible comment that 'ecumenism leads to confusion—and to communism.'"[16] Clearly, the hierarchy had an up-hill struggle if they were to pressure this goal of making the church relevant to the reality of revolutionary Cuba.

The Catholic hierarchy, along with the generally more progressive Protestant church leaders, launched a two-pronged attack aimed at raising the awareness of their followers and at convincing the revolutionary government of the church's commitment to reform. Bit by bit, nostalgia for the old days and the prerevolutionary religious life gave way to an appreciation of Cuba in its contemporary context. Proof of the hierarchy's commitment to renewal was its willingness to change itself. The death in 1968 of the formidable archbishop of Santiago, Pérez Serantes, and the resignations of Msgr. Evelio Díaz (Havana) in 1970 and of Msgr. Alfredo Müller (Cienfuegos) in 1971 gave the church the chance to replace the old guard with bishops in their thirties, like Pedro Meurice (Santiago) and Francisco Oves (Havana), more attuned to the church's needs in Cuba's current context.

These structural changes in the hierarchy were accompanied by a campaign by church leaders, eager to develop social activism among the clergy. During this period, Catholic and Protestant seminarians, for example, were encouraged to participate in various forms of "voluntary work" and in particular to help with the sugar harvest. Since so many other Cubans were undertaking harvest work, church leaders wanted to show that Christians, too, felt a profound identification with their patria and, despite occasional political differences of opinion, wanted to contribute on a practical and symbolic level. While not universally appreciated in church circles, social activities soon became standard church strategy. Indeed, many priests and pastors joined their students in this labor, a practice that continues and that has been extremely successful in breaking down barriers between Christians and atheists. The importance of this move was not lost on the revolutionary government, many of whose members were taken aback by the church's action.

Equally shocked were mainline Catholics and Protestants, long accustomed to seeing their ministers only in church delivering spiritual messages. It was all part of the deliberate strategy by church leaders to emerge from the catacombs into the post–Vatican II world, and it was extremely successful in the difficult process of establishing credibility. Pastor Javier Naranjo, explaining his reasons for choosing this new direction, said, "I am doing volunteer labor because I am a citizen of Cuba. . . . Also, because I believe that the minister should not withdraw from reality but immerse himself in the society to which he ministers. What testimony can we give if we remain in our parishes preach-

ing, or in the seminary studying?'"[17] Such decisions by a determined
and influential minority of Protestant and Catholics to combine the
religious mission with practical Christian witness were turning rhetoric into action. The question was whether this wedding of theology and
practical witness would trickle down to the membership at large, a
substantial number of whom were still in shock.

At first it seemed that social activism backfired on the church: "A
1971 survey of Presbyterians, regarded as the most liberal denomina-
tion, revealed that most were critical of the general direction of Cuban
society and progressive Church leaders."[18] Similar concerns had been
voiced more frequently in the Catholic church since the publication
of the 1969 pastoral letters, often aimed at the progressive young hierarchy and at nuncio Zacchi in particular. From a historical perspective,
however, this action was necessary if the church were to exorcise its
pre–Vatican II heritage and the prerevolutionary silence of many of
Cuba's church leaders. To convince the revolutionary government that
the church's social activism was here to stay, the hierarchy had to per-
severe in spite of criticism from within. The ordination of sixteen Cubans in 1971, "an unprecedented number even in the most favorable
days of the prerevolutionary period," according to the somewhat conservative *Area Handbook for Cuba*,[19] suggested the existence of a nucleus of Cubans keen on this radical approach to religious life.

Throughout the 1970s, the Catholic and Protestant churches struggled along this difficult path of concientización, or consciousness-
raising, seeking to realize the potential of social activism while trying
not to alienate the old guard. Along the way a series of enlightened declarations and documents were issued, the most daring among them
being the 1977 Confession of Faith of the Presbyterian-Reformed
church: "The conclusion of all of this: 'The Church lives joyfully in
the midst of the socialist revolution.' The reason for this is that 'the
revolution has concretely and historically inaugurated a series of values in human relations that make possible the whole modern
technical-scientific development of the service of the full dignity of the
human being'."[20] Even more controversial for many Christians was
that, far from following the traditional position on the dangers of
Marxism, the Confession of Faith spoke of the advantages that Christianity might reap by emulating aspects of that philosophy: "The
church teaches that the 'atheism' of the ideology sustained by the Socialist Revolution makes more clearly evident the atheism of the 'believers' who are not capable of 'discerning the signs of the times' in
the midst of the new society being constructed, in which the radical
transformation of the unjust structures makes possible the creation of
a more integrally reconstructed human being. The most important

thing, in this case, is that the atheist-communists serve as an inspiration to us because of their readiness and willingness to live sacrificial, solidary and effective love."[21]

For its part, the Catholic hierarchy, while following a liberal political line, nevertheless preferred to restrain its identification with the revolutionary process—perhaps for fear of losing the support of the rather large traditional sector. Although less radical than the extraordinary Confession of Faith of the Presbyterian-Reformed church, it did consistently produce documents that, in contrast with its previous efforts, were markedly progressive. In August 1976, for example, its "Toward Community Renewal: Evangelized and Evangelizing" called for social participation and church renewal. In November of that year, following the bombing by a Cuban exile group of a Cuban airliner and the death of its seventy-three passengers, the bishops condemned all such barbarous acts of terrorism. The importance of such documents lies in recognizing that, given the inherently conservative stance of the Catholic hierarchy, such rather innocuous statements would have been impossible in Cuba in the 1960s.

The most convincing evidence, however, that the new and dynamic direction of the hierarchy would continue came with preparations for the CELAM meeting in Puebla, Mexico, in 1979. Since the publication of the dramatic conclusions and theses reached at the 1968 meeting in Medellín, Colombia, the general secretary of CELAM, Alfonso López Trujillo, had repeatedly tried to make the organization nullify them or at least revert to a more conservative position on them. Toward this end, a preparatory document was circulated among Latin American bishops, indicating the conservative direction to be pursued at Puebla—one that encouraged returning to purportedly spiritual values and turning away from the social activism that had flourished in church circles throughout Latin America since the 1968 CELAM meeting. Another integral feature of this preparatory document was a rejection of communism and a request that all churchpeople pull together against this common enemy to defend the endangered faith. For any conservatives in the Cuban hierarchy it represented the perfect opportunity to stop the progressive church in its tracks. Yet the Cuban bishops stood firm, criticizing the document's superficial nature and simplistic interpretation. Msgr. Carlos Manuel de Céspedes, secretary of the Permanent Council of Cuban Bishops, noted: "In all six dioceses there was agreement in their critique of the document's position toward atheism. The view of atheism in that document was very negative. We insist on having a more positive view of atheism in general, and the possibilities of collaboration with different kinds of atheism. The document doesn't speak much about Marxism, some, but not much. We think in the development of our country we must take into account these people (Marxists) without this narrow view."[22]

In addition to this statement, a group of Cuban laity released their own sharply worded critique. Less diplomatic than the response of the hierarchy and more in touch with the thrust of the Confession of Faith of the Reformed-Presbyterian church, this critique was direct in its criticism of the narrow view of Marxism reflected in CELAM's preparatory document: "On one hand, Christians have to accept our responsibility for the origin, development and manifestation of contemporary atheism. . . . On the other hand our Communist comrades need to realize that the problem between religion and atheism is not of primary concern for the development of a new society and the needed infrastructure. We can all agree with the militant priest Camilo Torres when he asserted that whether the soul is immortal cannot be discussed when hunger is mortal."[23]

Within the Cuban Catholic hierarchy, perhaps nobody better symbolized the commitment to a new dynamic church seeking to rejoin Cuban society than Monsignor Francisco Oves. Deported by the revolutionary government in 1961, he returned to Cuba in 1964 prepared to make a significant contribution to the new church strategy. A sociologist by training and progressive by nature, he rapidly earned the support of his colleagues. In 1970 he was appointed to replace Msgr. Evelio Díaz in the Archdiocese of Havana. Widely respected in church and government circles alike, he followed the lead of nuncio Zacchi, pursuing this rapprochement until health problems forced his resignation. Nowhere did he more clearly express his philosophy on the necessity of social integration than in his words of welcome to young delegates at the XI Youth Festival, held in the summer of 1978 in Cuba.

At this festival, Archbishop Oves went out of his way to underline the positive attributes of the Cuban Revolution, many of which, he stressed, were in complete harmony with Christian beliefs. In particular he singled out health care, "given freely, without any discrimination, as befits the Christian concept in its demands for fraternal support to all"; free education; an economy "which refuses to be motivated fundamentally by the desire for profits, preferring instead to support the clear needs of the people, all of which is in harmony with the evangelical maxim that one cannot serve both God and money"; and Cuba's classless social structure.[24]

Critical of "the imperialist forces," the archbishop also expressed his concern at the way in which religion had been used as a counterrevolutionary arm, pointing out how the church had benefited from Marxist analysis in coming to terms with this fact.[25] Emphasizing again the value of the Marxist social sciences as a tool for analyzing society, he said Christians must make a commitment to work for social justice, a commitment in which old prejudices against Marxists had no place and in fact were totally counterproductive: "It is our objective, based on our Christian identity, to develop our activities and direct them toward encouraging a responsible and sincere participation in this, our socialist society, and we trust at all times in the progressive elimination of difficulties, as well as the surmounting of fixed plans ['esquemas fijos'] which, in our opinion, do not contribute to the irreversible and positive progress of the world in which we've been placed."[26] The church hierarchy's position had undergone a remarkable change.

Toward Peaceful Coexistence?

At the 1972 Christians for Socialism meeting in Chile, the Cuban representatives were extremely harsh in their criticism of the Cuban church, describing it as unrealistic and shortsighted, focused narrowly on sacramental and spiritual concerns.[27] They noted that the former allies of the church had long since departed Cuba and that society had been radically restructured, with little appreciation from the church, so that "the Church's problem is not really with atheism: it is with the new, changed world that it is pitifully unprepared to deal with. The problem of the Church in Cuba is not a Cuban problem, but the problem of the universal Church."[28]

While a fair amount of truth remains in this interpretation, the report by the Christian socialists in the early 1970s apparently failed to take into account several factors. Their dismissal of the importance of the 1969 pastorals. for instance, seems to underestimate grossly the letters' dramatic effect on Cuban Christians. The advantages of hindsight and geographical distance suggest that the church in revolutionary Cuba had indeed experienced a crucial decade. It was precisely during this period that Protestant and Catholic church leaders finally realized that the revolution was not a passing phenomenon and based plans for the first time upon this hypothesis. In addition, urged along by the papal nuncio and guided by a new, young, dynamic, Cuban hierarchy, the church decided not only to accept this reality but to cooperate with it. Although greeted coolly by the Communist Party, the hierarchy persevered throughout this period. While acting to a certain extent in response to Fidel Castro's own overtures, it is to the credit of this church leadership that by the end of this period hostility began to ebb. In its place there lay the opportunity for the church to restore its tarnished credibility and build the foundation for a new church-state relationship.

Many factors worked against such a development, from the PCC as well as from the church membership itself. The wording of the various party documents and resolutions on religious life and the general disregard of religious life by the state-controlled media were disheartening. Yet the decade had its positive features. The press's benign neglect of church activities was a major improvement on its frequent criticism and denunciation in the early 1960s. The new constitution's recognition of the right to religious choice, the Protestant and Catholic church leaders' forceful documents on pressing social concerns (and the role of the church vis-à-vis these concerns), and the normalization of relations with the Vatican in 1975 were positive moves in this developing church-state relationship. Similarly, the stand taken by Archbishop Oves at the XI Youth Festival and that of the Episcopal Conference on the rather simplistic Preparatory Document for the 1979 CELAM conference at Puebla were important gestures. Finally in this progressive vein one can cite the annual trek of seminarian students and pastors to cut sugarcane alongside members of the Juventud Comunista organization—a far cry from the UMAP camps of the mid-1960s—and the religious procession accompanying the installation of the new bishop of Pinar del Río in 1979, the first procession of its kind in nearly two decades. Despite objections by zealots in the party and church structures, a successful modus vivendi between government and church leaders seemed to be in the offing. Interviewed in late 1971, Archbishop Oves put the essence of this potential institutionalization of relations in its revolutionary context: "Our mission is . . . to help Christians to take up in a positive fashion their commitment to participate in the construction of this new society, and to recognize those human and evangelical values at which, among us, Christianity and socialism converge, but without neglecting the guidance resulting from the fundamental rights of an upright religious conscience."[29] It was a major step forward for the church that left two fundamental questions unanswered: Would the faithful as a body respond positively to the bishops' acceptance of socialist Cuba? Just as important, would the government?

7

The Beginnings of Dialogue,

1979–1987

The most beautiful gift God has given me is my meeting with President Fidel Castro.

Mother Teresa of Calcutta,

Havana, July 1986

The years from 1979 to 1987 span the period in the Latin American political scene dominated by discussion of a "new Cuba," namely Nicaragua. The revolutionary phenomenon in this tiny Central American nation (3.2 million) has marked the Cuban psyche and served as a catalyst for the thinking of both the Cuban government and the church, due in large part to the collective memory of Cuba's own fight for survival against a mighty foe. Cuban views on a host of cultural, political, and social matters have been shaken up. (Among the targets of the ensuing self-critiques has been the rather dogmatic view of religion held by the powerful policy-making sectors of the PCC. In 1985 Msgr. Jaime Ortega Alamino, archbishop of Havana, told me that virtually all of these members of the old guard had been educated in private, Catholic schools and had been deeply scarred by the memory of rigid pre–Vatican II dogma and authority. By comparison, he pointed out, Cuba's present bishops had all been educated in state schools.) The influence of the Nicaraguan revolution has helped the church and the government to adjust to the shifting sands of their particular cosmovision and has contributed to their mutual understanding.

The events of this eight-year period have moved faster than most churchpeople might have predicted, despite the encouraging words of Archbishop Oves at the 1978 Youth Festival (noted earlier). Three factors internal to Cuba have influenced the rapid development of church-state dialogue: the actions by which the Catholic hierarchy—and indeed the church as a whole—have shown the revolutionary government that a new cooperative spirit now imbues church activities; the government response, which has been generally supportive of the initiatives taken by the Christian sector; and the dramatic personal involvement of Fidel Castro, motivated by his personal interest in the religious question. Other influences include the constant example of the Consejo Ecuménico Cubano (in many ways a rival of the Catholic hierarchy in the field of "religious emulation"), the nucleus of committed churchpeople from a variety of faiths who continue to bear Christian witness by working within the socialist system, and the development of a rich and varied theological expression in the mainstream of other, better known strains of liberation theology.

Many diverse external influences and concerns have also contributed to this developing dialogue. Common to the two most widely held interpretations of these influences is a belief that the dialogue had its basis in convenience, that the relationship allows both church and state to exploit their partner while furthering their own ends. For many churchpeople, the Castro government's encouragement and support have been undertaken only to improve international political relations with (Catholic) Latin America. For many diehards in the PCC, the church's new interest in social concerns derives simply from its desire to camouflage, temporarily, deeper spiritual goals and a master plan to win souls away from the Cuban revolution. While there is some substance to these allegations, attributing too much importance to them downplays both the churchpeople's genuine initiative to come to terms with the revolution and the consistency of Fidel Castro's interpretation of religion. Moreover, the church's appeal in Latin America would continue apace with or without the blessing of the Cuban government, while Cuba's relations have never been better than in the mid-1980s with Latin American governments (especially with Argentina, Brazil, Peru, and Venezuela, with which traditionally there have been strains). Beyond the superficial validity of these claims regarding mutual exploitation, therefore, more genuine and fascinating elements are at work.

The Church's Commitment

Having emerged from the catacombs between 1969 and 1978, in the following years the church moved toward even greater commitment to the socialist process in Cuba, as evidenced by statements and declarations of, or supported by, the church hierarchy. (It remains to be seen, however, how the rank-and-file feel about the path their spiritual leaders are blazing, although a subjective, firsthand survey indicates wide acceptance among young Catholics and more suspicion among older ones.) Focusing on observations and actions of the hierarchy must in many ways distort the internal dynamics of the church in Cuba. In fact, to a great extent the hierarchy has reacted to rather than originated the demand for change within the church. Nevertheless, studying some of the positions taken by church leaders offers the opportunity to plot an interesting graph of their steady radicalization, to understand their present position, and to predict their future direction.

To begin to appreciate just how far the church has come during this period, one might compare events in Cuba in February 1986 to earlier phases of the church's role and influence. In that month, the Catholic church realized its first national conclave, attended by Cardinal Eduardo Pironio, representing the Vatican, and several U.S. and Latin American bishops. Concluding with a mass attended by government officials, the church encounter "expressed support for the socialist objectives of the Cuban revolution, though not for the program of the Communist Party," and praised the social advances of the Cuban system. At the same time, signaling a new self-confidence, church leaders asked for some concessions, among them an end to militant atheism in Cuba's school curriculum and to all forms of discrimination (although church spokesmen acknowledged that discrimination had radically diminished); greater access to the media for church groups (apparently church and government leaders have been negotiating access to state radio and importing printing equipment for the church sector); and the right to undertake church work in prisons. These concessions can be summed up by what the official church document commemorating the conclave termed the need for "more space to develop the Church's pastoral work."[1] The importance of these requests, all reasonable enough, resides in their being made in the first place— particularly in view of the church-state tradition of tension and mutual recrimination. As recently as a few years ago it would have been impossible to imagine, for example, church and revolutionary government representatives discussing the possibility of broadcasting mass on state-controlled stations. Yet those discussions have taken place.

The conclave (the Encuentro Nacional Eclesial Cubano, or National Encounter of the Cuban Church) is by far the best evidence to date of the new spirit of dialogue running through the mainstream church. Based on an idea of having a "Puebla in Cuba" (referring to the landmark meeting of Latin American bishops in Puebla, Mexico, in 1979), 181 delegates met in 1986 for undoubtedly the most important church meeting since the revolutionary victory. The tone for the meeting was set by Mgr. Adolfo Rodríguez, president of the Cuban Episcopal Conference, in his opening address as he explained the kind of church they hoped to establish in Cuba: "A church that wants to be a missionary church, since otherwise it would be merely a sect. . . . A church that wants to be a real part of our people, because if it didn't follow this path, then it would indeed be the 'opiate of the masses,' and would cease to be the real church. . . . The Cuban church of necessity, then, has to be the church of openness (la iglesia de la apertura), the church of dialogue and participation, with its hand extended—and its doors open."[2]

A study of the document proper (more than 200 pages of single-spaced, legal-size material) reveals four basic themes: pastoral shortcomings and goals; a basic acceptance of the socialist objectives of the revolution and a desire to cooperate within the revolutionary process; a constructive criticism of many of Cuba's social problems that still remain to be addressed; and the church's determination to update its approach and insert itself into Cuban society. Individually they would be important statements worthy of detailed scrutiny. Together, they represent a valuable critique and self-critique, such as has never been produced by the Cuban church.

One of the most difficult matters before the Episcopal Conference during the initial year of this period was the question of the Cuban exiles, who at this time were allowed by President Jimmy Carter to return to Cuba to visit their families.[3] It was a calculated gamble by the Cuban government, designed to bring in much-needed "hard" currency and to show exiles that their relatives had survived the rigors of socialism. It succeeded on both levels. On the other hand, the exiles' abundance contributed to the general malaise of many Cubans, disillusioned by twenty years of adversity with no apparent relief in sight. The result was the mass exodus of more than 125,000 Cubans through the port of Mariel in the spring of 1980.

While welcoming the Carter administration's decision to allow Cuban exiles to visit the patria, in a collective pastoral released 27 September 1979 the Cuban bishops issued some rather stern warnings about the social and spiritual dangers of the exiles' return and criticized the U.S. government. Moreover, the bishops commended the revolutionary government for freeing many political prisoners and took issue with the responses of countries to which the exiles were to be sent: "The governments of the countries which are to receive the exiles have been, in our opinion, rather slow in giving refuge to these people who need a place to live and who are so desirous of beginning a new stage of their lives."[4]

The document deemphasized the atheist nature of the government and stressed nationalistic pride. Indeed, returning members of the community were invited to rediscover the dignity of their Cuban roots and to seek a rapprochement with the patria. Missing was the emphasis of earlier pastorals on the disastrous nature of Cuban society under the communists.

Behind the ecclesiastical rhetoric lay some pointed warnings aimed at the members of the Catholic community. A sincere church-state dialogue was essential if the patria, and indeed the United States, were to benefit. A halfhearted or selfish manipulation of the dialogue, warned the bishops prophetically, would have negative social consequences: "And so if anybody abroad, in addition to wanting to see their beloved friends and relatives, does not attempt a serious, respectful rapprochement with the reality of Cuba; or if anybody in Cuba, without any humanitarian or other reasons, encourages the hope that this communication will principally help his or her personal plans to abandon the country, then this progressive rapprochement which is developing would remain marked by opportunism, and would have no possibility of developing and advancing" (4).

As a means of realizing this important exchange, the bishops cautioned returning exiles against flaunting their possessions acquired abroad and advised Cubans not to covet these goods. They reminded Cubans of their Christian roots as "followers of Jesus of Nazareth, regarded by all as 'the carpenter's son' who always shared the fate of his people" (6). It was a time, the bishops suggested, for accepting a somewhat austere life-style, one that nevertheless sought to provide the basics for all Cubans.[5] At all costs, unrestrained consumerism was to be avoided: "Let not, then, the experience lived during these years in which we have learned to base our faith on such far-reaching human and Christian values, be tarnished by immoderate desires for material goods" (6). Instead, the pastoral letter urged restraint and encouraged all Cuban Christians to live out their faith, "which stimulates us to imitate the simplicity of the life which Christ preached, through his own example" (7).

Far from encouraging its flock to flee the Marxist onslaught, the church in 1980 sought to dissuade Catholics from making the ninety-mile crossing to Florida—a remarkably changed scenario from the early 1960s, when church leaders urged Cuban Catholics to flee godless communism and find refuge in exile in a Christian society. Fiery denunciations of life under totalitarianism by such influential churchmen as Archbishop Pérez Serantes led to the 1960s exodus of Cuba's middle class and destroyed the substructure of all church activities. Behind this radical change in strategy in 1980 lay improved church-state relations and, by extension, a lack of fear of religious persecution, a steady increase in the social prestige of the church as a body, and a belief in the potential for apertura, or diplomatic opening. A massive exodus, it was widely feared, would jeopardize these conditions and thus was to be rejected. A final factor in the formulation of this new strategy was a tacit admission that, in the volatile period of twenty years earlier, the church had simply been wrong in its analysis and had subsequently paid the price for its errors. At all costs, a repeat of this course of action was to be avoided.

The message was quietly passed through the church communities that leaving the country was not recommended by church leaders—an effort that in general seems to have been successful.[6] In the face of the exodus the Youth Secretariat (Secretariado de Jóvenes) in the traditionally conservative diocese of Camagüey circulated an open letter to members of the Christian community in May 1980, asking them *not* to consider leaving the country for the allegedly greener pastures of Miami. The importance of the document can be gauged by the decision by high-ranking church officials in the archdiocese of Havana (Mariano Vivanco and Carlos Manuel de Céspedes—both vicar generals—and Alfredo Petit, chancellor secretary) to reproduce it immediately and circulate it in Havana.

The Youth Secretariat's letter pulled out all the stops to encourage Cubans to remain on the island. They were reminded that no decision should be taken "without studying the Gospel, without looking at Christ himself who undertook a commitment ("se comprometió") toward man, with all the consequences." They were urged to remember the last letter of José Martí to his mother in 1895, in which he noted that "the duty of a man is to be found where he is most useful." Concrete advice was given to Catholics tempted to leave for Florida, and the official church position was made abundantly clear. The letter told how many Christians truly concerned with their patria and their "Church, always young," had been able to discover "the hand of God, his call to continue serving in this land full of promise and virtue." Cuban Catholics were urged to remember that they were part of a community that needed their active support. "For you, as for us, and all Christians, there is a duty of offering the best of ourselves, of generously giving our lives to the service of others. We hope, then, that these lines will help you to reflect. The Christian community, a community of faith and love, needs you.'"[7]

A complete reversal of the position of twenty years earlier had taken place: instead of fleeing, Christians were now urged to remain in Cuba and work actively within the revolutionary process. This position conformed to the central thrust of the developing church-revolutionary dialogue. Once again the Catholic hierarchy was signaling in a straightforward fashion its designs to participate in the revolution.

Other official documents and presentations by representatives of the hierarchy prove that these letters were not isolated examples of the hierarchy's commitment to developing the role of the church in revolutionary Cuba. On 20 August 1981, for instance, the Comité Permanente de la Conferencia de los Obispos de Cuba (Permanent Committee of the Cuba Episcopal Conference) produced a press release on the production of the neutron bomb which clearly illustrated the pragmatic path being followed by the hierarchy. Citing the magisterium of Vatican II, as well as the work of Paul VI and John Paul II, the committee condemned the arms race in general and denounced U.S. plans to build the neutron bomb in particular: "We don't believe it necessary to stop and analyze an argument which has also been used to support the construction of the neutron bomb: it only destroys human lives, leaving material installations intact. It seems incredible for men to say that! The most sophisticated and contemporary techniques not at the service of mankind, but rather built to ensure our destruction! What sense does it make for mankind to produce, if we are to be destroyed?"[8]

In a similar vein was a presentation by one of Cuba's most articulate

and most balanced church representatives, Msgr. Carlos Manuel de
Céspedes (secretary of the Cuban Episcopal Conference, and vicar general of the Archdiocese of Havana), at an ecumenical forum in November 1980. The "Ecumenical Meeting in Solidarity with the Cuban People in the Face of the Threats of U.S. Aggression" was designed to draw
attention to the U.S. military buildup in South Florida and to the increase in anti-Castro rhetoric emanating from Washington. Fears of a
North American invasion of Cuba caused territorial militias to be
hastily formed and trained, and for several months the island remained
on a war alert. Speaking at the ecumenical forum, de Céspedes outlined the church position on the need for peace and referred back to
the memorable April 1969 collective pastoral which denounced "the
unjust situation of the blockade." Little had changed in the intervening years, he concluded sadly, largely because of the hardening position
and ignorance of successive U.S. administrations: "Twelve years later,
instead of the disappearance of the blockade, they are now threatening
us with fortifying it and even talking about more violent measures of
a military nature, something which would only place new burdens of
suffering on the shoulders of our people. How can we not express our
view that such measures represent an undeniable contradiction of the
most elemental notions of Christian ethics in the realm of international relations?"[9]

Positions such as those taken in these two documents, far removed
from those taken by the church hierarchy in the early stages of the revolution, are concrete reflections of the newfound determination of
church leaders to come to terms with their deficiencies and errors and
to seek to improve the credibility of the church within revolutionary
Cuba. In both goals they have been fairly successful: the "Church of
Washington" has become a thing of the past.

Church initiatives to strengthen this credibility have continued to
this day: interviews with church representatives (some from abroad,
some local) have appeared with great frequency in the Cuban media;
declarations and proclamations on terrorism, the invasion of Grenada,
and military repression in Latin America have been issued by the
church; and communication with the revolutionary government has
noticeably improved. In many ways the 1984 visit to Cuba of the black
churchman Rev. Jesse Jackson helped to solidify the gains made in recent years. The occasion was a service to pay homage to the memory
of the black human rights activist Martin Luther King. Organized by
the Protestant churches in Cuba, it brought together, in a Havana
Methodist church, leaders of the Christian faith and Fidel Castro himself (apparently in a Cuban church for the first time in nearly two decades). Rapid developments followed the Jackson visit, in part due to

the energetic role played by Msgr. Jaime Ortega Alamino, archbishop of Havana, who, in the spring of 1984 was invited by U.S. bishops to conduct a retreat in New York for Hispanic priests.

Building upon the base of this successful experiment and of Jesse Jackson's visit to Cuba, the church and state made 1985 an exceptional year, certainly the most productive for church-state relations since Castro's 1959 victory. The Cuban Episcopal Conference took the initial step by inviting representatives of their U.S. equivalent to Cuba. As a result, visiting Cuba in late January were Bishop James Malone of Youngstown, Ohio, president of the U.S. Bishops' Conference, accompanied by the archbishops of Boston (Msgr. Bernard Law) and San Antonio (Msgr. Patrick Flores), Msgr. Daniel Hoye (general-secretary of the conference), and Father David Gallivan (of the Latin American Secretariat of the conference). They celebrated mass in Santiago de Cuba and in Havana and met with government officials, including a five-hour meeting with Fidel Castro.

The visit of the U.S. clergy, as Bishop Malone stressed in his press conference statement, was essentially a pastoral one. Yet political capital was made for the church and revolutionary government alike. On a national level, relations between the Cuban bishops and Fidel Castro were clearly strengthened. Attending a reception in the nunciature for the U.S. clergy, for instance, were Vice-President Carlos Rafael Rodríguez and government ministers and members of the politbureau of the PCC. The following day, President Castro hosted a reception for the clergymen, as well as for the members of the Cuban Episcopal Conference, the superiors of religious orders in Cuba, and the pro-nuncio. These celebrations were on a far greater scale than one would have expected for a delegation of visiting clergy and clearly represented the intent of the revolutionary government and the church leaders themselves to solidify their working relationship.

Bishop Malone's final communiqué reflects this desire on the part of the church. Although the communiqué cited such problems as religious discrimination, the need for family reunion programs with Cuban exiles, difficult travel arrangements between Cuba and the United States, and political prisoners whose freedom was requested by the U.S. bishops, its general tone was extremely positive. Bishop Malone praised the "marked improvements" in education and health care in Cuba and noted the "limited, but real, improvements in communications between the Church and the government." Of the six observations summarized at the end of the Bishop's presentation, two spoke warmly of "the new dialogue between the Cuban bishops and the government," while Msgr. Malone's final point summarized the expectations of the church sector: "We believe it is significant that the bishops of Cuba and the highest authority in the government may soon meet to dialogue in an intensive and ongoing manner about the situation of the Church in Cuba. While there have been improved communication possibilities in recent times, this new level of discussion is a real sign of hope for the Church in Cuba."[10]

Since the visit of the representatives of the U.S. Episcopal Conference, several key developments have occurred. In August 1985 the Cuban bishops published a position paper, "Ecclesiastical Teachings on the Foreign Debt and the New International Economic Order," and with other Latin American church representatives played a major role in the conference on Latin America's foreign debt, held in Havana that year. In September 1985, Archbishop Jaime Ortega Alamino (Havana), together with Bishop Adolfo Rodríguez (Camagüey), head of the Cuban Episcopal Conference, Bishop Pedro Meurice (Santiago de Cuba), and Msgr. Carlos Manuel de Céspedes (secretary general of the conference), traveled to the United States at the invitation of the U.S. bishops to continue their international dialogue. Before leaving for the United States they met with Fidel Castro, whose continued interest in a church-state dialogue favorably impressed Msgr. Ortega Alamino: "The meeting with President Castro has been very positive, not only because of the concrete points discussed and the clear, frank atmosphere in which it was held, but because it seemed to me that, in what Fidel said, there was a desire for this dialogue to extend beyond the Catholic hierarchy and government to encompass concrete changes of attitude on the part of all our people along stretches of the path that must be traveled."[11]

Prior to 1985, representatives of the church hierarchy had frequently argued that Cuban government authorities talked a lot about meeting with them but were notoriously slow in following up. It had been many years since Fidel Castro had actually sat down with church leaders, yet in 1985 he did so on several occasions. In November of that year Fidel also met leaders of the Protestant church and talked once again with their Catholic counterparts.

On this occasion major progress was made in formalizing closer ties between church and state. It was decided, for example, to hold similar meetings every four to six months. A 200-page document published to mark the improved relations served as a working paper for the February 1986 national church enclave, the importance of which has been noted. Although the document criticizes many aspects of Cuba's political system, it represents a major step toward normalizing relations with the church's move "from acceptance of the reality of the socialist revolution and a decision not to oppose socialist objectives, to agreement with the government on its basic social goals: education, public health, jobs for all, the meeting of basic needs, etc." Church leaders, the document added, "have now committed themselves to foster 'national reconciliation' between Marxists and Catholics and to play an active and positive role in Cuba's future."[12]

Proof that the church has emerged from the catacombs but has not sold out to the Partido Comunista de Cuba lies in the self-confidence behind church leaders' demands at the February 1986 conclave, among them, "that education should abandon its militant atheism and ensure respect for religious beliefs," "an end to any form of discrimination against Christians," "greater access to the media," and "the resumption of Church work in gaols."[13]

This is not a church that has been bought off with material benefits but one that has gradually come to terms with the reality of present-day Cuba and decided to participate more fully in the revolutionary process of its country. Its leadership has taken some bold initiatives (reciprocated and at times supplemented by government action) based apparently on an analysis by Msgr. Jaime Ortega Alamino:

> The life of the Church in Cuba in the future depends on how much Catholics, as well as everyone in Cuba, including the authorities, are aware of what the Church is. That is not only bishops and priests, but rather that it encompasses the entire Catholic people.
>
> It is necessary that Catholics recall the 2nd Vatican Council and realize that the Church is nothing more than the Catholic part of the people of which they are a part.
>
> The Catholics, it is fundamental that the people in general and the authorities come to have this vision of them.[14]

Although events since the monsignor's 1984 statement suggest that his vision has captured the Cuban imagination, it remains to be seen to what degree this climate of open dialogue, of sensitizing the revolutionary leadership and the masses to the church's mission, will translate into actual benefits for the church. Since 1979, and in particular since 1984, remarkable gains have been made in establishing the credibility of the church. The test of this developing relationship between church and state will undoubtedly come with the debates in the central committee of the Communist party concerning the possibility of Christians becoming members of the PCC. With the next party congress scheduled for 1990, it is too early to predict results, but the actual consideration of the issue in a serious fashion within the revolutionary leadership is in many ways miraculous. For the first time in twenty-seven years, a suitable working base exists along with a rhythm of communication and mutual comprehension. What remains to be seen is how this climate of goodwill is converted into concrete actions.

The Government's Role in the Dialogue

The role of the Cuban government in the religious question can be analyzed at various levels: official declarations of the PCC; coverage of religious affairs in the government-controlled media; diplomatic initiatives toward the church and reaction to the church's own initiatives; and the role of Fidel Castro in these matters. A study of some of the more pertinent actions and reactions of the revolutionary government shows that what has evolved, gradually but unquestionably, is a definite policy of bland encouragement for church activities and a genuine desire for rapprochement.

An appropriate place to begin this analysis is the record of the PCC and its various *resoluciones* on religion at party congresses, especially those in 1975 and 1980 when the religious question was examined in detail. Comparing resolutions of the 1980 congress with the earlier dogmatic and critical party line on religious belief reveals some interesting, albeit minor, developments. In chapter 6 several examples were given of the doctrinaire and rather dated approach to religion in the 1975 congress. In 1980, by comparison, one finds a distinctive change of tone: examples of the increase in religious delegations to and from Cuba, the "relations which are, to our satisfaction, normal" enjoyed by the state and the vast majority of religious institutions in the country, and the existence of "an increasingly large number of Christians professing different religious criteria, who are undertaking the tasks of the revolution in the construction of socialism." The positive tone is continued as the document records "the significant process of numerous and active groups of Christian organizations, including elements of clergy from the Catholic faith and other denominations, joining the struggles for national liberation, and for social justice, of the peoples of Latin America, such as in Nicaragua, El Salvador and other countries." As a result of these conditions, the PCC recommended "the convenience of continuing to contribute to the successive consolidation of the common front for the benefit of the indispensable structural transformations in our hemisphere and throughout the world."[15]

The strictly doctrinaire level of the 1975 document has clearly been replaced by a more cooperative tone. The massive Christian participation in the Nicaraguan revolution and the ferocious treatment meted out by the military in Central America to the Christian sector (including the murders of Archbishop Oscar Romero, the American women religious, several priests, and tens of thousands of Salvadorans and Guatemalans) were slowly alerting the PCC to the idea that Christian militancy was no fleeting phenomenon. Even taking into account the "convenience" of the strategic alliance between the Christian and Marxist sectors—as outlined by Fidel Castro—there appear in the 1980 *resoluciones* the initial seeds of appreciation for the possibilities of a new working relationship with church leaders. Between 1975 and 1980, then, the basis had been laid for a fresh appreciation of the church's contribution to life, not only in socialist Cuba but also—and this of course was much more important—throughout Latin America. As the church leadership took up the challenge and showed itself able to respond articulately and practically, the revolutionary leadership, seeing that to a certain extent its bluff had been called, found itself drawn into the continuing process of dialogue.

An interesting parallel to the level and nature of this cooperation was the increase of news coverage of religious matters in state-controlled media since the late 1970s. After a decade of neglect, a policy obviously in tandem with the official government line, religious coverage experienced a resurgence, having great public visibility given it:

> What does strike the observer who has been in touch with religious life on the island during the 1970s and '80s is the increased *visibility* of religious people and institutions. Full-page spreads in *Granma* for religion-related stories are a phenomenon of the last two or three years, even though the kinds of activities reported in the articles . . . have been going on in Cuban Church circles for far longer. Five or ten years ago, the Cuban media might "mention" a statement, dealing with, say, solidarity with Central American struggles, or a response to a Cuban national crisis or event like the migration from Mariel in Cuba.
>
> Expanded news features on religious people or topics, however, were the exception. Why, then, the new public visibility of Church people and religious activity? What developments in Cuban Church or secular life have led to a wider publicizing of the activities of the faith community?[16]

One rather obvious explanation for this increased coverage is that the revolutionary government has decided to make some fundamental concessions to the church and to convert talk about a practical dialogue into something more tangible. The result is a large number of articles designed to show the role of the church in promoting social justice, denouncing imperialism, participating in the revolutionary struggle in Central America, sharing voluntary agricultural work, and undertaking internationalist service.[17] Radically different from previous coverage, this treatment reflects the government decision to push for a long-term strategic alliance with the church. (Also in contrast with a quarter-century ago, when government media commonly denounced the church, it is now virtually impossible to find criticisms of the church.) Perhaps what best sums up the rationale for this enlightened government policy toward the media is the subtitle of a recent article based on an interview with a priest based in Miami: "The Church-state dialogue is more promising now than ever before."[18]

From a historical perspective, it is interesting to look at the evolution from twenty-five years ago, when the church used its own controlled media to turn people against the revolutionary process, through the nationalization of church media (with the exception of the Protestant church, which has its own press), to the present situation, where the government in its controlled media is promoting a favorable profile of the church and the "Church and the revolutionary leadership are now discussing the possible import of modern printing equipment and the right to broadcast mass on the State radio."[19] This all represents a dramatic shift that is clearly laying the basis for an unusual—indeed unique—relationship between the church and the revolutionary government.

The official decision to present a more balanced view of the church in the media is one of a series of government initiatives, designed since the late 1970s to lessen church-state tension. Many of these are of a symbolic nature, with little of substance at risk, and often the initiative was the result of input from the church as well as from the government. Among these gestures was the 1979 installation of the new bishop of Pinar del Río, which was accompanied by the first religious procession in nearly two decades. Also in 1979, Dr. José Felipe Carneado, the government representative responsible for religious matters, accepted an invitation to address the annual assembly of the Cuban Ecumenical Council—another first. Such apparently unimportant incidents laid the foundation for the increasing spiral of mutual—if still somewhat superficial or limited—goodwill. Followed by the noticeably different tone in the 1980 resoluciones on the religious question at the Second PCC Congress, they constitute a useful working basis on which to construct a more friendly and mutually beneficial relationship between party and church.

Another symbolic and mutually beneficial gesture initiated by the revolutionary government has to do with the extensive restoration work being undertaken in several colonial church buildings in Havana. The completion in 1985 of repairs to the *palacio arzobispal*, the headquarters of the archdiocese of Havana, is a case in point. The repairs were undertaken by some of Cuba's finest craftsmen, and the quality of workmanship—as at the San Carlos and San Ambrosio Seminary, the cathedral, and several other churches in colonial Havana—is excellent. Repairs such as these are paid for not only by the local and international church, as one would expect, but also by the state. By completing these needed repairs, the state assists the church and at the same time supplements its own ambitious and successful renovation program in Old Havana. The gesture is appreciated by the church and is also a visible national and international symbol of active cooperation between the church and the revolutionary government.

Gestures of this kind continued throughout the early 1980s, a process reinforced by a positive media image. One can cite, for example, the visit of Msgr. Jean Vilnet, president of the French Episcopal Conference, or that of Hans Peter Kolvenbach (superior general of the Jesuits) and the cooperation of the Catholic Committee against Hunger and for Development, which assists state schools for the handicapped. It was, however, the visits of Rev. Jesse Jackson in 1984 and Bishop James Malone in January 1985 that accomplished huge improvements in church-state relations. The 1980 party congress had increased the potential for a significant breakthrough, the continued example of Christians participating in the Central American revolutionary process demonstrated the compatibility of committed political and religious activities, the media contributed to the growing popular acceptance of the church, and Fidel Castro was impressed by Christians involved in the Nicaraguan struggle against the Somoza dictatorship. The groundwork was laid for the whirlwind of activity in 1985.

Although Msgr. Jaime Ortega Alamino (archbishop of Havana), in particular, and the Cuban Episcopal Conference, in general, took the initiative in developing closer ties with the church in the United States, the revolutionary government helped to ensure the success of this initiative. One significant step was taken at the eleventh plenum of the Central Committee of the PCC on 13 January 1985, when an Office of Religious Affairs attached to the secretariat was instituted, to be headed by Dr. José Felipe Carneado, who prior to this time had been head of the Education, Science and Culture Department of the Central Committee—through which position he had been the de facto liaison of the government dealing with the church sector. This office will play a major role in the debate over religious matters. Widely respected by church representatives for his fairness, approachable nature, and access to the highest levels of the government, Carneado was a logical choice, despite his traditional, pre–Vatican II interpretation of the church. His appointment as the director of this newly formed office indicates a new stage in the revolutionary government's appreciation of the religious question.

The actual visit later that month (21–25 January) of the U.S. bishops was taken very seriously by the Cuban government. In a country where a function's importance can be gauged by the rank of people attending, a reception given at the nunciature was attended by Vice-President Carlos Rafael Rodríguez, Jesús Montané (from the politbureau of the PCC), several government ministers, the president of the National Assembly of "Poder Popular," and other high-ranking officials—suggesting the importance assigned the visit by the government. The following day another reception was hosted by President Castro himself. Castro was determined to ensure that the bishops were fully aware of the potential implications of their visit not only for domestic church matters but also for international diplomatic affairs. (Had they been bishops from Spain or Great Britain, for example, one doubts if the same attention would have been forthcoming.) That Fidel Castro spent five hours with the U.S. bishops in frank discussion on a variety of church-related matters and on U.S.–Cuban relations is also extremely important. The red carpet treatment given to the North American church representatives was meant to signal a very different interest in church-state relations than has traditionally been the case. The empty platitudes of the 1970s about the need for dialogue and for frank meetings between church and government representatives (which rarely occurred) were now rapidly giving way to a remarkably pragmatic approach. Pressure was mounting to develop a mechanism for wide-ranging and influential discussions, the outcome of which could have a significant impact on the future of church-state relations in Cuba, and both sides knew it.

This continuum of goodwill and communication stretched into the summer of 1985 at the meeting on the international debt crisis held in Havana and organized by Fidel Castro. Although not many Latin American leaders attended, what was surprising was, first, the fact that more than a hundred religious figures, among them representatives of the Cuban Episcopal Conference, participated and, second, their role in the conference proceedings, as the Cuban bishops themselves noted: "The fact that the Cuban Church for the first time in 25 years was invited to a meeting sponsored by the government of our country, that the Cuban Bishops' Conference accepted the invitation and that the subject of the meeting was one so apparently removed from the mission of the Church as the foreign debt, can only come as a surprise to many Catholics, bringing joy to many, hope to the majority and perhaps concern to a few."[20]

Certain quarters in the Cuban government must have felt profound concern at Fidel Castro's inviting not just delegates from the Cuban Episcopal Conference and the (Protestant) Cuban Ecumenical Council but more than a hundred Latin American religious, including Cuernavaca's retired ("red") bishop, Sergio Méndez Arceo, Bolivia's Bishop Jesús López Lama, and Brazil's outspoken Frei Betto (who read a document strongly supporting the goals of the meeting from Cardinal Paulo Arns, archbishop of Sao Paulo). As one journalist pointed out, "the presence of over a hundred religious figures in Havana—some of whom were quite militant—upstaged Castro at his own meeting." In this test of fire for the Cuban church and for the possibilities of active church cooperation within the revolutionary process, the religious delegations—including that from the Cuban Episcopal Conference— were remarkably consistent in their criticism of the international problem, leading Méndez Arceo to remark, "I have heard Christ's name very often, whilst Marx has been mentioned only three or four times."[21] Members of the PCC who suspected that church support of revolutionary goals was merely transient and self-serving must have had some of their suspicions allayed by the role played by church representatives at the International Debt Conference, apparently the first time since the revolution that the Catholic bishops had taken part in a major official state event.

Fidel Castro continued this initiative by meeting with the Cuban bishops twice in subsequent months, on 8 September, the feast day of Cuba's patron saint, the Virgen de la Caridad del Cobre, and on 12 November. The first meeting was held the day before representatives of the Episcopal Conference were to leave for a meeting with their U.S. colleagues. The main purpose of the visit was to make a presentation about church life in Cuba to the standing committee of the U.S. Bishops' Conference, although the conference had also arranged meetings with U.S. government officials and representatives of the Cuban Interests Section in Washington. Another concern was the release of seventy-five prisoners, many of whose names had been on a list given to Fidel Castro by the U.S. bishops on their January visit to Cuba. (The problem, as Msgr. Jaime Ortega pointed out, was that "Cuba is willing to release them, but there have been difficulties in obtaining U.S. visas.")[22]

On 12 November, Fidel Castro, together with Vice-President Carlos Rafael Rodríguez and Dr. Carneado of the Religious Affairs Office of the Central Committee, talked with seven Cuban bishops on a wide range of topics in a meeting described by Msgr. Carlos Manuel de Céspedes, secretary general of the Cuban Episcopal Conference, as "warm and positive." Perhaps the most significant development of the meeting, though, was the note issued afterwards by church representatives; it stated that this was just the second in an ongoing process of reunions with "the top authorities in the country, and there will be others which should be viewed as part of the normal proceedings in the relations between the Catholic Church and the Cuban State."[23]

Two days later, the same Cuban government leaders met with representatives of the Protestant church, their "first formal meeting with top government officials" and one described by the Rev. Adolfo Ham, president of the Cuban Ecumenical Council, as "a historic meeting which transpired in a cordial climate."[24] A government that had been remarkably reticent in meeting with church leaders throughout the entire revolutionary process now seemed prepared to make the effort to develop a solid working relationship with church leaders. One reporter caught the sense of this important session:

> In the meeting, Castro acknowledged that his government was interested in creating "a climate of understanding," the president of the ecumenical council, Adolfo Ham, told us. Castro emphasized that "we must go beyond coexisting and living in peace; we must achieve an environment where remaining problems disappear."
>
> Protestant leaders took President Castro by surprise, though, by asking about the possible admission of Christians in the Communist Party. Castro replied that it is "a historical question which we are not yet ready to solve," one participant told us. But, he added, "perhaps that can happen in the future."[25]

Thus the government itself reciprocated the major initiatives being pursued by the church hierarchy. The major catalyst from the government side was no less than Fidel Castro, who—gradually—is winning his more skeptical colleagues in the PCC to his view. In this internal campaign, the most significant development has been the Council of State's publication—also in 1985—of a remarkable book of interviews with the president by Brazilian cleric Frei Betto. This study, *Fidel y la religión*, is having a tremendous impact on the national consciousness, and Fidel Castro himself believes it will help "in Cuba as well as in other countries"[26] to overcome prejudices against Christians. This will not be an easy task, however, given the traditional skepticism of party cadres toward the church. At the 1986 PCC congress, held in February, substantial resistance arose to the modernizing trend suggested by Fidel Castro: "The Congress' final report showed the Party had accepted Castro's line in domestic policies, but it did not share the enthusiasm of cordial relations with Christians at home and abroad. Legal reforms granting all Churches similar status—at present the non-Catholic churches are considered private corporations—won support, but the final report did not reflect Castro's warmth towards liberation theology or Christians."[27]. With more than a million copies of *Fidel y la religión* sold in several editions, and the continued interest of Fidel Castro in this question, the years leading to the 1990 PCC congress should see some vigorous debate on the subject.

Fidel y la religión

The answer to whether Cuban Christians as well as the government of Fidel Castro would respond positively to the church hierarchy's acceptance of socialist Cuba appears to be a qualified yes. Urged on by their political and spiritual leaders, respectively, the PCC cadres and the mainstream faithful have warily edged toward a more meaningful relationship. Fidel Castro has been of paramount importance in laying the groundwork for their mutually beneficial dialogue. Indeed, if, as seems likely, church fortunes do rise in Cuba, the person to whom Christians will owe the greatest debt of gratitude may not be Pérez Serantes or Ortega Alamino but Fidel Castro.

For many Cuban Catholics, especially those living abroad, such a claim may appear wildly far-fetched. However it was the Cuban president who has traditionally battled for the rights of the Christian sector, encouraging his colleagues in the PCC to adopt a less doctrinaire position. Through his excellent lines of communication with Vatican nuncio Zacchi, Fidel Castro consistently supported church activities (albeit in a superficial way), urging government tolerance of Christians' spiritual needs as well as church tolerance for the material goals of the revolutionary process. In full agreement with the modernizing spirit of Vatican II and the goals of the theology of liberation, influenced by his own Jesuit training, Fidel Castro more than anyone has prepared the ground so that the various initiatives of the 1980s might come to fruition. Mexican bishop Sergio Méndez Arceo, summarizing social reform in Cuba, suggests, "There is but one History—and God is present in all men. That is the basis of our faith." He concludes that Fidel Castro is in fact a man "inspired by God."[28]

Although Fidel Castro's thinking on the role of organized religion has remained consistent over the last twenty-five years, the unity of Marxist, Christian, and nationalist sentiments in the Nicaraguan struggle against the Somoza dynasty offered him new food for thought. In July 1980, for instance, upon returning from the celebrations of the first anniversary of the Sandinista victory, he spoke at length about the importance of the example of the convergence of these three currents.

He sought to explain to Cubans that in other Latin American countries religion played a far more important role than in Cuba:

> Nicaragua is a country where religious feelings go far deeper than they did in Cuba, therefore, the support given to the revolution by those religious sectors is very important.
>
> In Chile once, and also in Jamaica, we spoke of the strategic alliance between Christians and Marxist-Leninists. . . . If the revolution in Latin America were to take on an antireligious character, it would split the people. In our country, the Church was, generally speaking, the Church of the bourgeoisie, of the wealthy, of the landowners. This is not the case in many Latin American countries, where religion and the Church have deep roots among the people. . . .
>
> If we bear in mind that Christianity was, in the beginning, the religion of the poor, that in the days of the Roman Empire it was the religion of the slaves, because it was based on profound human precepts, there is no doubt that the revolutionary movement, the socialist movement, the communist movement, the Marxist-Leninist movement, would benefit a great deal from honest leaders of the Catholic Church and other religious returning to the Christian spirit of the days of the Roman Slaves. . . . What's more, Christianity would also benefit, along with socialism and communism. . . .
>
> And some religious leaders in Nicaragua asked us why strategic alliance; why only strategic alliance; why not speak of unity between Marxist-Leninists and Christians? . . .
>
> I don't know what the imperialists think about this. But I'm absolutely convinced the formula is highly explosive.[29]

From a subsequent visit to Nicaragua in January 1985, it is clear that Fidel Castro was surprised at the role of the Christian sector in the Nicaraguan revolution.[30] The massive involvement in the struggle against Somoza and the continued support of the revolutionary program of the FSLN (Sandinista Front for National Liberation) by a sizable portion of Nicaraguan Christians are conditions foreign to the Cuban context. In part because of his own respect for revolutionary Christianity, President Castro has learned to appreciate the value of this relatively new form of church activism. He has tried with limited success to sensitize his fellow citizens to the outdatedness of their resistance to the concept, which must change before they can appreciate its importance throughout Latin America. Toward this end, he agreed to a series of interviews with a Dominican friar from Brazil, Frei Betto.

The result, *Fidel y la religión*, released in late 1985, became an immediate best-seller with the first runs of 200,000 copies sold out within a few days.[31] Published by the Council of State, this 379-page volume represents not only a major symbolic olive branch extended to the church by a sector of the Communist party hierarchy but also an extraordinary personal appeal by the Cuban president himself.

By means of a personal analysis the Cuban president, in *Fidel y la religión*, once again dons the mantle of national mentor, primarily to show his fellow revolutionaries that religion is far more important on the Latin American mainland than most of them can imagine. Consequently, even though Cuba may be the major sports power in the Americas, and may enjoy the lowest inflation rate and best employment record, and with justification can boast of superb achievements in health care and education, its reputation remains tarnished by the continental perception of its dogmatic stand on religious matters. Castro delicately seeks to explain the reasons for the Cuban suspicion of religion, the realistic potential that religion offers in the Cuban context, and (for the benefit of the PCC) the political value of a church-state alliance in the eyes of Latin America, where 95 percent of the population are baptized Catholics and where, by the year 2000, the majority of the world's Catholics will live. In short, he provides a more objective, "continentalist" appreciation of the religious question. The book is thus an attempt to forge a more relaxed policy among the revolutionary policy makers, as well as the story of a personal odyssey begun a quarter of a century ago.

A striking facet of *Fidel y la religión* is the similarity between Castro's current positions and arguments on religion and those he put forward in the initial years of the revolutionary process (before the major renovating influence of Vatican II, it is worth noting). Also of interest are the Cuban president's personal observations of religion-related topics, including his own religious training (at home and at school), the roots of the earlier troubled relations between the church and the revolutionary government, the post–Vatican II church in general, popular religiosity, and the roles of various pontiffs. Together they throw a fascinating light on the complex nature of the religious question and constitute a valuable insight into the psyche of one of the major protagonists of this matter. Concerning religious issues, the work can be divided into four categories: Fidel Castro's own religious upbringing; the roots of tension between church and state in the revolutionary period, including a look at the traditionally more progressive role of Protestants throughout this period; the current state of relations between the church and revolutionary government, including the existence of popular religiosity and the need for a practical form of religion in the "here and now"; and the need for church and state to coexist and work in harmony.

Fidel Castro's early religious experiences were in many ways typically Cuban, at least for rural Cubans. "There couldn't be the kind of religiosity which accompanied going to church," Castro wrote, "because in the region where I was born out in the middle of the countryside—there were no churches."[32] The young Fidel, baptized at the age of five or six, saw a priest only once a year, when the *cura* made the annual trip from Mayarí twenty miles away. Among the workers on his father's estate "there were all kinds of beliefs and superstitions: spirits, phantoms, animals that could help to predict the future, the lot. Those were the religious parameters that I remember" (103–4). Fidel's mother was a traditional Catholic, "a fervent believer, who prayed every night, and always lit candles to the Virgin and the saints. She would ask favors, request their help in all circumstances, and make promises to help any member of the family who was sick, in any difficult situation. And she didn't just make promises—she kept them too" (104).

His experiences at Catholic schools, the La Salle college, and subsequently at two Jesuit institutions, the Colegio de Dolores and the prestigious Belén College, undoubtedly helped form his career but also fostered a strong skepticism concerning religious matters. He criticizes the social and racial discrimination found in these schools, although he retains a soft spot for the Jesuits and their devotion to teaching. The conservative leanings of these teachers, most of whom were Spanish, concerned him, as did their penchant for corporal punishment, although he is appreciative of their pedagogical intent. Fidel Castro's most biting criticism, however, is reserved for the religious instruction and religious life in general of the various colleges. He had to attend mass daily before breakfast and is extremely critical of the mechanical way in which students were obliged to recite prayers, particularly since they were in Latin or Greek.[33] Regarding his Catholic education, Castro had little sympathy for the message preached and much less for the method by which it was realized:

> It wasn't possible, however, to inculcate a solid religious faith into me, since in explaining things, everything revolved around dogma: you had to believe this because that was the way it was; and not believing it was a terrible thing, a major sin that deserved the most horrible punishment.
>
> If you really have to accept things because they tell you to, you can't even argue over them, or reason about them. Moreover, if the element and the fundamental argument that they use revolve

around rewards or punishment (and indeed usually more punishment than rewards), then it's impossible to develop your reason-
ing and your feelings that could prove to be the base of a sincere
religious belief. (133)

This insight into Fidel Castro's experience with religious training casts
a valuable light not only on the church of his youth and the kind of
education available to Cuba's prerevolutionary bourgeoisie but also on
the feelings and prejudices of the revolutionary leader in his dealings
with the church. It is by far the most intimate portrait to date of Fidel
Castro. More important, it represents an excellent synthesis born of
one (highly influential) man's view of the role of the church in Cuba
and of the obstacles to be overcome if church-state relations in revolutionary Cuba are to become solidly established.

The book offers little new insight on the initial struggles between
the church and the revolutionary government. The Cuban president
outlines the much-needed social reforms introduced in 1959 and describes the reaction of the bourgeoisie: "The revolutionary laws began
to produce conflicts, without any doubt at all, because the bourgeois
sector and the estate-owners, the wealthy sectors, changed their attitude toward the Revolution, and decided to oppose it. They were aided
by institutions at the service of these interests, which began a campaign against the Revolution. In this way there developed the first conflicts with the Church, because really these sectors attempted to use
the Church as an instrument against the Revolution" (208–9). Fidel
Castro suggests that this manipulation of the church by its closest ally,
the bourgeoisie, together with the Spanish and extremely conservative
traditions of the majority of the clergy, were the fundamental reasons for the early problems between the church and the revolutionary
government.

The Cuban president goes out of his way to indicate that the revolutionary government has always enjoyed better relations with the Protestant church than with the Catholic.[34] Their schools (in general more
accessible and less discriminatory than their Catholic counterparts)
produced many supporters of the revolutionary process and, with few
exceptions, have traditionally been more united in dealing with the
government. Castro speaks very highly of their practical form of religion and the difference in their approach to religious life: "In addition,
one could note a difference in the conduct of the Protestant Churches.
I was able to notice (indeed I always observed) that as a rule the Protestant Churches had developed especially among the poorer sections of
the population, and I also noted in them a more militant religious practice. By this I mean that I observed more discipline in the Protestant

Churches, seen in their interpretation, their style, methods, and means of praying" (214).

Fidel Castro believes that religious life can only garner respectability by serving the interests of those whose needs are greatest—hence his respect for the traditional service work of the Protestant church. He has always praised, in this regard, the dedication of nuns in Cuba engaged in service activities, particularly in hospitals, homes for senior citizens, the leprosarium, and the like. In a nationally televised session of the National Assembly, the Cuban president said, "I have always mentioned, precisely, the attitude of those nuns as true communist models, because I believe that they really possess those conditions which we desire for every militant communist" (266). It is this form of practical religion, as distinct from a vague, purely spiritual variety, that Fidel Castro has repeatedly praised—in Chile in 1971, in Jamaica in 1977, and in Nicaragua in 1979. It is this brand of religion that he has counterposed to the Christianity of others: "There are many people in this world who call themselves Christian, but who do terrible things. Pinochet, Reagan and Botha, to cite just a few examples, consider themselves to be Christian" (127).

In the book, Fidel reaffirms his traditional support for the concept of the "strategic alliance" between the religious sector and the revolutionary state, thereby limiting, critics would argue, the nature of each. While he admits that in Cuba there exists a fairly widespread popular religiosity, he believes "that no people in the history of humanity has ever existed that didn't have a diffuse religiosity" (211).[35] Still, government policy consistently imposes limitations on the extent of this Christian "integration." Castro's fundamental belief seems to be that, given the historical circumstances of the relationship of church and revolutionary government, the necessary conditions for an alliance are still not present.

This attitude surfaces in regard to the issue of allowing practicing Christians to join the PCC. Fidel Castro explains the historical development of the foundation of the party—that most of the opposition to the revolutionary government came from sectors allied to the church and that most of the actual revolutionaries had little or no religious faith. As a result, and in the face of pressure from the United States, a political orthodoxy was demanded of all party members. Christian revolutionaries were thus forced by circumstances to take a stand in one camp or the other.[36] At the same time that Castro admits grave shortcomings on the part of the revolutionary leadership in coming to terms with the new situation, he affirms that it is still too early for the PCC to admit Christians as full members: "Now, you were asking me if the conditions for this stage were present. I don't think so, because we haven't worked toward providing them; we should have worked more in that direction. If you ask me, 'Is that vital for the Revolution?,' I would tell you that it isn't—in the sense that our Revolution has an enormous strength, in political and ideological terms. However, if we don't succeed in constructing that climate, then we can't say that our Revolution is a perfect work because while the circumstances exist in which individuals, who for particular religious beliefs don't possess the same rights as others (despite fulfilling the same social duties as any other person), then our revolutionary work isn't complete" (247).

Beyond the mere coexistence of church and revolutionary government, Fidel Castro believes that "there should be closer, and better, relations, indeed there should be a relationship based on cooperation, between the Revolution and the Churches" (246). He lists three pragmatic reasons for this: "the confrontation between revolutions and religious beliefs is not useful, especially when reactionaries and imperialism can use religious beliefs as arms against the revolutions" (246); the existence—as hinted above—of such religious discrimination is proof that the revolutionary process has to mature in several areas;[37] and the realization that the church in Latin America has been undergoing fundamental changes over the past two decades.[38]

Fidel Castro also knows that if he is to go beyond the narrow bounds of coexistence, he requires the solid support of the leaders of the church. In the book, he thus outlines in great detail the similarities between Marxism and Christianity. He compares, for example, the moral values espoused by both, their predisposition to sacrifice and austerity (258); the similarities between the church's missionaries and the revolution's *internacionalista* workers scattered around the globe (263); the revolution's realization of the biblical parable of the loaves and fishes, "multiplying the loaves and fishes to feed our people, multiplying the number of schools, teachers, hospitals and doctors" (325); and the role of Christianity as a "revolutionary doctrine" for the Roman Empire (327) and as a philosophical doctrine (333). "From a strictly political viewpoint . . . I even think that one can be a Marxist, without ceasing to be a Christian, that it is possible to work together with the Marxist communist in order to transform the world. The important thing is that in both cases one should attempt to be sincere revolutionaries, prepared to suppress the exploitations of man by man, and to struggle for the just distribution of social wealth, and for equality, fraternity, and the dignity of all human beings. In other words, one should be a bearer of the most advanced political, economic and social awareness, even though the point of departure may be—as in the case of Christians—a religious concept" (333). He synthesizes his observations by repeating to Frei Betto what he told the U.S. bishops during their January 1985 visit: "If the Church were ever to create a State based upon these principles, it would organize a State like ours" (263).

In this uphill struggle to convince church leaders and fellow members of the PCC that they must cooperate to improve socioeconomic conditions throughout Latin America, Castro is at pains to remind them that their differences are limited, the potential for such joint action unlimited. If only they could understand that the opportunity exists for a unique model, different and better than the Polish or Italian models. If they could only see the advantages of such potential in the broader Latin American context. United action, however, requires courageous leadership from the erstwhile reluctant vanguard of the PCC and from the church hierarchy that Fidel suggests would prove politically advantageous to both.[39] Above all, he emphasizes the need to realize that much has happened since the early hostility between church and revolutionary government. He openly admits that his earlier insistence on "total purity" among members of the party made it impossible to be a practicing Christian and member of the PCC and is convinced that, at that particular juncture, his action was justified.[40] Nevertheless, the central thrust of this position in *Fidel y la religión* is toward meaningful cooperation. It is time "for us to create the conditions for some advances in these matters, because of course it's been 26 years since the revolutionary victory" (248).

Church-State Maturity and Leadership

The years from 1979 to 1987 have seen the development of maturity and leadership on the part of the revolutionary government and the Catholic church (gradually catching up to the less influential but more progressive Protestant church). The Catholic hierarchy has, belatedly, realized that its obligation is to be with the people; if the people are supporting the revolution, then the church must work within that reality. To do otherwise might preserve pre–Vatican II teachings but little else. Finally, if the church wants to improve its material base, have access to media, and print church teaching materials, then it needs to cooperate with the system. The church has learned these difficult lessons only gradually.

Mindful of their prerevolutionary influence and social status, church leaders have struggled long and hard to come to terms with their reality. Indeed, many Cubans (largely of the older generation but including a fair sprinkling of younger people) still have difficulty accepting the liberal views now espoused by their hierarchy. Many exiled Cubans, who remember the Cuba of yesterday, must find it even more difficult to accept the Catholic hierarchy's position. Perhaps most practicing Christians in Cuba lie somewhere between the two extremes, worried about the government control that permeates every facet of life yet not hostile to the gains of the revolutionary process that are apparent throughout Cuba.

The church in Cuba during these years has begun to pursue with vigor a policy of dialogue and cooperation with government leaders, a policy of constructive rapprochement. Prepared to cooperate with government leaders (and, just as important, to be seen to be cooperating), these Catholics have developed this newfound mutual understanding. While it is still too early to evaluate gains made by the church, it is significant that church leaders have had such access to Fidel Castro (who seems more than disposed to meet the bishops' concerns), while government concern about the Christian threat has lessened substantially. In sum, the risks engendered by this church policy seem thus far to have been accompanied by noteworthy gains, although it remains to be seen just what tangible benefits will result.

The Catholic leadership's maturity in seeking a fresh dialogue has been more or less matched by its government counterpart. Spurred on by Fidel Castro, the revolutionary government has loosened control over the media, a process that has resulted in a consistently favorable profile of church activities not seen in the past twenty-seven years. Moreover, the Cuban president has sought to coax the PCC to recognize that it regards the church through a filter that is a quarter of a century out of date. Finally he has attempted to show that Cuba's doctrinaire interpretations of the religious question can only do the country a great disservice in Catholic Latin America, which—given the nature of clerical activism—understandably looks askance at Cuba's outdated views. If Cuba wants to continue impressing Latin America with its revolutionary leadership, then it must come to terms with radically different and rapidly evolving world circumstances.

The reaction on the part of the PCC cadres, particularly the old guard, has been slow but encouraging—although they have been less eager to take up the challenge than Fidel Castro would probably have liked. The potential advantages of rapprochement with the church must in some ways pale in comparison with the power that they already wield. The result has been a series of limited major concessions to church leaders, although their position has become noticeably softer. The most important yardstick for measuring this missionary activity of Fidel Castro will come at future congresses of the PCC, with the discussion of resolutions on religious activities, including the thorny issue of practicing Christians as party members.

   The prevalent note of church-state relationships during this period is one of hope and accord. For the first time in nearly three decades there is the apparent desire to make the relationship succeed and, to differing degrees of acceptance, to move to the next stage, from open dialogue to action. Moreover, given the leadership shown by the Catholic hierarchy as well as Fidel Castro's own remarkable role in the process, there is every chance that this comparatively small grouping (maybe 100,000–160,000 practicing Christians out of a population of 10 million) will indeed succeed in establishing its identity within the revolutionary process, a feat never realized in Cuba's history. Writing in January 1986, Christian Reformed pastor James C. Dekker described this ability to retain a Christian identity yet work wholeheartedly within the revolutionary system as "Christian citizens": "We Christians in the U.S. and Canada are constantly in danger of confusing our governmental system with God's will because long ago we blurred the distinction between *right* and *privilege*. Our Cuban brothers and sisters live in a less privileged but much more honest situation. We can learn from them, if we dare, how to be Christian citizens. They know how to render Caesar his due."[41]

8

Toward a Rapprochement

> The Revolution has been very careful with the Church: it very carefully
> has set up the ties that allows [sic] its definite strangulation. The Revo-
> lution has been patient with the Church; it patiently has been waiting
> for time to do its work, and has not wasted any occasions to promote
> its demise.
>
> Froilán Domínguez,
> exiled Cuban priest, 1981[1]

> We are not a martyred or suppressed Church but we have lost all the
> privileges and comforts of Churches who were part of and responsible
> for the Establishment. . . . But we have learned the hard lesson that
> only when the Church is a servant—when the Church can be fully
> identified with the needs and spirit of the people, is when she can be
> the Church.
>
> Adolfo Ham,
> chairman, Cuban Ecumenical Council, 1983[2]

The radically differing opinions reflected in the epigraphs give some indication of the continuing debate within church circles of the role and nature of church-state relations in revolutionary Cuba. In many ways they serve as a fitting summary for this study, since they represent two views, each held by a fairly large Christian constituency, of the church's mission in Cuban society. It would be easy to disregard both opinions, the first because it comes from an exiled, embittered cleric and the second because the Cuban Ecumenical Council's progressive opinions do not necessarily reflect mainstream Christian thought. Nevertheless, they both need to be taken into account if we are to assess properly the meaning of the church in Cuba more than a quarter-century after Fidel Castro proclaimed the Marxist-Leninist nature of the revolution.

Before analyzing the current scene, it is worth reflecting on the tradition of church life, both Catholic and Protestant, in prerevolutionary times. The Catholic church started badly in colonial Cuba: never fully integrated into what rapidly degenerated into a backwater of the Spanish drive for profit in the Americas, the church gradually developed into the protector of vested interests. Defending the status quo— including slavery—the church (with a few exceptions) sought to gain respectability for itself by adhering tenaciously to its Spanish roots. This unswerving identification with things Spanish might have had some value during most of the colonial period—the period of nineteenth-century liberalism excepted—but in the Cuban context it represented an anachronistic stance that would never be forgotten.

With the upsurge of nationalist feelings in the mid-nineteenth century, the church misread historical trends, seeking at all costs to support the interests of the madre patria, Spanish settlers, and itself. Unfortunately this tendency to misread inevitable political change would continue to plague the church through most of the twentieth century. In the case of Cuba in the 1860s and again in the 1890s, by which time all of Spanish America had won its independence, the church's disregard of political currents would lead to grave political repercussions within the church itself, pitting Spanish against Cuban clerics— in many ways similar to the split in the church's ranks in Cuba in the 1950s.

At a time when most Cubans were becoming increasingly disenchanted with the motherland's crude domination of the island, this persistent identification with Spanish values and, more important, political aspirations by the body politic of the church could only work to the church's detriment. Despite the noble tradition of liberal native clergy who supported the struggle of the mambises, in some cases with their lives, the church as a whole became branded as the legitimizing agent of Spanish repression that continued to deny Cuba the rights already enjoyed by her sister republics. In the wake of the overthrow of the Spanish forces, two bishops, along with a large number of priests, requested immediate repatriation. As in the 1860s, and again a century later in the 1960s, this obsessively pro-Spanish conservative tradition would continue to haunt the church's search for acceptance among the Cuban population.

While still nominally a Christian people, Cubans were far less religious than any of their Latin American counterparts—particularly if one takes into account the widespread popularity of syncretic ("Afro-Cuban") religious practices. Religious penetration had exercised a limited impact on Cuban society as a whole, and indeed it was limited largely to the white urban bourgeoisie. As the twentieth century progressed, this trend became more deeply ingrained—particularly in Catholic circles—as the church's influence remained limited by its active role in private education, supporting in this process an easily identified, albeit economically powerful, minority. The ensuing accommodation with this political elite was in many ways a repeat of its siding in the 1890s with the Spanish settlers in the face of a universal clamor for greater freedom and socioeconomic improvements. Once again the church lost the credibility it so desperately sought. Once again, despite the example of many Catholics and Protestants who fought against the Batista regime, the church not only was exceptionally slow in taking the nation's pulse but was seen—because of the hierarchy's supine stance on the dictatorship—as the defender of oppression.

By the 1950s the church was again socially acceptable, having rescaled the pinnacle of material and political well-being. True, the Cuban church's wealth was nowhere near that of the church in other Latin American nations, but it had once again assumed a position of respectability among the influential. As a result, while many members of the clergy and Acción Católica, and similar Protestant organizations, were pushing for the church to assume a more activist position in the face of government repression by Batista's forces, the hierarchy—with the notable exception of Archbishop Pérez Serantes of Santiago de Cuba—feared that such activism would put at risk this newly garnered respectability. Once again, the church gambled on the political currents of the day—and lost.

Summarizing four centuries of Catholic evangelization and sixty years of Protestant missionary work brings into focus many aspects of the church's identity encountered in the revolutionary period. One was an honest if misguided attempt to import religious models—in theory to save the souls of the entire population but in practice for the benefit of a powerful middle-class minority. (Protestant missionaries, possibly because they arrived more recently and were thus compara- tively unhampered by the baggage of the colonial experience, were somewhat less guilty of this tactic.) The vast majority of Cubans were simply not influenced or greatly affected by organized religion. More- over, having seen church fortunes improve after many difficult dec- ades, the Catholic church preferred not to cause problems for itself by criticizing the government of the day, repeatedly falling back on the premise that theirs was a mission of spiritual, and not political, leader- ship. With the onset of the revolution in 1959, this corporate position—not withstanding the valor of many individual Catholics— would always be remembered.

In the almost three decades since Fidel Castro addressed the crowds in Santiago de Cuba's central square following Batista's flight, much has happened to the church—both in Cuba and, more important, in the world. To a certain extent the problems of the church in Cuba have been the problems of this worldwide body, seeking to come to terms with the momentous changes unleashed by the Second Vatican Coun- cil (1962–65), the spirit of modernization of faith in the context of the modern era and of disparate traditions and histories. The renewed politicization of religious faith, both from the so-called fundamentalist interpretation on the one hand and from that of "liberation theology" on the other, is a result of this process—both by those who vehemently re- ject this aggiornamento and those who welcome it as long overdue.

This modernization of church practice and the controversy it has generated have been well received by the Cuban clergy, although the first decade of church-state relations was marred by mutual recrimina- tion, constant pressure, and resulting isolation. Urged by the Vatican, though, and energetically encouraged in Cuba by the papal envoy, Msgr. Zacchi, the Cuban church (as opposed to the earlier "church in Cuba") has in the past two decades emerged from the catacombs fol- lowing a long period of introspection and self-evaluation. Aided by the Cubanization of clergy, an enlightened hierarchy emphasizing the val- ues and benefits for the church of cooperation rather than confronta- tion as well as the need to enter the post–Vatican II world, the increas- ing rejection among Cuban Christians of the earlier martyrdom complex, and a less hostile response in government circles (and in par- ticular the major initiative of Fidel Castro), a gradual thawing of an icy relationship has occurred.

Church statistics provide a useful, if somewhat misleading, indica- tion of the decline in church membership in revolutionary Cuba. From a high of 89.3 percent of Cubans regarded (incorrectly) as Catholic in 1960, by 1983 the percentage of Catholics had dropped to 38.9 percent of the population, with only one priest for every 43,000 nominal Catholics. The 1960 figure of 723 priests and 2,225 nuns had shrunk by 1980 to 213 priests and 220 nuns.[3] One has to treat these statistics with some distance, however, for while 89.3 percent of the population might be regarded in prerevolutionary times as nominal Catholics, the number of practicing Catholics was optimistically put at between 4 and 10 percent of the population.[4] In other words, the ratio of priests (224 in 1985) to practicing Catholics in Cuba in the mid-1980s (generally estimated to be between one-half and one percent—or 100,000),[5] might in fact be superior to that of other predominantly Catholic Latin American nations.[6] In addition there are more than forty Protestant denominations, with a total of 60,000–90,000 followers (estimates vary) and approximately 1,000 Jews.[7]

While it may be easy to juggle statistics on priest-communicant ratios, it is nevertheless abundantly clear that while the number of Cubans practicing Christianity has dropped to approximately 1–2 percent of the population, the quality of their practice, carried on many years in extremely adverse conditions, with a great deal of negative societal pressure and discrimination, has risen dramatically. This vitality can be seen most readily in the clergy, more than one-half of whom are young Cubans ordained since the revolution.[8] Indeed, 102 new priests have been ordained since 1970, and approximately 40 others are presently studying for the priesthood at the Catholic seminaries in Havana and Santiago de Cuba.[9] The average age of seminarians has increased from 21.4 years in 1971 to 26.5 in 1982, an indication that candidates entering the seminaries are in general more mature than their predecessors, often young professionals seeking a more meaningful existence than that offered by contemporary society. Finally, a low annual dropout rate of 15 percent also indicates a promising future for the Cuban church.[10] All this transpires in a society where entering the priesthood does not correspond to a desire for upward social mobility or for an education (often the case in other Latin American countries) and where there is absolutely no social prestige in being a priest—at times seminarians risk being mocked by their peers. In sum, the vitality of the faith far outweighs the relatively small number of communicants. This religious foundation can be seen in the 1–2 percent of the population who practice their faith regularly, despite social pressure ranging from discrimination in employment and education, to general suspicion and a distrust among neighbors, to alternative activities for children on Sundays, to limiting the practice of religion to church buildings. The strength of the faithful can also be gauged by the 100,000 and more who turn out for popular religious ceremonies like the San Lázaro procession every year or the approximately 50 percent of the population who request a religious ceremony to accompany burials at Havana's Colón Cemetery. Given nearly three decades of the revolutionary process and the extremely limited religious penetration in prerevolutionary times,[11] these are major achievements.

The intriguing questions that remain to be answered tend to relate not to the quality of religious life but to the reasons why the rapprochement between church and government leaders has been developing in recent years and precisely what this change means for both the church and the government of Fidel Castro.

The first question—why the rapprochement—is perhaps the more difficult to answer, since it involves evaluating and interpreting decisions taken by leaders of the church and revolutionary government. Nevertheless, certain obvious benefits for both institutions are results of the current rapprochement. In a recent press conference, Bishop Adolfo Rodríguez Herrera of Camagüey (president of the Cuban Episcopal Conference) noted that "the Church does not want to remain confined to the vestries, and is concerned over the number of people who 'do not know Jesus,' and over the existence of Cuban towns without churches."[12] An earlier report of the bishops had cited three fundamental goals for the church in Cuba: "involving the Church in the problems of society; strengthening Christians' relationship with God; and spreading Catholicism throughout society."[13] In order to realize these goals, the church continues active promotion of dialogue with the Castro government—much to the chagrin of conservatives in the church.[14]

For his part, Fidel Castro obviously stands to gain internationally by his decision to assist the church—far more than their approximately 100,000–150,000 members would normally expect. To a certain extent this diplomacy may be directed at showing North America how reasonable the Cuban government is, although a far more likely target is Latin America. Cuba's diplomatic relations have improved dramatically in recent years with countries like Argentina, Venezuela, and Brazil, and a policy of dialogue with the church can only assist this process. Moreover, if Cuba is to appear as the socialist alternative in Latin America, it behooves the revolutionary government to develop this policy of apertura, or diplomatic opening. But one should not see this approach as merely a cynical manipulation of the religious question by Castro, for the Cuban president's observations on the role of the church have remained extremely consistent for nearly three decades. Perhaps, then, it is in many ways the church that has moved, not Fidel Castro.

A study of religion and politics in Cuba over nearly thirty years of this revolutionary process shows that the church has consistently sought to discover a niche for itself, a secure platform from which to undertake its mission of evangelizing. Faced with a dramatic loss of influence, impeded by a generally foreign and somewhat elitist outlook—"theological orphans in a rapidly changing Church"—and located in a country that was probably the least Christian of Latin America, the church has had to come to terms slowly with its reality. Prodded by the reforms of Vatican II, the church set itself four basic goals: "political reinsertion or breathing space in the prevailing system . . . doctrinal reintegration into the post-Conciliar Church . . . transnational interaction within the Church . . . [and] ecumenical dialogue."[15] For many years this was a lonely, uphill struggle against a combination of a hostile political climate and the church's own inability to change. The mid-1980s have witnessed the beginning of a new and meaningful dialogue, however—in many ways the culmination of this struggle. In the spring of 1959, Angel del Cerro, in an article significantly entitled "La Iglesia tiene que resucitar" ("The Church Has to Resuscitate"), urged all Catholics to come to terms with the reality of Cuba's new, and unique, context:

> Faced with this irrefutable reality, there are two clear positions to consider. Some cling with passive nostalgia to the old privileges, while attempting to fight back with arguments that could very well be true, but which in practical terms are inoperable. . . . Others adapt to the new conditions and strive to give to the Christian message a modern sense, at once lively and effective. . . .
>
> Valiantly and honestly, the Church has to recognize its errors, human errors after all, and give way to the reinvigorating strength of the revolution.[16]

Almost three decades after this eloquent plea was written the thrust of del Cerro's argument is now being taken seriously: the spirit of Vatican II has finally taken root in Cuba.

Notes

Introduction

1. This expression (literally "the marvelous real element") is used to describe the "larger-than-life" phenomenon of works by such writers as Carpentier and Gabriel García Márquez. In essence they claim that the reality of Latin America, where twentieth-century technology exists alongside medieval living conditions and customs, is an amalgam of such extraordinary and contradictory material that often what we in the so-called First World see as fantastic, above reason, is in fact a real facet of life in Latin America.

Chapter 1. The Colonial Period, 1492–1898

1. See Torres-Cuevas, "El obispado de Cuba," 75–76.

2. Figueroa y Miranda, *Religión y política*, 13.

3. See the Reflexión Eclesial Cubana, "Comisión de Historia," 21 (hereafter cited as REC Com).

4. Leiseca, *Historia Eclesiástica de Cuba*, 18, 19.

5. Lewis Hanke, *The Spanish Struggle for Justice in the Conquest of America* (Philadelphia: University of Pennsylvania Press, 1949).

6. Thirty years later, Charles V followed the advice of Las Casas and introduced similar progressive legislation designed to revoke Spanish settlers' rights to Indian service and tribute. The predictable result: rebellion against the 1542 legislation, including the capture and murder of the Peruvian viceroy by enraged *encomenderos*, and the demand by Spanish settlers throughout the Americas that the new laws be revoked. The clergy in Cuba were conspicuously silent.

7. Hernán Cortes, the great conquistador of New Spain, reputedly refused a huge land grant in Hispaniola, claiming, "I came to get gold, not to till the

soil like a peasant." In a detailed study of the encomienda system, Lesley Byrd Simpson notes that most of the conquistadores of Mexico and South America had already served in Cuba and Hispaniola, where their attitude toward the Indians hardened as they saw the widely accepted exploitation. Therefore "they (along with the Church, legislators, judges and colonists) thought that the Indians were given to Spain by Providence—and that they could dispose of them as they pleased" (*The Encomienda in New Spain: The Beginning of Spanish Mexico* [Berkeley: University of California Press, 1950], xii).

8. See "Relación del primer viaje de Cristóbal Colón," in Pichardo, ed., *Documentos para la historia de Cuba*, 1:15.

9. Jorge Ibarra, *Historia de Cuba* (La Habana: Dirección Política de las F.A.R., 1967), 45.

10. See Testé, *Historia Eclesiástica de Cuba*, 4:3.

11. Ibid., 76.

12. Irene Aloha Wright, *The Early History of Cuba, 1492–1586* (New York: Octagon Books, 1970), 317–18.

13. See Bishop Sarmiento's "Carta del Obispo al Emperador dando cuenta de la visita hecha á las villas é iglesias, y del estado en que se hallan," in Pichardo, ed., *Documentos para la historia de Cuba*, 1:99, 100, 101. (The Puerto del Principe cleric, Alonso de Tolosa, had apparently not received any funding from the government for more than two years.)

14. Wright, *Early History of Cuba*, 53.

15. Quoted from the bishop's "Testimonio de la visita que hizo a su diócesis Juan del Castillo, Obispo de Cuba—2 de agosto 1569 a abril 1570" in Leiseca, *Historia Eclesiástica de Cuba*, 34.

16. Leiseca, *Historia Eclesiástica de Cuba*, 57.

17. Cited in Maza, "The Cuban Catholic Church," 15.

18. Ibid., 21.

19. Testé, *Historia Eclesiástica de Cuba*, 2:54.

20. Maza, "The Cuban Catholic Church," 26–27.

21. Leiseca, *Historia Eclesiástica de Cuba*, 105.

22. José Martí, *Obras completas* (La Habana: Editorial Nacional de Cuba, 1963–66), 5:249.

23. Maza, "The Cuban Catholic Church," 32.

24. REC Com, 3.

25. Martí, *Obras completas*, 4:418.

26. REC Com, 8.

27. Ibid.

28. Maza, "The Cuban Catholic Church," 28.

29. Ibid.

30. Leiseca, *Historia Eclesiástica de Cuba*, 122–24.

31. Hugh Thomas, *Cuba*, 62–63.

32. Ibarra, *Historia de Cuba*, 129.

33. REC Com, 2.

34. Ibarra, *Historia de Cuba*, 104.

35. REC Com, 9.

36. Ibid.

37. Pichardo, ed., *Documentos para la historia de Cuba*, 1:318.

38. Franklin W. Knight, *Slave Society in Cuba during the Nineteenth Century* (Madison: University of Wisconsin Press, 1970), 112.

39. Figures taken from Leiseca, *Historia Eclesiástica de Cuba*, 119, 139–40. By 1819, this population would increase to 553,000 (143) and by 1827 to 704,487 (149).

40. Leiseca, *Historia Eclesiástica de Cuba*, 129.

41. REC Com, 12.

42. Maza's analysis therefore seems valid: "The transformation of Cuba into an important sugar producer had grave consequences for the Catholic Church, particularly the convents and religious orders. They became banking institutions, lending the initial money for promising sugar ventures including slave traffic. The Church also provided the ideological justification for slavery, since it made Christians out of the Blacks, showing them the way to salvation" ("The Cuban Catholic Church," 102).

43. See, for example, Kenneth F. Kiple, *Blacks in Colonial Cuba, 1774–1899* (Gainesville: University Presses of Florida, 1976), 43n.21, who notes that burials cost between $5.00 and $7.50 and baptism as much as $17—an extraordinary amount for a slave.

44. Thomas, *Cuba*, 82.

45. Knight, *Slave Society in Cuba*, 106–7.

46. Thomas, *Cuba*, 151.

47. Ibid., 40.

48. Martín Socarrás Matos, *La Necrópolis Cristóbal Colón (Investigaciones preliminares)* (La Habana: Instituto Cubano del Libro, 1975), 10.

49. Figueroa y Miranda, *Religión y política*, 28.

50. Ibid., 44.

51. Ibid., 95.

52. Cited by Cintio Vitier in his excellent and insightful study, *Ese sol del mundo moral: para una historia de la etnicidad cubana* (México: Siglo Veintiuno, 1975), 18.

53. Raymond Carr, *España 1808–1939* (Barcelona: Ediciones Ariel, 1969), 176.

54. REC Com, p. 15.

55. Ibid.

56. Hageman and Wheaton, eds., *Religion in Cuba Today*, 20.

57. REC Com, 15.

58. Ibid., 15, 16.

59. Ibid., 17.

60. Thomas, *Cuba*, 151.

61. Franklin W. Knight, for instance, quotes a visitor in the 1840s who commented on this feature: "With this [his income from a coffee estate] he supported his family, for he joined in the custom observed by his brother priests in Cuba; but he was not the less respected as a man, while his house was visited by all the neighboring gentry" (*Slave Society in Cuba*, 109).

62. Maturin M. Ballou, *History of Cuba; or Notes of a Traveller in the Tropics* (Boston: Phillips, Sampson and Co., 1854), 81.

182
Notes to Pages 28–42

63. Ibid., 93.
64. Richard Henry Dana, Jr., *To Cuba and Back, A Vacation Voyage* (Boston: Ticknor and Fields, 1859), 58.
65. Ibid., 239.
66. Alfred L. Padula, Jr., "The Fall of the Bourgeoisie: Cuba, 1953–1961" (Ph.D. diss., University of New Mexico, 1974), 419.
67. REC Com, 23.
68. Quoted in Maza, "The Cuban Catholic Church," 46–47.

Chapter 2. The Church in Search of a Constituency, 1898–1959

1. Cited in Miguel Luis and Diego Barros Arana, *La Iglesia Frente a la Emancipación Americana* (La Habana: Instituto del Libro, 1967), 11.
2. For an insightful discussion of this dilemma, see E.E.Y. Hales, *The Catholic Church in the Modern World: A Survey from the French Revolution to the Present* (Garden City, NY: Doubleday, 1958), 82–83.
3. See Lucas Ayarragaray, *La Iglesia en América y la dominación española: Estudio de la época colonial* (Buenos Aires: J. Lajouane y Cía., 1920), 186–88.
4. Raymond Corrigan, S.J., *The Church in the Nineteenth Century* (Milwaukee: The Bruce Publishing Company, 1938), 56.
5. For another view, see E. E. Y. Hales: "Leo XIII had been at special pains to repeat what his predecessors had said, namely that the Church believed, certainly, in social order, and therefore in obedience to legitimately constituted authority, but as to forms of government she was neutral" (*Church in the Modern World*, 191).
6. I. Grigulévich, *El Papado: Siglo XX* (Moscow: Editorial Progreso, 1982), 33.
7. Dewart, *Christianity and Revolution*, 33.
8. Ibid., 93.
9. Cited in Neblett, *Methodism's First Fifty Years*, 11.
10. Thomas, *Cuba*, 462.
11. Ibarra, *Historia de Cuba*, 523.
12. Cited in Pichardo, *Documentos*, 2:79. For a discussion of this topic, as well as for a comparison of points in earlier revolutionary constitutions, see Philip Foner, *The Spanish-American War and the Birth of American Imperialism, 1895–1902* (New York: Monthly Review Press, 1972), 2:550–53.
13. Leiseca, *Historia Eclesiástica de Cuba*, 212.
14. In 1912, Pius X created two new dioceses, Camagüey (to which a Spanish prelate was assigned) and Matanzas (where Charles Warren Currier, an American, became bishop). See Leiseca, *Historia Eclesiástica de Cuba*, 222.
15. Crahan, "Salvation through Christ or Marx," 160.
16. For a study of the ACU, see Hernández, *Agrupación Católica Universitaria*.
17. Cited in Hageman and Wheaton, eds., *Religion in Cuba Today*, 19.
18. Maza, "The Cuban Catholic Church," 61.
19. Leiseca, *Historia Eclesiástica de Cuba*, 96. Maza cites the 1919 census

to show an increase in clergy since the turn of the century to the comparatively large figure of 880 in 1919, one-half of whom lived in Havana ("The Cuban Catholic Church," 56). Of these, 657 were men and 213 women; significantly, two-thirds of the men were born in Spain, one-third in Cuba.

20. "The Church had little to say in the early days and years of the Republic. As the overthrow of Machado and the revolutionary days of 1933 appeared, the Church was still suffering from the pro-Spanish role it had played during the nineteenth century. The Church was socially relevant among the Spaniards, the children of the sugar barons and the well-off people living in the Vedado and Miramar, but it lacked any significant meaning for the peasants and workers . . . a Church limited in its actions and reduced to a small circle in its social relevance" (Maza, "The Cuban Catholic Church: True Struggles and False Dilemmas," 55).

21. Cited by Aurelio Alonso Tejada, "La religiosidad y las instituciones religiosas en la sociedad cubana actual," unpublished paper, December 1986, 9–10. Batista, however, seems also to have gained the sympathy of Protestant groups, for a leading Methodist, Sterling Augustus Neblett, cited Batista's response to a Catholic request for the introduction of religious education into the Cuban schools: "The Republic has been tolerant, is tolerant, of religious activities of every sort. The Cuban State must continue to respect freedom of worship. As to education, I think the same thing. Officials must remain free of religious preponderances and influences of every sort just as at present. Cuba is not faced with conflicts of this nature. To provoke them would be imprudent: to create them would be criminal" (*Methodism's First Fifty Years,* 207).

22. Crahan, "Salvation through Christ or Marx," 161.

23. Marimón, "The Church," 400.

24. See Maza, "The Cuban Catholic Church," 62–63.

25. All figures from this survey are from Oscar A. Echevarría Salvat, *La Agricultura Cubana, 1934–1966: Régimen Social, Productividad y Nivel de Vida del Sector Agrícola* (Miami: Ediciones Universal, 1971), 13–17, 24.

26. "The general attitude of organized Catholicism was first opposed to the usurpation of power by force, and later opposed to the exercise of that power by illegal means and by increasing violence," Marimón writes, and cites "the frequent public denunciations of the Batista regime by Catholic Youth: the similar but private attitude of nearly all the secular clergy and of many groups of regular clergy (i.e., the Franciscans); the active militancy of Catholic students, leaders in the National Workers' Front (FON); the participation of Catholic professionals in the Civic Resistance movement; and, finally the participation of Catholic Youth in the Alliance of Civic Institutions" ("The Church," 402–3).

27. "The great majority of the predominantly Cuban secular clergy, however, had no hesitation as to where their duty and their sympathies lay. Most of them were at one time or another molested by the *batistianos*; many were arrested and interrogated; several were tortured. At one point despite his earlier collaboration, Manuel Cardinal Arteaga, an ailing, elderly man was struck by the brother of Batista's Chief of Police, who searched the Cardinal's resi-

dence while looking for documents incriminating the rebels. (Having found none, he took $30,000 in diocesan property instead.) The incident was glossed over when Batista's wife called the next day and apologized on her husband's behalf" (Dewart, *Christianity and Revolution*, 104).

28. See Padula, "Fall of the Bourgeoisie," 431–39, for a more detailed study of this phenomenon.

29. See "Catolicismo: La Cruz y el Diablo," 98–100.

30. Ibid., 100.

31. Ibid.

32. Ibid.

33. Crahan lists the criticisms that could be leveled at the churches of this time: "elitism, lack of concern with socioeconomic justice, autocracy, over-preoccupation with financial matters, using charitable gestures to avoid confronting the structural bases of poverty and exploitation, cowardice in the face of political repression and corruption, overdependency of foreign and domestic political and economic elites and failure to assume a prophetic role in a highly inegalitarian society. In addition, the Churches were scorned for racism, pietism, pacifism, triumphalism, enclavism, puritanism, paternalism, individualism and escapism" ("Salvation through Christ or Marx," 170).

34. Cited in "Catolicismo: La Cruz y el Diablo," 100.

35. Delofeu, *Notes of the Cuban Mission*, 15.

36. Ibid.

37. Ibid., 32.

38. Davis, *Sugar Economy*, 53.

39. Ibid., 205.

40. Witness, for example, the tone of Sterling Neblett: "Unlike 10 of the 12 spies whom Moses sent into Canaan, the Methodist explorers unanimously echoed the report of Caleb and Joshua, 'Let us go up at once and possess it, for we are well able to overcome it.' The plan outlined for Bishop Candler called for the immediate occupation of Havana and Matanzas on the north coast, and of Cienfuegos and Santiago de Cuba on the south coast. As soon as it should be 'feasible', the remaining provincial capitals, Pinar del Río, Santa Clara and Camagüey, were to be occupied. Proceeding from these strategic centers the evangelistic responsibility of Methodism would be discharged as opportunity, forces and the guidance of the Spirit might direct" (*Methodism's First Fifty Years*, 16–17).

41. Crahan, "Religious Penetration," 204.

42. Ibid.

43. Crahan notes how missionaries "stressed the advantage of establishing schools in order to influence the 'very best people', that is, the political and economic elite. In this they were successful. As early as 1900 a Methodist school in Havana had enrolled the children of the governor of the province as well as those of a number of leading doctors, lawyers and merchants" (ibid., 219).

44. Neblett, *Methodism's First Fifty Years*, 81.

45. Crahan, "Religious Penetration," 210.

46. Neblett, *Methodism's First Fifty Years*, 170.

47. Ibid., 141–42.

48. Cited in Crahan, "Religious Penetration," 213.

49. Davis, *Sugar Economy*, 78.

50. "Of these perhaps the most influential was Candler College which by the time of the 1959 revolution had an enrollment of close to 1,000 on the elementary and secondary level and 150 on the university level. Perhaps the most substantial role that Candler played was preparing English-speaking functionaries for U.S. businesses and the Cuban government. As early as 1910 Candler in response to a meeting in Havana of prominent bankers and businessmen calling for the establishment of an adequate business school took upon itself the task of filling that need" (Crahan, "Religious Penetration," 220).

51. Davis, *Sugar Economy*, 55.

52. This decline was accounted for by several factors: societal pressure against religion as an appropriate activity for male Cubans; the lack of a church hostel for students in Havana, where there were an estimated 340 Protestant students, and racial tension, for as one respondent to Davis noted: "Our churches do not have rooms or facilities for social and recreational work. The auditorium offers the only available space and our pastors oppose using this for secular purposes. In many churches negro members make difficulty. Our white youth will worship with them, but do not want to mix socially with them" (ibid., 84).

53. Ibid., 13.

54. Crahan, "Protestantism in Cuba," 69.

55. Ibid., 62.

56. Robertson, "Political Role," pt. 1:2.

57. Ibid., 3–4.

58. Robertson notes that, among others, Faustino Pérez was named to the cabinet of President Urrutia, Rev. Raúl Fernández Ceballos became head of the literacy program, Rev. Daniel Alvarez was appointed to a key position in the Department of Social Welfare, and José Naranjo, a Protestant layman, was first appointed governor of Havana province, and later became secretary of the interior in the Urrutia cabinet.

Chapter 3. From Euphoria to Despair, 1959–1960

1. Enrique Pérez Serantes, "Vida Nueva" ("A New Life"), 3 January 1959, in Testé, *Historia Eclesiástica de Cuba*, 5: 540.

2. Ibid., 544.

3. Ibid., 542.

4. Enrique Pérez Serantes, "El justo medio" ("The Just Means"), 29 January 1959, in Testé, *Historia Eclesiástica de Cuba*, 5: 546–47.

5. Ibid., 545.

6. Cited in Robertson, "Political Role," pt. 1: 4–5.

7. Enrique Pérez Serantes, "La Enseñanza Privada" ("On Private Education"), 13 February 1959, in Testé, *Historia Eclesiástica de Cuba*, 5: 548.

8. Ibid.

9. Evelio Diaz, "Al Pueblo de Cuba: Circular del Episcopado Cubano" ("To the People of Cuba: Communiqué of the Cuban Bishops"), 18 February 1959, in Testé, *Historia Eclesiástica de Cuba*, 5: 597.

10. Ibid., 598.

11. Ibid., 599.

12. Evelio Díaz, "La Iglesia Católica y la Nueva Cuba" ("The Catholic Church and the New Cuba"), 31 May 1959, in Testé, *Historia Eclesiástica de Cuba*, 5: 607.

13. Ibid., 608.

14. Alberto Martín Villaverde, "La Reforma Agraria y la Iglesia Católica" (The Agrarian Reform and the Catholic Church"), July 1959, in Testé, *Historia Eclesiástica de Cuba*, 5: 611–12.

15. Enrique Pérez Serantes, "La Reforma Agraria y el Arzobispado de Santiago de Cuba" ("The Agrarian Reform and the Archbishopric of Santiago de Cuba") [1959], in Testé *Historia Eclesiástica de Cuba*, 5: 552.

16. Ibid., 552–53.

17. Dewart, *Christianity and Revolution*, 48.

18. Thomas, *Cuba*, 1223.

19. Ibid., 1243.

20. Ibid., 1229.

21. Ibid., 1269.

22. For a more detailed study of this period, see ibid., 1288–93.

23. C. Alton Robertson claims that Protestants were well represented in Cuban society: "In fact, in January 1959, when Fidel Castro came to power after the flight of Batista, there were more Cubans who were Protestant ministers than Cubans who were Roman Catholic priests; a majority of all the church buildings and chapels on the island were Protestant; and the average attendance at the Protestant churches' Sunday services was approximately the same as the average attendance at Roman Catholic Sunday services. . . . Only 15 to 20 percent of the total Cuban population was active in either Protestant or Roman Catholic congregations. On the other hand, the Protestants of Cuba numbered more than 250,000 in 1959, and were a potentially strong political force. (The Communist party claimed only 20,000 members in 1959)" ("Political Role," pt. 1: 1).

24. Haselden, "Cuba's Revolution," 1438.

25. Robertson, "Political Role," pt. 1: 5.

26. Thomas, *Cuba*, 1267.

27. Leslie Dewart noted that both Fidel Castro and Osvaldo Dorticós attended the Congress but that the conservative media "practically suppressed" news of their attendance. Of the fifty-two pictures of the conference in the *Diario de La Marina*, for instance, not one showed Castro or any government official (*Christianity and Revolution*, 150).

During the Congreso, although liberal Msgr. Díaz praised the government claiming that "never has a [Cuban] government during the time we have been a prelate expended as many facilities to the Church," the dominant note was struck by Villanueva professor José Ignacio Lasaga: "Social justice, yes; Communism, no" (Dewart, *Christianity and Revolution*, 150).

28. Spanish ambassador Juan Pablo de Lojendio, Marqués de Vellisca, a strong conservative, had apparently pressured the Spanish clergy to oppose the revolutionary government and, after a bitter confrontation with Fidel Castro, was ordered out of Cuba. For further information, see ibid., 155–56, or Padula, "Fall of the Bourgeoisie, " 462–63.

29. Enrique Pérez Serantes, "Por Dios y Por Cuba" ("For God and for Cuba"), [1959], in Testé, *Historia Eclesiástica de Cuba*, 5: 562. Quotations from this letter in the text following are cited by page numbers in parentheses.

30. See Dewart, *Christianity and Revolution*, 158–59, and Claude Julien, *La Révolution Cubaine* (Paris: Julliard, 1961), 190–91.

31. "Circular Colectiva del Episcopado Cubano" ("Collective Communiqué of the Cuban Bishops"), 7 August 1960, in Testé, *Historia Eclesiástica de Cuba*, 5: 602.

32. Ibid.

33. See chapter 4, note 34, for the text of Fidel Castro's condemnation.

34. Enrique Pérez Serantess, "Ni traidores ni parias" ("Neither Traitors nor Pariahs"), 24 September 1960, in Testé, *Historia Eclesiástica de Cuba*, 5: 571.

35. Ibid.

36. See "Roma o Moscú" ("Rome or Moscow"), November 1960, in Testé, *Historia Eclesiástica de Cuba*, 5: 576.

37. Ibid., 572. Pérez Serantes developed this point, noting: "Communism is a seemingly powerful resource for many people who are bitter at life, and out of touch with society, and who often possess very little spiritual steadiness. The same is true for many people lacking in caution, and laden with illusions which fit easily into brains that are lacking in substantial values" (572).

38. Ibid., 573, 574. The bishop's praise was specific: "They say that the reason why communism hasn't lulled the entire world to sleep is because of the generosity of the American people who in the last 15 years have contributed the fantastic amount of 365,000 million dollars . . . in order to obtain the security of the world, and to stop the military advance of communism" (574).

39. "Carta Abierta del Episcopado Cubano al Primer Ministro" ("Open letter of the Cuban Episcopacy to the Prime Minister"), 4 December 1960, in Testé, *Historia Eclesiástica de Cuba*, 5: 605, 606.

40. Cited in Dewart, *Christianity and Revolution*, 161–62.

41. Padula, "Fall of the Bourgeoisie," 497.

42. In his 6 December 1969 pastoral letter, "La Voz de la Iglesia" ("The Voice of the Church"), Archbishop Pérez Serantes quotes from two exceptional pastorals of 1933, "Problemas del Momento" ("Problems of the Moment"), 23 October 1933, and "El Problema Obrero" ("The Problem for Workers"), 20 August 1933, to show that the church did have a social conscience (in Testé, *Historia Eclesiástica de Cuba*, 5: 577–82). It is only fair to say that these hardly represented the official church position. When the church did begin to pursue such an approach in the 1950s, its credibility rose. "The tragedy of the Cuban Church was that its renaissance came a decade too late, the revolution a decade too soon. Had the renaissance come earlier—and more vigorously—the revolution might have had to contend with a more socially conscious, active and pop-

ular Church, a Church more capable of defining—and defending—its interests. Had the revolution come later, it might have found a Church whose violent antagonism towards socialism had mellowed under the influence of Pope John XXIII and the Marxist-Christian dialogue of the 1960s" (Padula, "Fall of the Bourgeoisie," 496–97).

43. "Vivamos en Paz" ("Let Us Live in Peace"), in Testé, *Historia Eclesiástica de Cuba*, 5: 583.

44. Thomas, *Cuba*, 1211. Thomas also analyzes the rise of communist influence in Cuba at this time (1234–54).

45. Cited by Padula, "Fall of the Bourgeoisie," 457.

Chapter 4. Confrontation, 1961

1. Thomas, *Cuba*, 1316. In a later work, on the revolutionary period, Hugh Thomas compared Soviet and North American aid: "Soviet and other Communist *bloc* aid amounted to $M570 in 1961–62, or $40 a head; in comparison, U.S. aid to the rest of Latin America attained only about $2 a head" (*The Cuban Revolution* [New York: Harper and Row, 1977], 596–97).

2. For a discussion of Cuba's dependence on the U.S. market, see the recent excellent study by Medea Benjamin, Joseph Collins, and Michael Scott, *No Free Lunch: Food and Revolution in Cuba Today* (San Francisco: Food First Books, 1984), 11–13. U.S. domination of the Cuban market reached ludicrous proportions: "An exporter of raw sugar, Cuba imported candy. Cuba exported tomatoes but imported virtually all its tomato paste. Cuba exported fresh fruit and imported canned fruit, exported rawhide but imported shoes. It produced vast quantities of tobacco but imported cigarettes" (13).

3. Thomas, *Cuba*, 1348–49.

4. According to "El Latifundio del la Muerte," certain parts of the cemetery cost from 200 to 500 pesos per square meter (*Bohemia*, año 53, 1 [1 January 1961]: 70).

5. *Bohemia*, año 53, 12 (19 March 1961): 129.

6. Cited in Fernández, *Religión y revolución*, 106.

7. Ibid., 108.

8. Hageman and Wheaton, eds., *Religion in Cuba Today*, 67.

9. Enrique López Oliva, "La educación cristiana en Cuba: ¿un tema polémico?" (unpublished report to *Noticias Aliadas*, 1984), 3. Manuel Fernández provides different figures, but the thrust of his analysis is the same: "The superiors of the religious orders then opted to leave Cuba. Of the 723 priests who were there in 1960, 483 belonged to religious orders, and a large proportion of them were involved in teaching. There were also 2,255 nuns, most of whom were teachers." The former Cuban Catholic leader, citing the Anuario Pontificio de 1960, claims that there were in fact 339 Catholic schools, with an enrollment of 65,519 students (*Religión y revolución*, 111–12, 18).

10. "Primero de Mayo en la Revolución Cubana," *Bohemia*, año 53, 19 (7 May 1961): 67.

11. Cited in Fernández, *Religión y revolución*, 109–10.

12. "They will say, of course, that this 'heathen' government is opposed to religious education. . . . No señor! Can they give religious instruction? Yes, those priests who don't get involved in counterrevolutionary campaigns can give religious instruction in their churches—because religion is one thing, and politics is something else" (ibid., 110).

13. Alfred Padula has described the scene shortly after the May Day speech: "The great exodus began. Within a few days, some three hundred nuns and priests were escorted aboard the steamer *Covadonga*, bound for Spain. A month later, 109 Christian Brothers left by air for Miami" (*Fall of the Bourgeoisie*, 493).

14. Walfredo Piñera Corrales, "La Iglesia Católica en la Revolución (Borrador)," 16.

15. Pérez Serantes, 4 March 1961, in Testé, *Historia Eclesiástica de Cuba*, 5:625.

16. Eduardo Boza Masvidal, *Voz en el destierro, por el obispo expulsado Boza Masvidal*, ed. Revista Ideal (Miami: Revista Ideal, 1976), 59.

17. Dewart, *Christianity and Revolution*, 170.

18. Cited in "Acepto la revolución," *Bohemia*, año 53, 17 (23 April 1961): 95.

19. Cited in "Iglesia: De espaldas al pueblo," *Bohemia*, año 53, 21 (21 May 1961): 59. Father Biaín warned that "the Church was in grave danger of repeating before the socialist revolution the false posture it had assumed before the pseudo-liberal epic feats ["la gesta demoliberal"] of the late nineteenth century, since it was yet again persisting in showing itself supporting privilege, and opposed to the people" (59).

20. Cited in "Ante la prensa: Cristo y la revolución," *Bohemia*, año 53, 9 (26 February 1961) 66.

21. Fernández, *Religión y revolución*, 113.

22. "El alto clero no descansa en su actividad por difundir y confundir al pueblo cubano," *Bohemia*, año 53, 38 (17 September 1961): 68.

23. These clergy included eighty-six Spaniards, thirty-three Cubans, and twelve from a variety of countries, mainly Canada and France (Fernández, *Religión y revolución*, 115.

24. "The Church in Cuba," *Newsweek*, 9 October 1961, 94.

25. Prior to this period (throughout 1959 and 1960), while numerous references appeared to the "thugs in priest's clothes" ("esbirros en sotana") and "Falangist clergy," a remarkably large number of articles presented a positive view of the church.

26. See José Luis Massó, "Una obra humana en favor de los desamparados," *Bohemia*, año 53, 12 (20 March 1962): 76–78.

27. See Ricardo Solano, "Operación Bautizo Colectivo," 56–57, and the page 65 photograph in *Bohemia* (21 May 1961) of Father Sardiñas baptizing the child of some campesinos, with Fidel Castro's secretary and confidante, Celia Sánchez, in attendance as godmother.

28. See Dora Alonso, "¡Yo seré miliciano!" 56.

29. "Ahora alfabetizan," *Bohemia*, año 53, 20 (14 May 1961): 60.

30. The 17 September 1961 issue of *Bohemia* provided a symbolic overview of this situation for, in addition to a critical cartoon of the *cura falangista* say-

ing "Praying novenas to God and spraying bullets with our guns!" (70), it offered two positive treatments of church activities: see Solano, "Operación Bautizo Colectivo," 14–15, and "Las fiestas de la Caridad y la Virgen de Regla en la tradición popular," 56–57.

31. Hageman and Wheaton, eds., *Religion in Cuba Today*, 67.

32. Rev. Enrique Méndez, S.D.B., "Fidel Castro, 'Fiel amigo,' " *Diario de la Marina*, 1 February 1959, 5B (emphasis in original).

33. Fernández, *Religión y revolución*, 41.

34. Ibid., 82.

35. See "Fidel en tres discursos," *Bohemia*, año 52, 52 (25 December 1960): 83.

36. See "¡Eso sí es ser cristiano!," *Bohemia*, año 52, 51 (18 December 1960): 71.

37. "Did [the Cuban hierarchy] ever issue a pastoral against graft? Did any of you ever read a pastoral defending the sugar-plantation peasants? Or demanding schools for the children of peasants? Or condemning the murder of labor leaders and students? Or protesting against the [exorbitant] prices [charged by the] electric and telephone companies? Did they ever protest against politicking? Against profiteering in food? Against high rents? Against smuggling?

"They say their differences with us are ideological. [The real difference] is the difference between those who are allied with those things and those who are the enemy of those things. Not a single sermon, not a single pastoral defending the people, either recently or during the war of independence" (Dewart, *Christianity and Revolution*, 163).

38. Fernández, *Religión y revolución*, 104.

39. Rodolfo Riesgo, "Por culpa de los fariseos," *La Quincena*, año 7, 2 (31 March 1961): 47.

40. Dewart, *Christianity and Revolution*, 168.

41. Riesgo, "Acusaciones concretas," 6.

42. Aldo J. Büntig, "The Church in Cuba: Toward a New Frontier," in Hageman and Wheaton, eds., *Religion in Cuba Today*, 111.

Chapter 5. "De profundis . . . ," 1962–1969

1. Domínguez, "Cuban Catholics and Castro," 25.

2. Gendler, "Cuba and Religion," 1015.

3. See, for example, "Frustran al precio de sus vidas el secuestro de una semana," *Bohemia*, año 58, 13 (1 April 1966): 70–71, and the photo essay by Vicente Cubillas, "El fatídico vuelo 905," *Bohemia*, año 58, 14 (8 April 1966): 58–69.

4. For an opposing view of the Loredo affair, see Testé, *Historia Eclesiástica de Cuba*, 4: 68–73. Testé maintains that Father Loredo (termed the "Billy Graham cubano") was found guilty because of false evidence tendered at the trial. Following a similar line of argument is Clark, *Religious Repression in Cuba*, 23–26.

5. Ciro Pérez, "Capturado el asesino," *Bohemia,* año 58, 15 (15 April 1966): 68.

6. Angell, "Salomón Bolo Hidalgo," 80–81, 90; Salomón Bolo Hidalgo, "¡Viva Cuba!" *Bohemia,* año 54, 27 (6 July 1962): 81, 90.

7. Bayo, "Asia volcánica," 106–7, 111.

8. For example, Salvador Bueno, "Félix Varela, primer intelectual separatista," *Bohemia,* año 55, 9 (1 March 1963): 27–29, 82.

9. "Vaticano: 'Paz en la tierra,' " *Bohemia,* año 55, 16 (19 April 1963): 88–89: "Después de Juan XXIII la incógnita de Roma: Reforma o tradición?," *Bohemia,* año 55, 23 (27 June 1963): 60–62; "Vaticano: 'Papa Habemus,' " *Bohemia,* año 55, 26 (28 June 1963,): 89–90.

10. That criticism of the church continued is apparent in other *Bohemia* articles of this period, such as that by Luis Felipe Angell, "Nueva forma de penetración yanqui: Los padres Maryknoll," *Bohemia,* año 54, 30 (27 July 1962): 83.

11. "We explain religion as a product of the past, of ignorance and of man's impotence before nature. At the present moment, it is supported by the interest of the exploiting classes in possessing an ideological instrument to control the masses and make them submissive, and also by the inability of the individual to dominate the social forces which oppress him.

"We know that, once the causes for the original dependency have disappeared (as well as the forces and rationale which continue to support it), religion will disappear.

"Those are the basic criteria of Marxism-Leninism, the doctrine of our Party, on religion" (*Periódico 'Hoy': Aclaraciones* [Havana: Editorial Política, 1969], 2: 333).

12. Ibid., 331.

13. Anne Power, "The Church in Cuba." *Commonweal* 89, no. 22 (7 March 1969): 704.

14. Walfredo Piñera Corrales, "La Iglesia Católica en la Revolución (Borrador)" (manuscript, Havana, 1979), 40.

15. Frederick C. Turner, *Catholicism and Political Development in Latin America* (Chapel Hill: University of North Carolina Press, 1971), 156.

16. Fernández, *Religión y revolución,* 121–22.

17. Testé, for instance, cites one piece of canon law that automatically excommunicates "all who usurp or retain, personally or indirectly, the property or rights of the Church" (*Historia Eclesiástica de Cuba,* 5: 387).

18. The "most abject servilism" quotation in the subtitle, for instance, comes from ibid., 4: 695. See also his more extensive (and extremely harsh) treatment of the nuncio in 5: 493–500.

19. Cited in the excellent study by the former Acción Católica executive, Mateo Jover Marimón, "The Church," 405.

20. John Horgan, "An Irishman: What I Saw in Cuba," LADOC "Keyhole" Series, *Cuba* (Washington: LADOC, n.d.), 5.

21. Cardenal, *In Cuba,* 231.

22. Testé, *Historia Eclesiástica de Cuba,* 5: 493.

23. "It has been necessary for Msgr. Oddi, at present the Nuncio in Brussels, to come on a special mission of the Holy See. He was endowed with a particular authority to prevent everybody from leaving. Of more than three thousand religious in the country, at least 2,500 have left," François Houtart reported after interviewing Zacchi (Fernández, *Religión y revolución*, 121).

24. Ibid., 122.

25. Cited in Edward L. Cleary, O.P., *Crisis and Change: The Church in Latin America Today* (Maryknoll, NY: Orbis, 1985), 13–14.

26. Testé, *Historia Eclesiástica de Cuba*, 5: 494.

27. Fernández, *Religión y revolución*, 126.

28. Testé, *Historia Eclesiástica de Cuba*, 5: 495.

29. Ibid., 496.

30. "Well, here there is one party, the communist party, and its members undertake an important function in the concrete tasks of social development. I have no objection to a Catholic adopting Marxist economic theory and applying it to his conduct as a member of that revolutionary process" (ibid.).

31. Swaren, "Church in Today's Cuba," 212.

32. Fernández, *Religión y revolución*, 125.

33. Testé, *Historia Eclesiástica de Cuba*, 5: 496.

34. Fernández, *Religión y revolución*, 126.

35. Fidel Castro said in 1961, for instance, that Cuba's Catholic schools were staffed by "a scourge of louts dressed up in priest's vestments as well as mercenary teachers" and that "imperialism and the upper levels of the hierarchy were one and the same thing" (ibid., 104).

36. See "'En su lucha contra el imperialismo los pueblos de América tendrán la mayor solidaridad mundial'—Fidel," *Bohemia*, año 54, 4 (28 January 1962): 32.

37. Ibid., 223, 330.

38. Aldo J. Büntig, "An Argentinian: What I Saw in Cuba," LADOC "Keyhole" Series, *Cuba* (Washington: LADOC, n.d.), 34.

39. Ibid., 33–34.

40. Cardenal, *In Cuba*, 187.

41. Fernández, *Religión y revolución*, 128.

42. Walfredo Piñera Corales, "La Iglesia Católica en la Revolución (Borrador)" (manuscript, Havana, 1979), 39.

43. MacKay, "Cuba Revisited," 201; Gendler, "Cuba and Religion," 1013.

44. See, for example, J. Lloyd Mecham, (short title), 307; a note in *The Christian Century* of 27 June 1961, 801; and MacKay, "Cuba Revisited," 200–203.

45. Raúl Gómez Treto, "Algunas reflexiones sobre el III Congreso Mundial para el Apostolado de los Laicos," *Almanque de la Caridad: Directorio Oficial de las Diócesis de Cuba, (Año de 1968)* (La Habana: Iglesia de la Merced, 1968), 9.

46. See the article of the same title in *Bohemia*, año 51, 11 (15 March 1959): 64, 97.

Chapter 6. Emerging from the Catacombs, 1969–1978

1. Salvador Díaz Versón, He also called the letter "an adulteration of the historical truth of the horrifying Cuba drama" (Testé, *Historia Eclesiástica de Cuba*, 5: 460).

2. José R. Andreu, in an article significantly entitled "Obispos amarillos y pastorales apóstatas" ("Yellow Bishops and Apostate Pastorals"), wrote: "The pastoral letter of the bishops is a document which possesses the dialectical communist style. One has to read it, not as a product of Church dignitaries, but rather as literature which uses sophism in order to arrive, by means of respectable assumptions, at conclusions which lie.

"The prose smells more of soviet than of the sacristy" (ibid., 461).

3. Ibid., 489.

4. See the observations of Father Lucien de Wulf (ibid., 493). A well-placed church source advised me that Catholic reaction was more complex. Reactions ranged, he claims, from violent rejection to enthusiastic acceptance, although the general position was critical of the pastoral.

5. Fernández, *Religión y revolución*, 129; see also 119–30 for an extended discussion.

6. Domínguez, "Cuban Catholics and Castro," 24.

7. From an English translation of the April 1969 letter, "Cuban Bishops Call for End to Trade Blockade," in Hageman and Wheaton, eds., *Religion in Cuba Today*, 288–94. Quotations from this letter in the text immediately following are cited by page numbers.

8. "On Contemporary Atheism," ibid., 298–308. Quotations from this letter in the text immediately following are cited by page numbers.

9. Because of the importance of the visit to Chile (and the basic repetition of these elements in his speech to Jamaican clergy six years later), I have referred only to the first (and more developed) event. For a copy of Castro's Jamaican address and a subsequent question period, see Fidel Castro, "Christianity and the Revolution," *New Blackfriars*, 59, no. 695 (April 1978): 152–65. For comparison see Frei Betto's interviews of Castro, *Fidel y la religión*.

10. See Instituto Histórico Centroamericano, ed., *Fidel Castro y los cristianos revolucionario* (Managua: Instituto Histórico Centroamericano, n.d.), 10. Quotations from this source in the text immediately following are cited there by page numbers.

11. See the complete text of Article 54 in Alfonso, ed., *Acerca de la religión*, 3. Quotations from this source in the text immediately following are cited there by page numbers.

12. Writing in the 1970s, Nicaraguan priest (and minister of culture) Ernesto Cardenal quotes a young Cuban Catholic: "The Cuban Church is behind the times? . . . Well, you probably know this because you come from outside. We didn't know that we were behind the times" (*In Cuba*, 146). The Nicaraguan passed equally harsh judgment on officials of the Ministry of Foreign Affairs with whom he met, noting that they "did not know about the changes in the post-Council Church, and they were much surprised when I told them about

the transformations that Catholicism had undergone in its theology, morals, Biblical interpretation, liturgy" (152–53).

13. Domínguez, "Cuban Catholics and Castro," 26.

14. Cardenal, *In Cuba*, 250.

15. Montero Rodríguez, *Cristianos*, 54.

16. Peerman, "Church-hopping in Havana," 1435.

17. Andrade, "Protestant Pastors," 224.

18. Crahan, "Protestanism in Cuba," 65.

19. Jan Knippers Black, *Area Handbook for Cuba* (Washington: U.S. Government Printing Office, 1976), 132.

20. Robert McAfee Brown, "Living Joyfully in the Midst of the Revolution," *Cuba Review* 9, no. 1 (February 1979): 10.

21. Ibid., 12.

22. Kirkpatrick, "Cuban Church at Puebla," 19.

23. "Cuban Catholic Reflections," *Cuba Review* 9, no. 1 (February 1979): 22.

24. "Intervención de Francisco Oves," 6, 7.

25. "We have to confess with total honesty, with profound historical humility, human and evangelical, that the Christian faith has been an object of ideological manipulation. However, we have been able to gradually discern this manipulation, and in this process one of the elements which have helped us is the contribution of Marxist social sciences" (ibid., 8).

26. Ibid., 7.

27. "Today, our approximately 200 priests devote themselves almost entirely to parish affairs, celebrating Masses and dispensing the sacraments. Their own background, plus the sociological attitudes of their parishioners, cast them in the role of 'consolers.' Standing apart from the social and economic construction of the new society they see no way of allaying the pessimism and sectarianism around them. Infected by the mood of their people, they radiate it further, thus actually preventing the process of maturation in faith that the circumstances require from the Church." See "Can One Still Be a Christian in Cuba?" LADOC 2, no. 50 (Summer 1974): 17.

28. Ibid., 18.

29. Cited in Montero Rodríguez, *Cristianos*, 300.

Chapter 7. The Beginnings of Dialogue, 1979–1987

1. "Cuba: Church Demands 'More Space,' " 3.

2. "Discurso inaugural del ENEC pronunciado por Mons. Adolfo Rodríguez," Encuentro Nacional Eclesial Cubano, *Documento Final* (Havana: mimeo, 1986), 7. In the document proper, church delegates further defined the need for dialogue, calling for "a church that is prepared for dialogue with the civil authorities, and which hopes to overcome the historical obstacles between us" (214).

3. This family reunification program was part of a rare period of constructive dialogue between Cuba and the United States. Speculation has it that, had Carter been reelected, relations between the countries might have normalized.

4. "Circular de la Conferencia Episcopal Cubana sobre las Relaciones con la Comunidad Cubana Residente Fuera de Nuestro País," (Havana, 27 September 1979, mimeographed), 2. Quotations from this letter in the text immediately following are cited by page numbers.

5. "Our specific situation as a small country which should make every effort in order to obtain its full development also results in the need for material limitations, while we struggle with tenacity to obtain that greatly desired well-being shared by all and to which, as Christians, we should aspire. But there are moments in the historical process which impose upon us the duty of assuming an austere life. Specifically, with regard to the consumption of material goods, Christians should feel capable of fulfilling the biblical command to 'dominate the land' (Gen. 1, 28) so that it will produce goods for mankind, while at the same time they should not ask God the Father for 'riches' (2 Cr. 1, 11), but rather 'our daily bread' (Mat. 6, 11). All this is summarized in the message of the Beatitudes: Blessed are the poor in spirit, because the Kingdom of Heaven is theirs' (Mat. 5, 3)" (ibid., 6).

6. It would be appropriate to compare the percentage of practicing Catholics among the marielitos, with that of earlier "freedom flotillas." One would suspect that a small fraction of Cuba's Catholics left in 1980 compared to the percentage that left twenty years earlier.

7. Secretariado de Jóvenes, Diócesis de Camagüey, open letter to Cuban Catholics (no formal title given) (mimeographed, 9 May 1980).

8. Comité Permanente de la Conferencia de los Obispos de Cuba, "Nota de Prensa sobre la Fabricación de la Bomba de Neutrones" (Havana: mimeographed, 20 August 1981).

9. See Carlos Manuel de Céspedes's presentation to the "Encuentro ecuménico de solidaridad con el pueblo cubano ante la amenaza de agresión por parte de EE.UU." (Havana: mimeographed, 14 November 1985), 3.

10. "Press Conference Statement by Bishop James Malone" (Havana: mimeographed, 25 January 1986), 3, 5.

11. "Cuban Bishops Visit United States," 7.

12. "Castro Meets the Bishops," 5.

13. "Cuba: Church Demands 'More Space,' " 3.

14. Oliva, "Interview with Ortega Alamino," 12.

15. See the "Resoluciones sobre la política en relación con la religión, la Iglesia y los creyentes," in Alfonso, ed., *Acerca de la Religión,* 46.

16. Elice Higginbotham, "Religion in the Cuban news," *Cubatimes,* November–December 1983, 8–9.

17. A random sampling of these articles includes: Javier Navarro, "Christians in the Revolution," *Síntesis Informativa* no. 35 (August 1981): 23–27; Susana Lee, "Cuban Christians Speak Out Against U.S. Aggressions, Threats and Interventions Against Cuba, Central America and Caribbean," *Granma Weekly Review,* 22 November 1981, 3; Enrique López Oliva, "The Progressive Christian Movement: A Revolutionary Force," *Granma Weekly Review,* 24 October 1982, 7.; Jorge Timossi, "Mexican Bishop Méndez Arceo: A Champion of the Poor and Oppressed," *Granma Weekly Review,* 14 November 1982, 3; Luis M. Arce, "Cuban Christians at Work in Kampuchea," *Granma Weekly*

Review, 20 February 1983, 7; José Gabriel Gumá, "Sergio Méndez Arceo in Cuba: 40-Minute Conversation with a Bishop Who Defends the Poor and the Dispossessed," *Granma Weekly Review*, 27 February 1983, 9; Enrique López Oliva, "¡Unámonos a favor de la Paz!" *Paz y soberanía* 3 (1983): 24–31; Milagros Oliva, "Cuban Christians Take Part in Voluntary Labor in Agriculture: 'Ours is a modest contribution, but we can cooperate in the construction of socialism,'" *Granma Weekly Review*, 6 March 1983, 7; Jean Stubbs, "British Religious Delegation Visits Cuba: A Church Concerned with This World," *Granma Weekly Review*, 13 March 1983, 4; Milagros Oliva, "'We Christians and the Cuban Revolution have many things in common to struggle for together'—Reverend Raúl Fernández Ceballos," *Granma Weekly Review*, 3 April 1983, 9; Raúl Gómez Treto, "Los cristianos y la paz," *Paz y Soberanía* 11 (1983), 7–13; Anon., "Carlos Rafael Rodríguez Meets with over 100 Theologians and Social Scientists," *Granma Weekly Review*, 11 December 1983, 5; Anon., "U.S. Religious Groups Ready to Organize Human Shield Between Honduras and Nicaragua to Prevent Attack on Sandino's Homeland," *Granma Weekly Review*, 11 December 1983, 1; Mirta Balea, "2nd International Meeting of Theologians and Social Scientists Held in Cuba," *Granma Weekly Review*, 18 December 1983, 5; Anon., "Christians from 30 Countries Discuss Options of the People's Liberation Struggle and the Need for Social Change," *Granma Weekly Review*, 1 April 1984, 5; Milagros Oliva, "Valoran delegados de Norteamérica y el Caribe la integración de cristianos cubanos en la construcción de la nueva sociedad," *Granma Resumen Semanal*, 18 March 1986, 5; H.C. Moya, "The Salvadoran People's Church: Priests with the People in Arms," *Granma Weekly Review*, 1 January 1984, 10; Milagros Oliva, "Interview with Monsignor Jaime Lucas Ortega Alamino, Archbishop of Havana; More and More Catholics are becoming involved in efforts, struggles and day-to-day activities of people as a whole," *Granma Weekly Review*, 27 May 1984, 12; Mirta Balea, "Cristiano y revolucionario: Entrevista con Monseñor Sergio Méndez Arceo," *Prisma* 3 (1984): 23–24; Alberto Rabilotta, "Iglesias solidarias: Denuncian política norteamericana en Centroamérica," *Prisma* 138 (February 1984): 7–8; Anon., "Interview with Miami-based Priest Felipe Estévez: The Church-State Dialogue Is More Promising Now than Ever Before," *Granma Weekly Review*, 23 March 1986, 4; Arturo Chang (Ain), "*Fidel y la religión*: 'Va a fortalecer la unidad y la lucha'—Asegura el presidente de la Iglesia Presbiteriana Reformada de Cuba," *Bohemia*, año 78, no. 2 (10 January 1986): 39–40; Reinaldo Peñalver Moral and Susana Tesoro, "Encuentro Eclesial: Concluyó con una Misa en la Catedral de La Habana," *Bohemia*, año 78, no. 9 (28 February 1986): 48–49; Ana María Radaelli, "Conversación con Frei Betto," *Cuba Internacional*, año 18, no. 197 (April 1986): 26–29; Javier Rodríguez, "El Cardenal Evaristo Arns," *Prisma*, año 12, no. 164 (April 1986): 7; Ana María Ruiz, "Congreso eclesiástico: el deseo de renovar," *Prisma*, año 12, no. 164 (April 1986): 11–12; Anon., "Cuban Bishops Visit United States Invited by U.S. Episcopate," and "Declaration by Cuban Bishops on the Foreign Debt and the New International Economic Order," *Granma Weekly Review*, 27 October 1985, 7; Milagros Oliva, "President Fidel Castro's Second Meeting with Cuban Bishops 'Warm and Positive,'" *Granma Weekly Review*,

24 November 1985, 3; Félix Pito Astudillo, " 'Historic' Is how Fidel's Meeting with Ecumenical Council and Protestant Dignitaries Described," *Granma Weekly Review,* 24 November 1985, 3; Anon., "U.S. Religious Delegation Deplores Its Country's Anti-Cuba Policy," *Granma Weekly Review,* 24 November 1985, 3; Mireya Castañeda, "U.S. Council of Churches Advocates Normalization of Cuba-United States Relations," *Granma Weekly Review,* 5 May 1986; Milagros Oliva "'The Most Beautiful Gift God Has Given Me Is My Meeting With President Fidel Castro', Nobel Laureate Mother Teresa of Calcutta Said at the End of a Brief Visit to Cuba," *Granma Weekly Review,* 20 July 1986, 1; Anon., "There Are Many Similarities Between the Black Church and the Cuban Church," *Granma Weekly Review,* (20 July 1986), 9; Milagros Oliva, "U.S. and Caribbean Christians Condemn Reagan's Central American Policy," *Granma Weekly Review,* 29 July 1986, 9; Milagros Oliva, "Donation of Bibles to Cuban Catholic Church," *Granma Weekly Review,* 28 September 1986, 6; Milagros Oliva and Mireya Castañeda, "Monsignor James Malone, President of U.S. Bishops Conference, Arrives in Havana," *Granma Weekly Review,* 21 January 1985, 1; Anon., "Mexican Bishop Awarded Cuban Order of Solidarity," *Granma Weekly Review,* 12 January 1987, 1; Anon., "22nd Anniversary of Father Sardiñas' Death," *Granma Weekly Review,* 18 January 1987, 4; Milagros Oliva, "Dr. Emilio Castro, Secretary-General of the World Council of Churches Arrives in Cuba," *Granma Weekly Review,* 30 August 1987, 9; Milagros Oliva, "Cuban and Foreign Religious People Honor Frank País," *Granma Weekly Review,* 6 September 1987, 3; Milagros Oliva, "Latin American and Caribbean Religious People Against U.S. Ideological Blockade in Region," *Granma Weekly Review,* 6 September 1987, 9; Anon., "Cuban Archbishop Confirms Authenticity of Virgin of El Cobre," *Granma Weekly Review,* 13 September 1987, 1; "Church-State Understanding in Cuba," *Granma Weekly Review,* 20 September 1987, 3; Enrique Capablanca, "The Parish Church in Sancti Spíritus Restored," *Granma Weekly Review,* 15 November 1987, 4; Senén Conejeros A., "Cardinal Silva Henríquez, Human Rights Defender," *Granma Weekly Review,* 6 December 1987, 2; Anon., "Freedom of Worship in Cuba, Say Religious People," *Granma Weekly Review,* 6 December 1987, 3; Gregorio Selser, "Liberation Theology Under Attack," *Granma Weekly Review,* 6 December 1987, 11; Gladys Blanco, "The Mystifying Bayamo Altarpiece," *Granma Weekly Review,* 27 December 1987, 2; Marisol Marín, "Two Nuns in El Salvador Recount Nightmare," *Granma Weekly Review,* 17 January 1988, 11; Emilio Surí Quesada, "The King of Palmira," *Granma Weekly Review,* 24 January 1988, 3; Camilo Egaña Villamil, "Payment of the Foreign Debt Is Ethically Unjustifiable Just as the Present International Economic Order Is," *Granma Weekly Review,* 31 January 1988, 3; Gladys Blanco, "Churches and Worshipers in Cuba," *Granma Weekly Review,* 14 February 1988, 12; Milagros Oliva, "Traditions Born Anew," *Granma Weekly Review,* 21 February 1988; Milagros Oliva, "European Participation in Central American Peace Process Encouraged: Statements in Havana by Reverend Oscar Boliodi, Latin American Director of the National Council of Churches of the United States," *Granma Weekly Review,* 28 February 1988, 3; Anon., "4th Congress of Orisha Tradition and Culture Scheduled to Take

Place in Havana," *Granma Weekly Review,* 28 February 1988, 1; Milagros
Oliva, "'The Foreign Debt Weighs Down the Lives of Peoples,' Says Father
Jean-Paul Marsaud, General Superior of the Sons of Charity Institute During
the Order's Meeting in Havana," *Granma Weekly Review,* 28 February 1988,
3; Milagros Oliva, "Foreign Debt Is Immoral and Anti-Christian: War Only Alternative to Esquipulas II, Say Members of Latin American Council of
Churches at Havana Meeting," *Granma Weekly Review,* 28 February 1988, 1;
Anon., "Monsignor Ortega Elected President of the Cuban Bishops Conference," *Granma Weekly Review,* 6 March 1988, 5; Anon., "Mass in Commemoration of Father Varela's Death," *Granma Weekly Review,* 6 March 1988, 5;
Gladys Blanco, "100 Years of Charity," *Granma Weekly Review,* 6 March
1988, 2; Luis Manuel Arce, "The Churches Are Always Open in Cuba: Inter-
view with Vice-President of Cuban Ecumenical Council, in Montevideo for
Synod of Vaudois Church and for Lecture Series," *Granma Weekly Review,* 13
March 1988, 3; Anon., "President Fidel Castro's Activities: Meeting with
Hans Peter Kolvenbach," *Granma Weekly Review,* 27 March 1988, 4.

18. "Interview with Miami-based priest Felipe Estévez," 4.

19. "Church Demands 'More Space,'" 3.

20. "Declaration by Cuban Bishops," 7. The position of the Cuban bishops
was similar to that of Fidel Castro: "Having accepted the invitation, we feel
that while the foreign debt is a financial, technical and political problem to
be handled by the experts, there is however a moral, ethical and humane side
to which the Church cannot remain and in fact never has remained indifferent.
Since this foreign debt problem is a moral responsibility, the Church cannot
remain neutral.

"The foreign debt is a complex problem caused by economic dependence:
by international aid given in the form of loans and by foreign investments.
All aid that creates dependency does not liberate; it oppresses and humiliates,
offends and impoverishes" (7).

21. "Bishops Support Debt Meeting," 5.

22. "Cuban Bishops Visit United States," 7.

23. Oliva, "Castro's Second Meeting." 3. Elsewhere it was reported that
these meetings would be held "every four or six months" ("Castro Meets the
Bishops," 5).

24. Pita Astudillo, "'Historic' Meeting." 3.

25. "Castro Meets the Bishops," 5.

26. Ibid.

27. "Castro Alters Course," 7.

28. Suárez, "Al Regresar de Cuba," 70.

29. "Fidel Dialogues with Nicaraguan Christians," *Lucha* 5, no. 1 (1980?):
31–32.

30. In an interview in January 1985, Fidel Castro talked about the difference
in the role of the church in Cuba and in Nicaragua and tendered a fascinating
offer to the Nicaraguan Episcopal Conference: "With regard to the Church, we
have no problems, and of course we don't want to have any. Besides, though,
the Church's influence was never as great in Cuba as it was in Nicaragua. Do

you know what I've said to Msgr. Vega during the inauguration of Daniel Ortega? I've invited him to visit us. And I've been in favor of suggesting that, if the Sandinista government gives the Church some land, we'll help to construct a new cathedral in Managua—since the old one was destroyed by the earthquake. If it's necessary, we'll bring some microbrigades of volunteers to build it." See Juan Luis Cebrián, "'América Latina está en una situación explosiva,'" *El País* (Internacional), 21 January 1985, 6.

31. Ostling, "Castro Looks at Christianity," 72.

32. Castro, *Fidel y la religión*, 90. Quotations from this work in the text and notes immediately following are cited by page numbers.

33. "Together with the mass were the prayers. For me they didn't have a positive effect—that's the best I can say about all this repeating a prayer a hundred times, with people mechanically repeating Hail Marys and Our Fathers. How many I must have said in my life, every year! But did I ever stop and think about what that prayer really meant? . . . it seems to me that all of these weren't really prayers: perhaps an exercise for the vocal chords, or the voice, or whatever, an exercise in patience if you like, but it isn't a prayer" (149).

34. "These problems that existed [with the Catholic Church], we never had them with the Protestant Churches, and our relations with these institutions have always been, and continue to be, excellent" (245–46).

35. Estimates of the annual attendance at the procession to San Lázaro's shrine on the outskirts of Havana vary between 50,000 and 150,000, indicating the extent of this cult.

36. "You may ask me the following: does it have to be like that? My response is that it doesn't have to be like that, and indeed historically it hasn't been like that at all. There are countries where Catholicism—as in the case of Poland—is supported by the immense majority of the population, and the Polish Communist Party has many Catholics among its ranks. In other words, this [exclusion of Catholics] isn't part of the tradition of the revolutionary movement, nor indeed of the communist movement, and it doesn't exist in Latin America" (245). In a recent article in the *Granma*, the general secretary of the Dominican Communist Party outlined the changing role of church-state relations in the Dominican Republic: "The church's grass roots and some intermediate levels are taking active part in the popular movement's struggles in land takeovers, for example. These are priests who openly defend the peasants' right to take over land, call strikes, call into question the established capitalist order. . . . We even have Christians in the Party. We're against dogmatism and inflexibility. We consider the revolutionary Christians to be as revolutionary as we are." See "Isa Conde Talks about Dominican Economic and Social Situation," *Granma Weekly Review*, 20 March 1988, 9. The fact that this should be published in the official organ of the PCC is important—indicating that this position continues to be assessed by the Cuban Communist Party.

37. "On principle, I cannot agree with any type of discrimination. Period. I tell you very frankly. If I'm asked whether a particular kind of subtle discrimination exists toward Christians, then I admit that's correct. I honestly have

to say so, since it's not something we've yet been able to overcome. It's not intentional, nor deliberate, nor is it specifically planned. It simply exists, and I believe that we have to overcome that stage" (249).

38. To a certain extent this is based upon his own growing understanding of the changing role of the church. See, for instance, his comments on meetings with churchpeople in Chile, Jamaica, and Nicaragua (274–77). Particularly significant are his comments on Ernesto Cardenal, Miguel D'Escoto, several Maryknoll sisters (including those assassinated in El Salvador), and Archbishop Oscar Romero.

39. "We would like to see a united Church, supporting the just claims of the nations of the Third World and of all humanity, and especially the people of Latin America where, given present growth patterns, the majority of the world's Catholics—and the poorest of them all—are located, or shortly will be. It doesn't seem correct for me that we should try to reform or improve the Church from outside its structures, nor does it seem correct to promote division from outside. On the other hand, the solidarity of a Church united over the most deeply felt aspirations of humanity does appear to us as politically proper" (308).

40. "I have explained to you how history—in which I participated—developed, and in those conditions they were criteria of mine, and not others, which decided the situation. Mine is the fundamental responsibility, then, and I don't deny it, because it was I who stated that . . . we have to demand total purity. We have to demand it because the United States is against us, and is threatening us, because we need a very united party, one without the slightest crack. . . . Because we have an enemy which has been using religion as an ideology against our Revolution, our position has to be this" (248).

41. Dekker, "Christian Reformed Churches in Cuba?," 8.

Chapter 8. Toward a Rapprochement

1. Clark, *Religious Repression in Cuba*, 99.

2. Ham, "A View from Cuba," 14.

3. See Fernández, *Religión y revolución*, 184–85. In 1960, by comparison, from the same source, there was a priest for every 9,400 Catholics. J. Lloyd Mecham notes that some three years earlier "the ratio of communicants to priests was 8,145 to one" (*Church and State in Latin America: A History of Politico-Ecclesiastical Relations* [Chapel Hill: University of North Carolina Press, 1966] 303).

4. See, for example, Mecham's analysis in ibid., 304: "Of a nominal Catholic population of over five million, scarcely 10 percent practiced the Catholic religion to any extent. The Church, which had never been as influential in the national life in Cuba as in other Latin American countries, was so powerless that active anticlericalism was not and never had been a problem." A pastor from the Swiss Reformed church, Theodore Buss, noted in a recent article that in prerevolutionary times "some four per cent of the population were regular churchgoers, compared with about one percent today" ("Swiss Visitors," 5).

5. "Cuba: Waiting for the Pope," 5.

6. A 1984 report, for instance, notes in Colombia "the shocking statistic that one priest serves 200,000 parishioners": Victor J. Schymeinsky, "Building Bridges," *Maryknoll* (November 1984), 63.

7. For estimates see Woolfson, "Havana Diary," 8, Briggs, "Communist-Christian Conflict," 3, and Wall, "Cuba, Hunger and Geopolitics," 539.

8. "Cuban Catholics Prepare Mini-Puebla," 3.

9. Pérez Riera, "Un Signe d'Espérance," 19. See also Maillard, "Cuba: The Changing Climate," 269, for a more pessimistic view.

10. Pérez Riera, "Un Signe d'Espérance," 20.

11. "A far greater threat to the Catholic Church than that presented by Masonry, communism, or Protestantism was the inability of the church to combat general apathy and indifference and thus retain a hold on its own 'nominal' communicants." See Mecham, *Church and State in Latin America*, 304.

12. "Bishops Defend Dialogue with Castro," 4.

13. Ibid.

14. "The Cuban Catholic Church has therefore decided to turn over the page of the dark years and to seize every occasion for dialogue without expecting any spectacular changes. 'For three or four years,' said Archbishop Ortega, 'there has been a current, a consistent tendency on the government's part to ease the tensions, to do away with discriminations. We transmit the cases brought to us to the government's Office of Religious Affairs. There are fewer and fewer, nearly all have been resolved'" (Maillard, "Cuba: The Changing Climate," 270).

15. Domínguez, "Cuban Catholics and Castro," 25.

16. del Cerro, "La Iglesia tiene que resucitar," 78.

Bibliography

Collected Church Documents and Publications

A. From the Conferencia Episcopal Cubana

"Exhortación Pastoral a los Católicos de Cuba" (13 May 1951). In *Cuba Diáspora, 1978,* q.v., 100–101.

"Exhortación Pastoral del Año Mariano" (11 February 1954). In *Cuba Diáspora, 1978,* q.v., 97–99.

"Resumen de las Respuestas del Episcopado de Cuba al Cuestionario de la S. Congregración Consistorial para la Conferencia de Latinoamérica en Río de Janeiro" (30 March 1955). Havana. Mimeographed.

"Exhortación del Episcopado en Favor de la Paz" (25 February 1958). In Ismael Testé, *Historia Eclesiástica de Cuba,* q.v., 5:596.

"Al Pueblo de Cuba: Circular del Episcopado Cubano" (18 February 1959). In Testé, q.v., 5:596–600.

"Circular Colectiva del Episcopado Cubano" (7 August 1960). In Testé, q.v., 5:600–603.

"Carta Abierta del Episcopado al Primer Ministro" (4 December 1960). In Testé, q.v., 5:603–6.

"Pastorales Colectivas de la Conferencia Episcopal de Cuba: Durante la República Hasta 1960." In *Cuba Diáspora, 1978,* q.v., 88–96.

"Comunicado de la Conferencia Episcopal de Cuba a Nuestros Sacerdotes y Fieles" (10 April 1969). In Manuel Fernández, ed., *Religión y Revolución en Cuba,* q.v., 216–21). Translated as "Cuban Bishops Call for End to Trade Blockade." In Hageman and Wheaton, eds., q.v., 288–94.

"On Contemporary Atheism" (3 September 1969). In Hageman and Wheaton, eds., q.v., 298–308.

"Exhortación del Episcopado Cubano a los Sacerdotes, Religiosas y Fieles" (30 April 1974). Havana. Mimeographed.

"Toward Community Renewal: Evangelized and Evangelizing." *LADOC* 8, no. 2 (November–December 1977): 40–45.

"Conferencia Episcopal Cubana, Habana, 22–2–1978." *Notitiae* 14, no. 143–44 (June–July 1978): 270–77.

"Circular de la Conferencia Episcopal Cubana sobre las Relaciones con la Comunidad Cubana Residente Fuera de Nuestro País" (27 September 1979). Havana. Mimeographed.

"Cuban Bishops' Peace Plea." *LADOC* 12, no. 5 (May–June 1982): 41–44.

"Líneas Generales de la Conferencia Episcopal Cubana para una Acción Pastoral con los Jóvenes" Havana ([1984?]). Mimeographed.

"Mensaje de Navidad de los obispos de Cuba al pueblo de Dias y a todos los hombres de buena voluntad." Havana, December 1987. Mimeographed.

B. From Other Sources

Consejo Diocesano de Pastoral. "Plan Pastoral Trienal: La Comunidad Christiana—Centro y Fuente de Comunión (1984–87)." N.d. Havana. Mimeographed.

Episcopal Commission of Pastoral Ministry. "Piedad Popular." Havana, 1979. Mimeographed.

Permanent Committee of the Cuban Episcopal Conference. "Cuban Bishops on Terrorism." *LADOC* 8, no. 2 (November–December 1977): 46–47.

————. "Nota de Prensa sobre la Fabricación de la Bomba de Neutrones." Havana, 20 August 1981. Mimeographed.

Publications and Communications of Individual Bishops (Unless otherwise indicated, all entries in this section may be found in Ismael Testé, *Historia Eclesiástica de Cuba*, q.v., vol. 5.)

A. By Eduardo Boza Masvidal

"Nuestro Deber en el Momento Presente" (1 March 1959), 615–16.

"¿Es Cristiana la Revolución Social Que Se Está Verificando en Cuba?" (1959), 612–15.

"Dios en Nuestra Constitución" (5 July 1959), 617–18.

"Nuestro Credo Social" (6 December 1959), 618–19.

"Sermón de Mons. Boza en la Misa de la Catedral." *La Quincena* 6, no. 14 (31 July 1960): 24–25.

"¿La Iglesia Defiende Dólares o Principios?" *La Quincena* 6, no. 22 (30 November 1960): 3.

"La Patria que Soñó Martí" (8 February 1961), 623–24.

"Carta Abierta a Don Sergio Méndez Arceo, Obispo de Cuernavaca" (1969), 529–31.

"Un Ejemplo para el Exilio." In *Cuba Diáspora, 1975*, q.v., 8–10.

Voz en el Destierro, por el Obispo Expulsado Boza Masvidal. Miami: Revista Ideal, 1976.

"Comunidades Cristianas Cubanas." In *Cuba Diáspora, 1976*, q.v., 31–32.

"¿Qué Quiere Dios de Nosotros, Aquí y Ahora?" In *Cuba Diáspora, 1977*, q.v., 7–9.
"Conservemos la Pureza de Nuestra Fe." In *Cuba Diáspora, 1978*, q.v., 13–14.
"El Pueblo Cubano Es Un Solo Pueblo." In *Cuba Diáspora, 1979*, q.v., 9.
"La Iglesia, Hoy." In *Cuba Diáspora, 1981*, q.v., 5–11.
"Raíces Históricas y Doctrinales de la Nación Cubana." In *Cuba Diáspora, 1981*, q.v., 17–27.

B. By Enrique Pérez Serantes

"Paz a los Muertos" (29 July 1953), 531–32.
"Carta al Coronel del Río Chaviano" (30 July 1953), 532–33.
"Al pueblo de Oriente" (28 May 1957), 533–34.
"Queremos la Paz" (24 March 1958), 534–35.
"Explosión del Polvorín de el Cobre" (16 April 1958), 535–36.
"Invoquemos al Señor" (22 August 1958), 536–37.
"Paseo Macabro" (7 October 1958), 537–38.
"Basta de Guerra" (24 December 1958), 539–40.
"Vida Vueva" (3 January 1959), 540–45.
"El Justo Medio" (29 January 1959), 545–57.
"La Enseñanza Privada" (13 February 1959), 548–52.
"La Reforma Agraria y el Arzobispado de Santiago de Cuba" (1959?), 552–53.
"Por Dios y Por Cuba" (1959?), 562–68.
"Oración por los Difuntos" (21 July 1959), 553–54.
"El Congreso Católico Nacional" (November 1959), 554–56.
"Lecciones del Congreso" (24 December 1959), 556–62.
"Por la Unidad de la Iglesia" (1 September 1960), 568–69.
"Ni Traidores ni Parias" (24 September 1960), 569–72.
"Con Cristo o Contra Cristo" (1960?), 585–90.
"La Santa Misión" (1960), 592–96.
"No Dejemos que el Comunismo Usufructúe Inmerecidamente la Revolución" (2 September 1960?), 620–23.
"Roma o Moscú" (November 1960), 572–77.
"Vivamos en Paz" (21 November 1960), 582–85.
"La Voz de la Iglesia" (6 December 1960), 577–82.
"Respeto y Justicia" (22 January 1961), 590–91.
"Carta Abierta" (11 February 1961), 591–92.
"¡Vamos Bien!" (4 March 1961), 624–27.
"La Madre Cristiana" (1964). Pastoral letter. Santiago de Cuba. Mimeographed.

C. By Other Bishops

Díaz Cía, Evelio. "La Iglesia Católica y la Nueva Cuba" (31 May 1959), 606–8.
———. "Nota de Prensa" (24 November 1959). Havana. Note.
Martín Villaverde, Alberto. "La Reforma Agraria Cubana y la Iglesia Católica" (July 1959), 609–12.

———. "Un Congreso en Defensa de la Caridad." In *Cuba Diáspora, 1975,* q.v., 66–67.

Müller, Alfredo. "Despedida de Monseñor Müller al Salir de Su Diócesis" (16 July 1970), 522–23.

Ortega Alamino, Jaime. "Orientations de Mgr. Jaime Ortega Alamino, Archevêque de la Havane, sur la Participation des Enfants à la Catéchèse." *Missions Etrangères* 21, no. 7 (February 1984): 14.

Oves Fernández, Francisco. "Havana Archbishop's Address at XI World Festival." *LADOC* 10, no. 2 (November–December 1979): 41–45.

Prego, Fernando. "Pastoral de Mons. Prego que Sustituye a Mons. Müller" (12 August 1971), 523–25.

Studies on the Church in Cuba

Abascal López, Jesús. "Diálogo sobre el Surco." *Cuba Internacional* 16, no. 181 (December 1984): 34–35.

Alfonso, Pablo M. *Cuba, Castro y los Católicos (Del Humanismo Revolucionario al Marxismo Totalitario).* Miami: Hispamerican Books, 1985.

Alfonso, Rosa, ed. *Acerca de la Religión, la Iglesia y los Creyentes.* Havana: Editora Política, 1982.

Alonso, Dora. " '¡Yo seré miliciano!' (Una Entrevista con el Padre Director del Colegio Salesiano de Guanabacoa)." *Bohemia* 53, no. 22 (28 May 1961): 56–58, 105.

Alonso Tejada, Aurelio. *Religiosidad e Instituciones Religiosas en la Sociedad Cubana Actual.* Havana: Centro de Estudios sobre América, 1982.

Alzaga, Florinda. "Dos Obispos Cubanos Desterrados Visitan al Papa." In *Cuba Diáspora, 1981,* q.v., 57–58.

Amado Blanco, Luis. "El Sermón Olvidado." *La Quincena* 5, no. 3 (February 1959): 29, 48.

Andrade, Joaquín. "Protestant Pastors Join a Work Brigade." *International Review of Mission* 60, no. 238 (April 1971), 223–31.

Andrews, Paul. "Fidel Turns His Thoughts to Religion, but How Sincere Is He?" Special feature of the *Open Doors News Service,* 5 May 1986, 1–7.

Angell, Luis Felipe. "Salomón Bolo Hidalgo, El Cura Revolucionario del Perú." *Bohemia* 54, no. 27 (6 July 1962): 80–81, 90.

Arce, Luis. "Cuban Christians at Work in Kampuchea." *Granma Weekly Review,* 20 February 1983, 7.

———. "The Churches Are Always Open in Cuba: Interview with Vice-President of Cuban Ecumenical Council, in Montevideo for Synod of Vaudois Church and for Lecture Series." *Granma Weekly Review,* 13 March 1988, 3.

Arce, Reinerio. "Intervención de Reinerio Arce, Dirigente del Departamento del Consejo Ecuménico de Cuba y del Movimiento Estudiantil Cristiano." In *Encuentro de los Jóvenes Creyentes,* q.v., 10–14.

Arce Martínez, Sergio. *La Misión de la Iglesia en una Sociedad Socialista: Un Análisis Teológico de la Vocación de la Iglesia Cubana en el Día de Hoy.* Havana: n.p. [1965?].

———. "¿Es Posible Una Teologia de la Revolución?" In *De la Iglesia y la Sociedad,* edited by Rubem Alves, Richard Shaull, et al., 227–53. Montevideo: Tierra Nueva, 1971.

———. "Voices from the Church in Cuba." In *New Mission for a New People: Voices from the Caribbean,* 123–25. New York: Friendship Press, 1977.

———. "Development, People's Participation and Theology." *The Ecumenical Review* 30, no. 3 (July 1978): 266–77.

———. "La Realización de la Paz y Práctica de la Justicia." In *La Justicia Producirá Paz (Material de Estudio),* 2–9. Matanzas: Serie 'Augusto Cotto, 'no. 2 [1981?].

———. "Evangelization and Politics from the Cuban Point of View." In *Evangelization and Politics,* edited by Arce Martínez and Odén Marichal, 33–64. New York: New York Circus, 1982.

———. "La Dialéctica Bíblica de Lo Nuevo y el Hombre Nuevo." *Cuba Teológica* 2, nos. 1–2 (January–December 1983): 12–40.

Arce Martínez, Sergio, et al. *Primer Encuentro Latinoamericano de Cristianos por el Socialismo.* Havana: Ediciones Camilo Torres, 1973.

———. *Cristo Vivo en Cuba.* San José, Costa Rica: Departamento Ecuménico de Investigaciones, 1978.

Argüello, Alvaro H., ed. *Fidel Castro y los Cristianos Revolucionarios.* Folletos Monográficos "Rutilio Grande," no. 6. Managua: Instituto Histórico Centroamericano, [1979?].

Assman, Hugo, ed. *Habla Fidel Castro Sobre los Cristianos Revolucionarios.* Montevideo: Tierra Nueva, 1972.

Azcoaga, M. "Los Más Extraños Guerreros del Mundo." *La Quincena* 5, nos. 1–2 (January 1959): 34–35.

———. "La Reforma de la Enseñanza Católica Va," *La Quincena* 5, no. 15 (15 August 1959): 32–38.

Azpiazu, Iñaqui de. "Religiosos Españoles a las Ordenes de un Embajador." *Bohemia* 52, no. 5 (31 January 1960): 42–43, 97.

Balea, Mirta. "2nd International Meeting of Theologians and Social Scientists Held in Cuba." *Granma Weekly Review,* 18 December 1983, 5.

Batista Guerra, Israel. "Chiese Protestanti e Rivoluzione." *IDOC Internazionale* 13, nos. 3–4 (March–April 1982): 63–68.

———. "Las Contribuciones del Movimiento Ecuménico Cubano al Pensamiento Social de las Iglesias en Cuba." *Cuba Teológica* 2, nos. 1–2 (January–December 1983): 70–94.

Bayo, Armando. " 'Asia Volcánica': Monjes Budistas con la Revolución Cubana." *Bohemia* 54, no. 52 (28 December 1962): 106–7, 111.

Beckler, Lavy M.. "The Jewish Community of Cuba." *Congress Bulletin* (May–June 1971): 3.

———. "Jews in Cuba." *LAWG Letter* 2, no. 6 (December 1974–January 1975): 21.

Beckman, Joseph. "The Future of Religion in Cuba." *LADOC* 9, no. 5 (May–June 1979): 24–30.

Betto, Frei. *See* Castro Ruz, Fidel

Biaín, Ignacio. "La Política Social No Es Sovietizante." *La Quincena* 5, nos. 5–6 (March 1959): 48, 65, 72.

———. "Opina un Sacerdote Franciscano: La Revolución Debe Consolidarse en Este Año de 1960." *Bohemia* 52, no. 3 (17 January 1960): 3, 119.

———. "Comunismo, Anticomunismo y Confusionismo." *La Quincena* 6, no. 7 (15 April 1960): 32–33, 44.

———. "5 Respuestas en torno a la Revolución Cubana." *La Quincena* 6, no. 8 (30 April 1960): 32–33, 47.

Blanco, Gladys. "Worship on the Island." *Granma Weekly Review*, 8 June 1987, 4.

———. "The Mystifying Bayamo Altarpiece." *Granma Weekly Review*, 27 December 1987, 2.

———. "Churches and Worshipers in Cuba." *Granma Weekly Review*, 14 February 1988, 12.

———. "100 Years of Charity." *Granma Weekly Review*, 6 March 1988, 2.

Briggs, Kenneth A. "Communist-Christian Conflict in Cuba Seems to Ease." *New York Times*, 19 April 1981, 3.

———. "In Atheist Cuba, Soft Spot for the Church." *New York Times*, 20 April 1981, 3.

Buss, Theodore. "Cuba: Swiss Visitors Meet a 'Thin, Healthy Church'." *One World*, no. 68 (July 1981): 4–5.

Caluff Pérez, Orlando. "Revolución Cubana y Revolución Cristiana." *La Quincena* 6, no. 9 (15 May 1960): 1, 57–58.

Calzón, Frank. "Jehovah's Witnesses in Cuba." *Worldview* 9, no. 12 (December 1976): 13–14.

Cantor, Aviva. "Being Jewish within the Revolution." *Cuba Review* 9, no. 1 (February 1979): 25–31.

Capablanca, Enrique. "The Parish Church in Sancti Spíritus Restored." *Granma Weekly Review*, 15 November 1987, 4.

Cardenal, Ernesto. *In Cuba*. New York: New Directions, 1974.

Caron, Hervé. "Ministère à Varadero." *Missions Etrangères* 21, no. 4 (August 1983): 15–18.

Carr, Raymond. "Castro Arrests Baptist Churchmen." *Christian Century* 82, no. 16 (21 April 1965): 485.

Carreras, Julio Angel. "Terratenientes e Iglesia en Cuba Colonial." *University of Havana*, nos. 196–197 (1972): 147–157.

Carty, Marjorie T., and James W. Carty, Jr. "Cuba Improves Ties with Religious Groups." *The Times of the Americas*, 27 March 1985, 11.

Castañeda, Carlos M. "Cuba Visto por un Sacerdote Vasco." *Bohemia* 52, no. 2 (10 January 1960): 60–61, 80.

Castañeda, Mireya. "U.S. Council of Church Advocates Normalization of Cuba–United States Relations." *Granma Weekly Review*, 5 May 1986, 1.

Castillo, Andrés. "Las Fiestas de la Caridad y la Virgen de Regla en la Tradición Popular." *Bohemia* 53, no. 38 (17 September 1961): 56–57.

Castillo Armas, Rubén. "La Vertical Actitud del Párroco de Bayamo." *Bohemia* 53, no. 24 (11 June 1961): 110–11.

Castro Ruz, Fidel. "Castro and Freedom of Religion in Cuba." *LADOC* 8, no. 4 (March–April 1978): 1–11.

———. "Christianity and the Revolution." *New Blackfriars* 59, no. 695 (April 1978): 152–65.

———. *Fidel y la Religión: Conversaciones con Frei Betto.* Havana: Oficina de Publicaciones del Consejo de Estado, 1985.

Cepeda, Rafael. "The Church in Cuba." *Reformed and Presbyterian World* 27, no. 6 (June 1963): 261–70.

———. ed. *La Herencia Misionera en Cuba.* San Jose, Costa Rica: Departmento Ecuménico de Investigaciones, 1986.

Cerro, Angel del. "La Iglesia Tiene Que Resucitar." *Bohemia* 51, no. 14 (5 April 1959): 78–79.

———. "Los Curas Son Reaccionarios." *Bohemia* 51, no. 16 (19 April 1959): 68–69, 97.

———. "Cuarenta Casos de Injusticia Social." *Bohemia* 51, no. 17 (26 April 1959): 72–73, 95.

———. "En Busca de Una Tercera Posición." *Bohemia* 51, no. 23 (7 June 1959): 75, 96.

———. "Ante el Congreso Católica Nacional." *Bohemia* 51, no. 47 (22 November 1959): 54–55, 90–91.

———. "Un Mar de Fe." *Bohemia* 51, no. 49 (6 December 1959): 98–99, 112–113.

Céspedes, Carlos Manuel de. " 'Les Croyents Se Sentent Exclus de la Vie Politique.' Affirme le Sécretaire de l'Episcopat." *Informations Catholiques Internationales,* no. 155 (October 1980): 23–25.

———. Talk given at the Encuentro Ecuménico de Solidaridad con el Pueblo Cubano ante la Amenaza de Agresión por parte de E.E.U.U. Havana, 14 November 1981. Mimeographed.

Chang (Ain), Arturo. "*Fidel y la Religion.* 'Va a Fortalecer la Unidad y la Lucha,' Asegura el Presidente de la Iglesia Presbiteriana Reformada de Cuba." *Bohemia* 78, no. 2 (10 January 1986): 39–40.

Chaurrondo, Hilario, ed. *Almanaque de la Caridad: Directorio Oficial de las Diócesis de Cuba.* Published annually. Havana: Iglesia de la Merced, 1955, 1957, 1959, 1960, 1961, 1963, 1964, 1968.

———. "Fidel Castro, de rodillas ante un sacerdote." *La Quincena* 5, no. 1–2 (January 1959): 21.

———. "Humanismo Igual a Cristianismo en Cuba." *La Quincena* 6, no. 1 (16 January 1960): 8–9, 57–61.

———. "Operación Suburbios: La Corona de Espinas de La Habana Católica." *La Quincena* 6, no. 7 (15 April 1960): 20–21.

Cherson, Samuel J. "José Antonio Echeverría: Héroe y Mártir." *Bohemia* 51, no. 11 (15 March 1959): 98–99, 104.

Ciencia y Religión: Selección de Artículos [from the section "Ciencia y Religión" of the journal *El Militante Comunista*]. Havana: Editora Política, 1981.

Clark, Juan. *Religious Repression in Cuba.* Miami: Institute of Interamerican Studies, 1985.

Clavijo Tisseur, Arturo. *En Honor de Su Eminencia El Cardenal Monseñor Arteaga.* Santiago de Cuba: Imprenta 'Arroyo,' 1946.

Conejeros A., Senén. "Cardinal Silva Henríquez, Human Rights Defender." *Granma Weekly Review,* 6 December 1987, 2.

Congreso Católico Nacional. Havana: Ponciano, 1960.

Consejo Ecuménico de Cuba. "Bando Evangelico Gedeón Reconstruye Templo." *Tribuna Ecuménica* 1, no. 2 (September 1983).

Cox, Harvey. "Thoughts on the Church in Cuba." *The Nation* (9 May 1987), 595, 606–12.

Crahan, Margaret E. "Religion: Cuba." *IDOC*, no. 69 (January 1975): 17–21.

————. "Religious Penetration and Nationalism in Cuba: U.S. Methodist Activities, 1895–1958." *Revista/Review Interamericana* 8, no. 2 (Summer 1978): 204–24.

————. "Salvation through Christ or Marx: Religion in Revolutionary Cuba." *Journal of Interamerican Studies* 21, no. 1 (February 1979): 156–84.

————. "Protestantism in Cuba." *PCCLAS Proceedings*, vol. 9 (1982): 59–70.

————. "Cuba: Religious Freedom and Liberty of Worship." Paper prepared for the Inter-American Commission on Human Rights, 1983.

————. "Cuba: Religion and Revolutionary Institutionalization." *Journal of Latin American Studies* 17, no. 2 (November 1985): 319–40.

Crawford, Don, and Brother Andrew. *Red Star over Cuba*. Wheaton, IL: Tyndale House Publishers, 1971.

Cros Sandoval, Mercedes. *La Religión Afrocubana*. Madrid: Editorial Playor, 1975.

Cuba Diáspora: Anuario de la Iglesia Cubana. Miami: Revista Ideal, 1975–81.

Cuban Ecumenical Council. "Statement by Cuban Ecumenical Council." *Granma Weekly Review*, 5 June 1983, 3.

Cubillas, Víctor, Jr. "El Aporte de la Iglesia Evangélica a la Causa Redentora." *Bohemia* 51, no. 5 (1 February 1959): 108–10, 112.

Cumín, Alfonso. *Cuba: Entre el Silencio y la Utopía*. Barcelona: Editorial LAIA, 1979.

David, René. "Para Una Teología y Pastoral de Reconciliación Desde Cuba." Havana, 1982. Manuscript.

Davis, J. Merle. *The Cuban Church in a Sugar Economy*. New York: International Missionary Council, 1942.

Dekker, James C. "How Can There Be Christian Reformed Churches in Cuba?" *The Banner* (27 January 1986): 6–8.

Delahoza, Tony. " 'Esta Revolucion Es Genuinamente Democrática y Cubana'." *Bohemia* 51, no. 5 (1 February 1959): 76–77.

Delofeu, Manuel. *Historical and Biographical Notes of the Cuban Mission*. Tampa: Morning Tribune Electric Print, 1899.

Dewart, Leslie. *Christianity and Revolution: The Lesson of Cuba*. New York: Herder and Herder, 1963.

Díaz, Mons. Evelio. "Habla Monseñor Evelio Díaz, Obispo Auxiliar del Cardenal Arteaga y Administrador Apostólico de La Habana." *Bohemia* 51, no. 22 (31 May 1959), 69.

Domínguez, Jorge I. "Cuban Catholics and Castro." *Worldview* 15, no. 2 (February 1972): 24–29.

————. "International and National Aspects of the Experience of the Roman Catholic Church in Cuba." 1987. Manuscript.

Dorta-Duque, Juan M. "Escuela Privada y Educación Cristiana." *La Quincena* 6, no. 1 (16 January 1960): 8–9, 57–61.

Dubelman, Abraham J. "Cuba." *American Jewish Yearbook* 63 (1962): 481–85.

Dubois, Claude. "Coup d'oeil sur Cuba." *Missions Etrangères* 21, no. 7 (February 1984): 3–7.

———. "Les P.M.E. à Cuba: Une Présence Encore Significative." *Missions Etrangères* 21, no. 7 (February 1984): 21–23.

Durr, Barbara. "Cuban Christians Support Dialogue with Exiles." *Cuba Review* 9, no. 1 (February 1979): 32–33, 35.

Efundé, Agún. *Los Secretos de la Santería*. Miami: Ediciones Cubamérica, 1978.

Egaña Villamil, Camilo. "Payment of the Foreign Debt Is Ethically Unjustifiable Just as the Present International Economic Order Is." *Granma Weekly Review*, 31 January 1988, 3.

El Futuro del que Obra Justica Es la Paz (Material de Estudio). Matanzas: Serie 'Augusto Cotto' no. 2 [1981?].

Encuentro de Jóvenes Creyentes por la Solidaridad Antimperialista, la Paz y la Amistad. Havana: n.p., 1978 [?].

"Escritos de los Sacerdotes Cubanos en la Diáspora al Señor Cardenal Secretario de Estado en la Santa Sede" (Caracas, 28 February 1969). In Testé, q.v., 5: 517–20.

Errasti, Mariano. "Reportaje del Congreso Católico Nacional: La Noche Más Luminosa de la Historia de Cuba." *La Quincena* 5, no. 23–24 (December 1959): 42–47, 54–55.

Fanfani, Amintore. "Los Ideales Católicos y los Ideales Capitalistas." *La Quincena* 6, no. 15 (15 November 1960): 26–27.

Fernández, Manuel. "Presencia de los Católicos en la Revolución Triunfante." *La Quincena* 5, no. 1–2 (January 1959): 10–16, 54.

———. "Un 'Barbudo' Fraile a Quien un Ciclón Llevó a la Sierra." *La Quincena* 5, no. 1–2 (January 1959): 4–7.

———. " 'Las Leyes del Gobierno Revolucionario Son Cristianas,' Dice el Dr. Andrés Valdespino." *La Quincena* 5, no. 10 (31 May 1959): 12–15, 36

———. "La Iglesia de Cuba ante Nuevas Perspectivas." *Cuba Diáspora, 1975*, q.v., 15–18.

———. "La Juventud Católica Cubana: Un Enigma Histórico." In *Cuba Diáspora, 1976*, q.v., 85–87.

———. "El Futuro de la Evangelización en Cuba." In *Cuba Diáspora, 1978*, q.v., 43–46,

———. *Religión y Revolución en Cuba: Veinticinco Años de Lucha Ateísta*. Miami: Saeta Ediciones, 1984.

Fernández Ceballos, Raúl. "Intervención de Raúl Fernández Ceballos, Presidente del Consejo Ecuménico de Cuba." In *Encuentro de los Jóvenes Creyentes*, q.v., 23–25.

Figueroa y Miranda, Miguel. *Religión y Política en la Cuba del Siglo XIX: El Obispo Espada visto a la Luz de los Archivos Romanos, 1802–1832*. Miami: Ediciones Universal, 1975.

Fonseca, Jaime, "Los Catolicos Dan la Solida." *Diario de la Marina*, 12 December 1959, 4A.

Forker, W. "Cuban Jews: Trial by Change." *Christianity Today* 15, no. 19 (18 June 1971): 34.

Forrest, A.C. "And Now a Sugar Cane Curtain Too." *Presbyterian Life*, 15 December 1960, 15–17, 28–33.

———. "A Sunday in Cuba." *Presbyterian Life*, 1 January 1961, 5–9, 33–34.

———. "The Lesson of Cuba." *Presbyterian Life*, 15 February 1961, 22–26.

Friguls, Juan Emilio. Various articles in *Diario de la Marina* and *Bohemia*, 15 September 1957–20 January 1960.

García, Sixto. " 'Nadie Tiene Más Amor' . . . El Martirologio Cubano." In *Cuba Diáspora*, 1981, q.v., 29–36.

García Franco, Raimundo. "Responsabilidad en la Educación Cristiana de Nuestros Hijos." *Mensaje* (Organo del Consejo Ecuménico de Cuba), 1983–84, 8–11.

García Tuduri, Mercedes. "La Iglesia y la Cultura Cubana." In *Cuba Diáspora*, 1976, q.v., 21–25.

García Valencia, G. "Opinan los Dirigentes de la JOC." *La Quincena* 6, no. 10 (31 May 1960): 26–27, 54–55.

Gendler, Rabbi Everett. "Cuba and Religion: Challenge and Response." *The Christian Century* 86, no. 31 (30 July 1969): 1013–16.

Genet, Harry. "Bible Smuggling Comes Home to Roost." *Christianity Today* 23, no. 21 (7 September 1979): 75.

———. "The Church Finds Its Role in a Socialist State." *Christianity Today* 23, no. 28 (21 December 1979): 40.

Gómez, Nacira. "Amamos a Nuestra Iglesia, a Nuestro Pueblo y a Nuestra Revolución." *Mensaje* (Organo del Consejo Ecuménico de Cuba), 1983–84, 21–22.

Gómez Treto, Raúl. "Algunas Reflexiones sobre el III Congreso Mundial para el Apostolodo de los Laicos." In Chaurrondo, ed. (1968) q.v., 9–14.

———. "Intervención de Raúl Gómez Treto del Secretariado Internacional de la Conferencia Cristianos por la Paz." In *Encuentro de los Jóvenes Creyentes*, q.v., 15–18.

———. "Monseñor Boza: ¡Qué Pena!" (supp. of *El IRD y Su Junta de Directores*.). Matanzas: Serie 'Augusto Cotto,' no. 1, folleto no.2 [1983?].

———. *La Iglesia Católica durante la Construcción del Socialismo en Cuba*. San José, Costa Rica: Departamento Ecuménico de Investigaciones, 1987.

González del Valle, Francisco. *Jose de la Lúz y los Católicos Españoles*. Havana: Sociedad Editorial Cuba Contemporánea, 1919.

———. "El Clero en la Independencia Cubana." *Cuba Contemporánea* 18, no. 2 (October 1918): 140–205.

Guillet, Claude, and Henri Beaudouin. "Révolution Cubaine et Religion." *Missions Etrangères* 15, no. 12 (November–December 1972): 20–24.

Gumá, José Gabriel. "Sergio Méndez Arceo in Cuba: 40-Minute Conversation with a Bishop who Defends the Poor and Oppressed." *Granma Weekly Review*, 27 February 1983, 9.

Hageman, Alice L., and Philip E. Wheaton, eds. *Religion in Cuba Today: A New Church in a New Society.* New York: Association Press, 1971.

Ham, Adolfo. "Evangelism in the Socialist Society of Cuba." *International Review of Mission* 66, no. 263 (July 1977): 279–84.

———. "A View from Cuba." *Caribbean Contact* (November 1983): 14.

Haselden, Kyle. "Cuba: Much Religion, Little Faith." *Christian Century* 77, no. 47 (23 November 1960): 1368.

———. "Cuba's Revolution: Yes and No." *Christian Century* 77, no. 49 (7 December 1960): 1438–39.

Hernández, José M. "*Agrupación Católica Universitaria: Los Primeros Cincuenta Años.* Miami: Agrupación Católica Universitaria, 1981.

Higginbotham, Elice. "Religion in the Cuban News." *Cubatimes* (November–December 1983): 8–10.

Horgan, John. "Cuba: Church and State." *The American Eccesiastical Review* 162 (1972): 373–82.

"Intervención de Francisco Oves, Arzobispo de La Havana." *Encuentro de los Jóvenes Creyentes por la Solidaridad Antimperialista, la Paz y la Amistad.* Havana, n.p., [1978].

Jover Marimón, Mateo. "The Church." In *Revolutionary Change in Cuba,* edited by Carmelo Mesa-Lago, 399–426. Pittsburgh: University of Pittsburgh Press, 1974.

———. "The Cuban Church in a Revolutionary Society." *LADOC* 4, no. 47 (April 1974): 17–36.

Juventud Demócrata de América. "Un Documento sobre la Revolución Cubana." *La Quincena* 6, no. 12 (30 June 1960): 9–10.

Kerien, José Luis. "Monseñor E. Pérez Serantes." In *Cuba Diáspora, 1977,* q.v., 39–40.

Kirk, John M. "Al borde del volcán: la Iglesia en Cuba pre-revolucionaria." 1983. Manuscript.

———. "Between God and the Party: The Church in Revolutionary Cuba, 1969–1985." *Canadian Journal of Latin American and Caribbean Studies* 9 (1986): 93–109.

———. "La Iglesia en Cuba, 1959–1969: ¿saliendo de las catacumbas?" *Nueva Antropología* 9 (1986): 23–48.

———. Religion and Politics in Revolutionary Cuba: A Bibliographical Guide." *Revista Interamericana de Bibliografía* 37 (1987): 327–43.

Kirkpatrick, Dow. "Cuban Church at Puebla." *Cuba Review* 9, no. 1 (February 1979): 18–20.

Kochanski, Mendel. "The Jewish Community in Cuba." *Jewish Frontier* 18 (September 1957): 25–27.

Laneuville, Roland. "Pour une Eglise Peuple de Dieu (Cuba)." *Missions Etrangères* 15, no. 12 (November–December 1972): 5–7.

———. "Cuba: 60 Jeunes Se Préparent à Devenir Prêtres au Grand Séminaire de La Havana." *Missions Etrangères* 18, no. 6 (November–December 1977): 15–19.

———. "Cuba: l'Eglise des Béatitudes." *Missions Etrangères* 18, no. 7 (January–February 1978): 8.

――――. "De l'Anathème au Dialogue." *Missions Etrangères* 21, no. 7 (February 1984): 15–16.

Lasaga, José Ignacio. "La Actual Ley Agraria Cubana y el Comunismo." *La Quincena* 5, no. 12 (30 June 1959): 17–19, 30.

――――. "La Caridad y la Justicia Social" [from the 1959 Catholic Congress]. In *Cuba Diáspora, 1975*, q.v., 68–72.

――――. "La Iglesia Cubana en el Marco de la Constitución Socialista de 1976." In *Cuba Diáspora, 1977*, q.v., 11–17.

Lebroc Martínez, Reinerio. *Episcopologio*. Miami: Ediciones Hispamerican Books, 1985.

Leclercq, Jacques. "La Actitud de los Cristianos ante los Bienes." *La Quincena* 5, no. 18 (30 September 1959): 38–42.

Lee, Susana. "Cuban Christians Speak Out against the U.S. Aggressions, Threats and Interventions against Cuba, Central America and Caribbean." *Granma Weekly Review*, 22 November 1981, 3.

Leiseca, Juan Martín. *Apuntes para la Historia Eclesiástica de Cuba*. Havana: Carasa y Cía. 1938.

Llano Montes, Antonio. "Habla para *Bohemia*, el Padre Ramón Talavera." *Bohemia* 52, no. 26 (26 June 1960): 58–59, 73.

Llinas, René. "Algo sobre los Dioses Negros de Africa y de su Reino Cubano." *Bohemia* 53, no. 35 (27 August 1961): 46–47, 74.

Lombardo Toledano, Vicente. "¿Comunismo o Cristianismo?" *Bohemia* 53, no. 31 (30 July 1961): 24–25.

López Oliva, Enrique. *Los Católicas y la Revolución Latinoamericana*. Havana: Instituto del Libro, 1970.

――――. *¿Revolución en la Teología?* Caracas: Fondo Editorial Salvador de la Plaza, 1973.

――――. "Solidaridad Cristiana Contra Agresividad Imperialista." *Revista Tricontinental* 77 (April 1981): 79–90.

――――. "La CIA Contra la Unidad Cristiano–Marxista." *OCLAE*, no.1 (1982): n.p.

――――. "The Progressive Christian Movement: A Revolutionary Force." *Granma Weekly Review*, 24 October 1982, 7.

――――. "¡Unámonos a Favor de la Paz!" *Paz y Soberanía* 3 (1983): 24–31.

――――. "Opción Cristiana por la Liberación y la Paz." *Iglesias* (December 1983): 21.

――――. Series of reports on religious matters filed to Noticias Aliadas News Agency, Lima, 1984.

Lowe, Kathy. "Pastor Converted to a New Society." *One World*, no. 73 (January–February 1982): 22.

Lucas Azcona, Clara. "Caridad y Fraternidad" [from the 1959 Catholic Congress]. In *Cuba Diáspora, 1975*, q.v., 73–78.

McAffee Brown, Robert, " 'Living Joyfully in the Midst of the Revolution'." *Cuba Review* 9, no. 1 (February 1979): 3–15.

――――. "Confessions of Faith of the Presbyterian-Reformed Church in Cuba." *Religion in Life* 48, no. 3 (Fall 1979): 268–82.

McCarthy, Edward. "La Iglesia en Favor de los Presos: Mensaje del Arzobispo de Miami, Edward McCarthy, al Exilio Cubano en la Ermita de la Caridad." In *Cuba Diáspora, 1979,* q.v., 17.

McCoy, John. "Cuba's Churches Wither but Hang On." *Seattle Post–Intelligencer,* 30 March 1985, A6.

Machado Garcia, Juan Manuel. "Une 'Force' Qui Se Manifeste dans la 'Faiblesse'." *Missions Etrangères* 221, no. 7 (February 1984): 24–27.

MacKay, John A. "Cuba Revisited." *Christian Century* 81, no. 7 (12 February 1964): 200–203.

———. "A Fresh Look at Cuba." *Christian Century* 81, no. 17 (5 August 1964): 983–87.

Maillard, Stanislas. "Cuba: The Changing Climate." *Commonweal,* 9 May 1986, 268–72.

Malone, James. "Press Conference Statement by Bishop James Malone." Havana, [25 January 1985]. Mimeographed.

Maresma, Leonel. "El Santa Cristo de Limpias y la Santísima Virgen María Me Salvaron de la Catástrofe del 4 de Marzo." *Bohemia* 52, no. 17 (24 April 1960): 54–55,71–72.

Marín, Marisol. "Two Nuns in El Salvador Recount Nightmare." *Granma Weekly Review,* 17 January 1988, 11.

Márquez y de la Cerra, Miguel F. "Viejas Creencias e Ideas Nuevas (La Verdad Católica sobre el Derecho de la Propiedad." *Bohemia* 52, no. 12 (20 March 1962): 1, 124–25.

Maspero. Emilio. "¿Qué es el Socialismo?" *La Quincena* 6, no. 10 (31 May 1960): 1, 57.

Matas, Julio. "Revolución, Literatura y Religion Afrocubana." *Cuban Studies/ Estudios Cubanos* 13, no. 1 (Winter 1983): 17–23.

Matheu, Hilda. "Les Oblats à Cuba: 'A la manière des laïques'." *Missions Etrangères* 21, no. 7 (February 1984): 17–18.

Maza, Manuel P. "The Cuban Catholic Church: True Struggles and False Dilemmas: The Historical Characteristics of the Cuban Catholic Church and Their Impact on the 1959–1960 Episcopal Documents," Ph.D. diss., Georgetown University, 1982.

Michel, Fils de la Charité. "Une Terre Sans Dieu?" *Missions Etrangères* 21, no. 7 (February 1984): 8.

Montero Rodríguez, Celso. *Cristanos en la Revolución Cubana.* Estella, Spain: Editorial Verbo Divino, 1975.

Montigny, Roger de. "30 Ans d'Histoire Missionaire: Les P.M.E. à Cuba." *Missions Etrangères* 15, no. 12 (November–December 1972): 8–15.

Montó Sotolongo, José. "El Día de las Misiones." *El Mundo,* 2 October 1958, B4.

———. "Motivos de Octubre." *El Mundo,* 4 October 1958, B4.

———. "Nuestra Señora del Rosario." *El Mundo,* 5 October 1958, B6.

———. "El Día Misional a la Vista." *El Mundo,* 8 October 1958, B4.

Moya, H.C. "The Salvadoran People's Church: Priests with the People in Arms." *Granma Weekly Review,* 1 January 1984, 10.

Muñoz Unsain, Alfredo. "Arzobispo de Habana Llama a Juego Limpio con Gobierno Cubano." *El Nuevo Diario* [Managua], 9 March 1983, [3?].

Neblett, Sterling A. *Methodism's First Fifty Years in Cuba.* Wilmore, Kentucky: Asbury Press, 1976.

Nodal, Roberto, and André Maud. "Dynamique de la Santería Afro-Cubaine." *Présence Africaine* [Paris], nos. 105–6 (1978): 109–22.

Norton, Chris. "Catholic Church in Cuba Learns to Live with 'Devil'." *Toronto Globe and Mail*, 11 July 1987, D3.

Novas, Benito. "'Existe una Quinta Columna en los Colegios Católicos,' Denuncian los Alumnos Expulsados de Villanueva." *Bohemia* 52, no. 48 (27 November 1960): 48–49, 71–72.

Odén Marichal, Pablo. "Testimonio: Una Experiencia Cubana." *Cuba Teológica* 2, nos. 1–2 (January–December 1983): 95–103.

O'Grady, Desmond. "The Church in Cuba." *Ave Maria* 97, no. 15 (13 April 1963): 5–8.

Oliva, Milagros. Various artcles in *Granma Weekly Review*, March 1983–1988.

Ostling, Richard N. "Castro Looks at Christianity." *Time*, 30 December 1985, 72.

Pageau, Louis. "Le Seminaire de la Havana, à Cuba: Apôtres pour un Monde Nouveau." *Missions Etrangères* 15, no. 12 (November–December 1972): 16–17.

Pardo Llada, José. "Sobre el Anticomunismo." *Bohemia* 53, no. 4 (22 January 1961): 78–79, 83.

Pastora Fernández, Sara. "Tomemos la Ofensiva Cristiana." *La Quincena* 6, no. 4 (29 February 1960): 17, 55–56.

Peerman, Dean. "Church-Hopping in Havana." *Christian Century* 88, no. 49 (8 December 1971): 1435–38.

Peñalver Moral, Reinaldo, and Susana Tesoro. "Encuentro Eclesial: Concluyó con Una Misa en la Catedral de la Habana." *Granma Weekly Review*, 28 February 1986, 48–49.

Pérez Riera, José Félix. "Un Signe d'Espérance: La Relève Sacerdotale et Religieuse." *Missions Etrangères* 21, no. 7 (February 1984): 19–20.

Pérez Varela, Angel. *Coronación Canónica de la Virgen de Regla.* Havana: Editorial 'Las Mercedes', 1956.

Pichardo, Hortensia, ed. *Documentos para la Historia de Cuba.* Havana: Instituto Cubano de Libro, 1973.

Piché, Gisèle. "Heureuses en Pays Socialiste." *Missions Etrangères* 15, no. 12 (November–December 1972): 18–19.

Piñera Corrales, Walfredo. "La Iglesia Católica en la Revolución (Borrador)." Havana, 1979. Manuscript.

Pita Astudillo, Félix. "'Historic' Is How Fidel's Meeting with Ecumencial Council and Protestant Dignitaries Described." *Granma Weekly Review*, 24 November 1985, 3.

———. "Unholy Propaganda for Holy Week." *Granma Weekly Review*, 17 May 1987, 2.

Plaza, Benjamín. "El Comunismo, Ataque a la Dignidad Humana." *La Quincena* 5, no. 19 (15 October 1959): 14, 44–47.

———. "El Capitalismo, Un Sistema Viciado." *La Quincena* 5, no. 19 (15 October 1959): 15, 47–49.

Power, Anne. "The Church in Cuba." *Commonweal* 89, no. 22 (7 March 1969): 704–5.

Radealli, Ana María. "Un Peregrino de la Vida a bordo de una Paradoja." *Cuba Internacional* 18, no. 197 (April 1980): 26–29.

Ramos Regidor, José. "I Cristiani Oggi a Cuba." *IDOC Internazionale* 13, nos. 3–4 (March–April 1982): 1–4.

Recabarren, Patricio. "La Iglesia en la Encrucijada." *La Quincena* 5, no. 8 (April 1959): 1, 45–48.

Reflexión Eclesial Cubana. "Una Mirada a La Historia de Nuestra Evangelización." In *Vida Cristiana* (Archdiocese of Havana Newsletter), 15 January 1984–26 February 1984 and 10 June 1984–24 June 1984.

———. "Comisión de Historia desde la Fundación de San Carlos hasta 1902." Havana [1980]. Mimeographed.

———. "Historia de la Evangelación en Cuba; Parte II: Período de 1899 a 1959." Havana, 1985. Mimeographed.

Rendon, Thomas. "*Fidel y la Religión* Signals New Era in Cuba." *Christian Century* 21–28 (May 1986): 508–9.

Riesgo, Rodolfo. Various articles in *La Quincena*, 28 February 1958–31 March 1961.

Rivero, José I. "A los Católicos de Cuba." *Diario de la Marina*, 27 November 1959, 1A.

Robertson, C. Alton. "The Political Role of the Protestants in Cuba—1959 to 1962." *Missionary Research Library Occasional Bulletin* 18, pt. 1 (January 1967): 1–9; pt. 2 (February 1967): 1–14.

Rodríguez, Elmer. "Con el Arzobispo de La Habana Rumbo a Puebla: Cara a Cara con la Iglesia Cubana." *Prisma Internacional* 5, no. 77 (January 1979): 34–37.

Rodríguez Fajardo, Juan. "¿San Lázaro o Babalu Aye?" *Bohemia* 52, no. 51 (18 December 1960): 66–67, 85.

Roig de Leuchsenring, Emelio. "La Iglesia Católica Contra la Independencia de Cuba." *Hoy* (25 December 1960): 10–11.

Rosado, Caleb. "Sect and Party: Religion under Revolution in Cuba." Ph.D. diss., Northwestern University, 1985.

Rose, Donna. *Santería (The Cuban–African Magical System)*. Miami: Mi-World Publishing Company, 1980.

Rosell, Mariano. "Sólo a base de Justicia Social se Podrá Combatir el Comunismo." *La Quincena* 5, no. 9 (17 May 1959): 6–7.

Ruiz, Ana María. "Congreso Eclesiástico: El Deseo de Renovar." *Prisma* 12, no. 164 (April 1986): 11–12.

Sagredo, Angel. "¿Catolicismo a Remolque?" *La Quincena* 6, no. 13 (15 July 1960): 9, 52.

Santamaría, Carlos. "Ningún Gobernante. . . . " *La Quincena* 4, no. 2 (31 January 1958): 4.

Sapir, Boris. *The Jewish Community of Cuba: Settlement and Growth*. New York: Jewish Teachers Seminary Press, 1948.

Secretariado General de la Conferencia Episcopal de Cuba. *Almanaque de la Caridad: Directorio Eclesiástico de Cuba, 1971*. Havana: Instituto Cubano del Libro, 1971.

Selser, Gregorio. "Liberation Theology Under Attack." *Granma Weekly Review*, 6 December 1987, 11.

Seoane Pliego, Higinio. "Comunismo, Anticomunismo y Justicia Social." *La Quincena* 5, no. 7 (April 1959): 20, 49–50.

Solano, Ricardo. "Operación Bautizo Colectivo." *Bohemia* 53, no. 38 (17 September 1961): 14–15.

Sosa, Juan M. "Santería." In *Cuba Diáspora, 1979*, q.v., 65–78.

Stubbs, Jean. "British Religious Delegation Visits Cuba: A Church Concerned with this World." *Granma Weekly Review*, 13 March 1983, 4.

Suárez, Luis. "Al Regresar de Cuba, Méndez Arceo Ratifica: ¡Fidel Castro es un Inspirado de Dios!" *Siempre* (23 August 1978): 28–29, 70.

———. "Is There Religion in the New Revolutionary Cuba?" *LADOC* 9, no. 3 (January–February 1979): 26–31.

Surí Quesada, Emilio. "The King of Palmira." *Granma Weekly Review*, 24 January 1988, 3.

Swaren, Beverly. "The Church in Today's Cuba." *America* 119, no. 8 (21 September 1968): 211–13.

Testé, Ismael. "Por Qué No Soy Comunista." *Bohemia* 51, no. 8 (22 February 1959): 43, 111.

———. *Historia Eclesiástica de Cuba*. 5 vols. Burgos and Barcelona, Spain: El Monte Carmelo and Artes Gráficas Medinaceli, 1969–1975).

Thomas, Hugh. *Cuba or the Pursuit of Freedom*. London: Eyre and Spottiswoode, 1971.

Torres Cuevas, Eduardo. "El Obispado de Cuba: Génesis, Primeros Prelados y Estructura." *Santiago*, nos. 26–27 (June–September 1977): 61–98.

Trigo, Pedro. "Una Svolta nella Politica Religiosa del Partito Comunista Cubano?" *IDOC Internazionale* 13, nos. 3–4 (March–April 1982): 43–48.

Tucker, Jimmy. "Summary Report of the 1976 Visit to Cuba." In *New Mission for New People: Voices from the Caribbean*, edited by David I. Mitchell, 118–22. New York: Friendship Press, 1977.

ULAJE–CUBA (Latin American Union of Ecumenical Youth of Cuba). "Ecumenical Cuban Youth Group Treats of Christian Vocation in Political Situations." *LADOC* 12, no. 5 (May–June 1982): 45–47.

Urquiaga, Pablo. "Nuestro Anti-Comunismo Negativo." In *Cuba Diáspora, 1976*, q.v., 19–20.

———. "Analogías de Dos Pueblos." In *Cuba Diáspora, 1979*, q.v., 32–35.

Valdespino, Andrés. "El Cristianismo de los Sepulcros Blanqueados." *Bohemia* 51, no. 11 (15 March 1959): 64, 97.

———. "Las Trompetas de Josué." *Bohemia* 51, no. 15 (12 April 1959): 53, 137–38.

———. "Carta a los Ricos de Cuba." *Bohemia* 51, no. 21 (24 May 1959): 68–69, 92.

———. "El Mensaje del Congreso." *Bohemia* 51, no. 49 (6 December 1959): 88–89, 97.

———. "Los Puntos sobre las íes." *Bohemia* 52, no. 9 (28 February 1960): 44–45, 81.

Valle, Raúl del. *El Cardinal Arteaga: Resplandores de la Purpura Cubana*. Havana: Impreso Ramallo, 1957.

———. "En torno a la Represión del Comunismo." *La Quincena* 4, no. 16 (31 August 1958): 26–27, 46–48.

Various authors. "El Manifiesto de las Asociaciones Catolicas." *La Quincena* 5, no. 4 (February 1959): 30.

———. "Cuba ante la Prensa Católica Internacional." *La Quincena* 7, no. 2 (31 March 1961): 10–13.

———. *Periódico 'Hoy': Aclaraciones.* 2 vols. Havana: Editora Política, 1964.

———. "Mensaje al Mundo de los Sacerdotes y Laicos Católicos Cubanos en el Exilio," 28 February 1969. In Testé, *Historia Eclesiastica de Cuba,* q.v., 5:520–22.

———. "Can One Still Be a Christian in Cuba?" *LADOC* 5, no. 50 (September 1974): 15–21.

———. "Escritos de los Sacerdotes Cubanos en la Diáspora al Señor Cardenal Secratario de Estado en la Santa Sede" (Caracas, 28 February 1969). In Testé, *Historia Eclesiastica de Cuba,* q.v., 5:517–20.

———. *Encuentro de Jóvenes Creyentes por la Solidaridad Antimperialista, la Paz y la Amistad.* Havana: n.p., [1978?].

———. "Confession of Faith" [Excerpts from the 1977 Confessions of Faith of the Presbyterian-Reformed Church of Cuba]. *Cuba Review* 9, no. 1 (February 1979): 3–14.

———. "Cuban Catholic Reflections." *Cuba Review* 9, no. 1 (February 1979): 20–24.

———. "Religion and the Revolution." *Cuba Review* 9, no. 1 (February 1979) [special issue on the subject].

———. "Cuban Protestant Theological Encounter." *LADOC* 10, no. 2 (November–December 1979): 46–48.

———. "Religion in Cuba." *Maryknoll,* no. 74 (August 1980) [special issue on the subject].

———. "Ciencia y Religión: Selección de Artículos" [from section "Ciencia y Religión"]. In *El Militante Comunista.* Havana: Editora Política, 1981.

———. *El Futuro del que Obra Justica Es la Paz (Material de Estudio).* Matanzas: Serie 'Augusto Cotto' no. 2, [1981?].

———. *Cristianos Contra Invasion Militar Norteamericana a Granada.* Havana: n.p., 1983.

———. "Chrétiens et Chrétiennes de Cuba après 25 Ans de Revolution." *Missions Etrangères* 21, no. 7 (February 1984) [special issue on the subject].

Vázquez Candela, E. "Imperialismo Yanqui e Imperialismo Romano: Dos Caras del Mismo Fenómeno." *Bohemia* 52, no. 52 (25 December 1960): 66–67, 90–92.

Viera Trejo, Bernardo. "La Caridad en Cuba Libre." *Bohemia* 51, no. 38 (20 September 1959): 62–65.

Walker, Janet. "Faith and Fidel: Reflections on Cuba." *Mandate* 17, no. 3 (April–May 1986): 17–19.

———. "Faith Holds in Cuba." *United Church Observer* 50, no. 1 (July 1986): 22–24.

Wall, James M. "Cuba, Hunger and Geopolitics." *Christian Century* 97, no. 18 (14 May 1980): 539–40.

———. "A New Use for the Miramar." *Christian Century* 97, no. 36 (12 November 1980): 1083–84.

———. "Worshipping God in a Communist State." *Christian Century* 98, no. 15 (29 April 1981): 467–69.

———. " 'Christ Will Not Leave Cuba.' " *Christian Century* 98, no. 16 (6 May 1981): 499–500.

White, David. "Cuba: Beautiful and Violent." *Christian Century* 76, no. 3 (21 January 1959) 74–76.

Woolfson, Susan. "Havana Diary: Jesus, Moses, and Marx in Cuba." *Worldview* 24, no. 7 (July 1981): 8–10.

Yergo Ugarte, Angel Felix. "La Accion Enérgica del 'Espriritualismo Militante'." *Bohemia* 52, no. 2 (10 January 1960): 38–39, 89–90.

Articles on the Church in Cuba (author unnamed)

"Visita el Cardenal Arteaga al Presidente de la República." *Alerta*, 3 May 1952, 5.

"Curas Patriotas." *Bohemia* 44, no. 26 (29 June 1952): 140.

"Inauguró el Gen. Batista la Nueva Iglesia del Guatao." *Diario de la Marina*, 4 February 1958, 1A, 9B.

"El Enigma de la Paz." *La Quincena* 4, no. 3 (15 February 1958): 1.

" 'Prestaron los Católicos de Cuba su Cooperación Decidida a la Causa de la Libertad'—F. Castro." *Diario de la Marina*, 7 January 1959, 1A, 2A.

"Catolicismo: La Cruz y el Diablo." *Bohemia* 51, no. 3 (18–25 January 1959): 98–100.

"Renunció a su Mitra el Obispo M. Dalmau." *Diario de la Marina*, 21 January 1959, 1A.

"Socorre el Santo Padre a las Víctimas de la Guerra en Cuba: Contribuye con Cinco Mil Pesos para Los que Tanto Padecieron." *Diario de la Marina*, 12 February 1959, 1A, 2A.

"Defiende Mons. Pérez Serantes la Libertad de Enseñanza y Pide al Gobierno Se Permita Enseñar Religión en las Escuelas Públicas." *Diario de la Marina*, 18 February 1959, 1A, 2A.

"Con Brillantez y Entusiasmo Celebró la Juventud Obrera Católica su XII Aniversario." *Diario de la Marina*, 22 February 1959, 1A, 2A.

"Entrevista con Mons. Evelio Díaz." *Diario de la Marina*, 30 May 1959, 1A, 2A.

"Despertar de la Conciencia Social." *La Quincena* 5, no. 16 (30 August 1959), supp., 3, 36.

"El Congreso Católico Nacional." *Bohemia* 51, no. 47 (22 November 1959): 59.

"Religión en la Escuela Desea el 95% en Cuba." *Diario de la Marina*, 24 November 1959, 1A, 2A.

"Analiza el Cardenal Cushing el Estado de la Iglesia en Cuba." *Diario de la Marina*, 24 November 1959, 1A, 6A.

"Aclara Mons. Díaz Afirmaciones del Cardenal Cushing." *Diario de la Marina*, 25 November 1959, 1A.

"Responde Monseñor Alfredo Müller al Cardenal de Boston." *Diario de la Marina*, 27 November 1959, 8A.

"Aclarando un Infundio: La Iglesia Católica y la Revolución." *Bohemia* 51, no. 48 (29 November 1959): 64–65.

" 'Justicia Social, Sí; Pero el Comunismo, No,' ' Fue el Unánime Grito en el Congreso Católico." *Diario de la Marina*, 1 December 1959, 1A, 20A, 5B.

"La Iglesia y la Cuestión Social." *Diario de la Marina*, 2 December 1959, 4A.

"La Verdad del Congreso Católico y las Mentiras del Comunismo." *Diario de la Marina*, 4 December 1959, 1A.

"Gratitud por la Gran Colaberación Brindada al Congreso Católico." *Diario de la Marina*, 4 December 1959, 1A.

"El Congreso Católico: Otra Victoria del Pueblo de Cuba." *Bohemia* 51, no. 49 (6 December 1959): 71.

"Gran Demostración de Fe popular, el Congreso Católico." *Bohemia* 51, no. 49 (6 December 1959): 72–78.

"Superiores Religiosos Hispanos en Cuba Recuerdan los Crímenes de los Comunistas en España." *Diario de la Marina*, 8 January 1960, 1A, 2A.

" 'Esta es la Hora del Cristianismo Social,' dice el P. Aspiazu." *La Quincena* 6, no. 1 (16 January 1960): 2–4, 62.

"La Consegración del Obispo de Pinar del Río." *Bohemia* 52, no. 14 (3 April 1960): 67.

"Los Católicos y el Comunismo." *Bohemia* 52, no. 16 (17 April 1960): 55, 76.

"Semana Santa Cubana." *Bohemia* 52, no. 17 (24 April 1960): 69.

"The Embattled Catholics." *Newsweek*, 30 May 1960, 56.

"Denuncian los Sacerdotes Vascos el Régimen Criminal de Franco." *Bohemia* 52, no. 25 (19 June 1960): 54–55, 76–77.

"Catolicismo y Comunismo Frente a Frente." *La Quincena* 6, no. 14 (31 July 1960), 1, 59–61.

"Church vs. State." *Newsweek*, 22 August 1960, 49–50.

"El Episcopado contra la Revolución." *Bohemia* 52, no. 52 (25 December 1960), 89.

" 'Curas Falangistas'—Fidel." *Bohemia* 52, no. 52 (25 December 1960): 88.

"Campaña Anticatólica." *La Quincena* 6, nos. 23–24 (31 December 1960): 8, 60–62.

"El Latifundio de la Muerte." *Bohemia* 53, no. 1 (1 January 1961): 70.

"Por Sacerdote y por Cubano." *Bohemia* 53, no. 7 (12 February 1961): 68.

"Ante la Prensa: Cristo y la Revolutión." *Bohemia* 53, no. 9 (26 February 1961): 65–67.

" 'El Cardenal Spellman Apadrina a los Criminales de Guerra.' Fidel." *Bohemia* 53, no. 14 (2 April 1961): 73.

" 'Acepto la Revolución.' " *Bohemia* 53, no. 17 (23 April 1961): 95–98.

"Ahora Alfabetizan." *Bohemia* 53, no. 20 (14 May 1961): 60.

"Iglesia: De Espaldas al Pueblo." *Bohemia* 53, no. 21 (21 May 1961): 59–64.

"Enforced Exodus." *Newsweek*, 2 October 1961, 52.

"The Church in Cuba." *Newsweek*, 9 October 1961, 94.

"Protestant Students Meet in Mexico." *Christian Century* 78, no. 45 (8 November 1961): 1327.

"Cristo-Marx: El Padre Pessoa, Líder de los Favelados de Belo Horizonte, Propone una Alianza de la Cristiandad con el Marxismo." *Bohemia* 53, no. 48 (26 November 1961): 32–34, 103.

"Cuban Churches Persist in Adversity." *Christian Century* 79, no. 26 (27 June 1962): 801.

"Castro vs. the Witnesses." *Newsweek*, 25 March 1963, 72.

"Church Endures in Cuba." *Christian Century* 80, no. 22 (29 May 1963): 702.

"Methodists Rally in Cuba." *Christian Century* 81, no. 11 (11 March 1964): 327.

"The Church in Cuba." *America* 11, no. 24 (12 December 1964): 769.

"News of the Churches: Presbyterian-Reformed Church of Cuba." *Reformed and Presbyterian World* 29, no. 5 (March 1967): 231–32.

"Church in Cuba." *Christian Century* 85, no. 5 (31 January 1968): 131.

"Approfondissement et Dialogue (Cuba)." *Missions Etrangères* 15, no. 1 (January–February 1971): 7–11.

"Fidel and Religion." *America* 138, no. 1 (7–14 January 1978): 4.

"Juan Pablo II Bendice a Sus Hijos de Cuba." In *Cuba Diáspora, 1981*, q.v., 47–49.

"Obispos de la Iglesia de Cuba." In *Cuba Diáspora, 1981*, q.v., 117–20.

"Nicaraguan Sugar Harvest: Cuban Priests Pitch In." *Granma Weekly Review*, 21 March 1982, 9.

"Cuba: Mesures Vexatoires Envers les Catholiques." *Diffusion de l'Information sur l'Amérique Latine* 816 (9 December 1982).

"Carlos Rafael Rodríguez Meets with Over 100 Theologians and Social Scientists." *Granma Weekly Review*, 11 December 1983, 5.

" 'L'Education à l'Athéisme: Tâche et Devoir de Tous': Un Article de la Revue, *Jeune Communiste*." *Missions Etrangères* 21, no. 7 (February 1984): 9–10.

"Un Christianisme Courageux." *Missions Etrangères* 21, no. 7 (February 1984): 11–14.

"Cuba: Waiting for the Pope." *Latin American Regional Reports (Caribbean)*, 22 February 1985, 5.

"Cuban Catholics Prepare 'Mini-Puebla'." *Latinamerica Press*, 25 July 1985. 3.

"Bishops Support Debt Meeting: Militant Christians Upstage Castro." *Latin American Regional Reports (Caribbean)*, 23 August 1985, 5.

"Declaration by Cuban Bishops on the Foreign Debt and the New International Economic Order." *Granma Weekly Review*, 27 October 1985, 7.

"Cuban Bishops Visit United States Invited by U.S. Episcopate." *Granma Weekly Review*, 27 October 1985, 7.

"U.S. Religious Delegation Deplores Its Country's Anti-Cuba Policy." *Granma Weekly Review*, 24 November 1985, 3.

"Castro Meets the Bishops: Cuba's Government and the Church Find Common Ground." *Latin American Regional Reports (Caribbean)*, 6 December 1985, 5.

"Castro Alters Course: Papal Envoy at Catholic Congress." *Latin American Weekly Report*, 21 February 1986, 6–7.

"Cuba: Church Demands 'More Space'." *Latin American Weekly Report*, 28 February 1986, 3.

"Bishops Defend Dialogue with Castro." *Latin American Regional Reports (Caribbean)*, 13 June 1986, 4.

"There Are Many Similarities between the Black Church and the Cuban Church." *Granma Weekly Review*, 20 July 1986, 5.

"Church Affairs: Bishops Approve One Year's Task." *Latin American Weekly Report*, 25 September 1986, 5.

"Cuban Archbishop Confirms Authenticity of Virgin of El Cobre." *Granma Weekly Review*, 13 September 1987, 1.

"Church-State Understanding in Cuba." *Granma Weekly Review*, 20 September 1987, 3.

"Freedom of Worship in Cuba, Say Religious People." *Granma Weekly Review*, 6 December 1987, 3.

"4th Congress of Orisha Tradition and Culture Scheduled to Take Place in Havana." *Granma Weekly Review*, 28 February 1988, 1.

"Monsignor Ortega Elected President of the Cuban Bishops Conference." *Granma Weekly Review*, 6 March 1988, 5.

"Mass in Commemoration of Father Varela's Death." *Granma Weekly Review*, 6 March 1988, 5.

"President Fidel Castro's Activities: Meeting with Hans Peter Kolvenbach." *Granma Weekly Review*, 27 March 1988, 4.

Index

San Carlos y San Ambrosio
College-Seminary, 12–15, 20,
25. *See also* Caballero, José
Agustín; Luz y Caballero,
José de la; Varela y Morales,
Félix
Santander y Frutos, Bishop, 36
Sardiñas, Guillermo, 48–49, 114;
criticism of hierarchy by, 101
Sarmiento, Bishop Diego, 8–9
Sbarretti, Archbishop Donato, 39
Slavery in Cuba, 15–20. *See also*
Cuban church
Soviet-Cuban relations, 65–66,
79, 91–92; visit of Anastasas
Mikoyan, 76–77, 80; economic
aid, 77, 92, 188n1; military
aid, 78. *See also* Mikoyan,
Anastas; U.S.–Cuban relations
Spanish colonial system in
Cuba, 4, 5, 24, 179–80n7; role
of Fernando V, 6; disputes be-
tween church and government
representatives, 7
Struggles for independence
(1868–78, 1895–98), 29;
church's reaction to, 4, 20,
29–30, 35–36

Tacón, Governor Miguel, 24.
See also Spanish colonial
system
Toledo y Armendáriz, Fray
Alonso Enríque de, 10
Torres, Camilo, 122, 141

UMAPS, 111–12
Unión de Católicos
Universitarios, 102
U.S.–Cuban relations, 42, 48, 71,
89, 91, 92–98; U.S. influence
as a result of Protestantism,
55, 56, 57; U.S.–Cuban–USSR

relations, 65–66, 76–79,
84–90; U.S. response to Cuban
nationalization of American
businesses, 75; CIA role in, 76,
78, 93; impact of Bay of Pigs
invasion on church-state relations, 94–102; U.S. per capita
aid to Latin America
(1961–62), 188n1; family reunification program, 194n3.
See also Bay of Pigs;
Eisenhower, Dwight; Kennedy,
John F.; Nixon, Richard;
Soviet-Cuban relations
Usera y Alarcón, Father
Jerónimo, 26

Valdés, Bishop Gerónimo, 11
Valdés, Ramiro, 103. *See also*
Boza Masvidal, Eduardo
Valdespino, Andrés, 126
Varela y Morales, Félix, 13–14,
113
Vatican: role of, 33; reaction to
independence movements,
33–36
Vatican II (1962–65), xix, 66,
107–8, 115, 116, 120, 122–23,
124, 125, 126, 127, 132, 135,
138, 154, 175, 178. *See also*
John XXIII; Zacchi, Cesare
Villalpando, Bishop Bernardino
de, 10
Villanueva University (Havana),
48, 50, 69, 77, 82
Villaverde, Alberto Martín, 47,
51, 116; opinions on agrarian
reform, 71, 72, 73
Virgin of Charity (Cuba's
national patron saint), 30,
44–45, 102

Wite, Bishop Juan de, 7